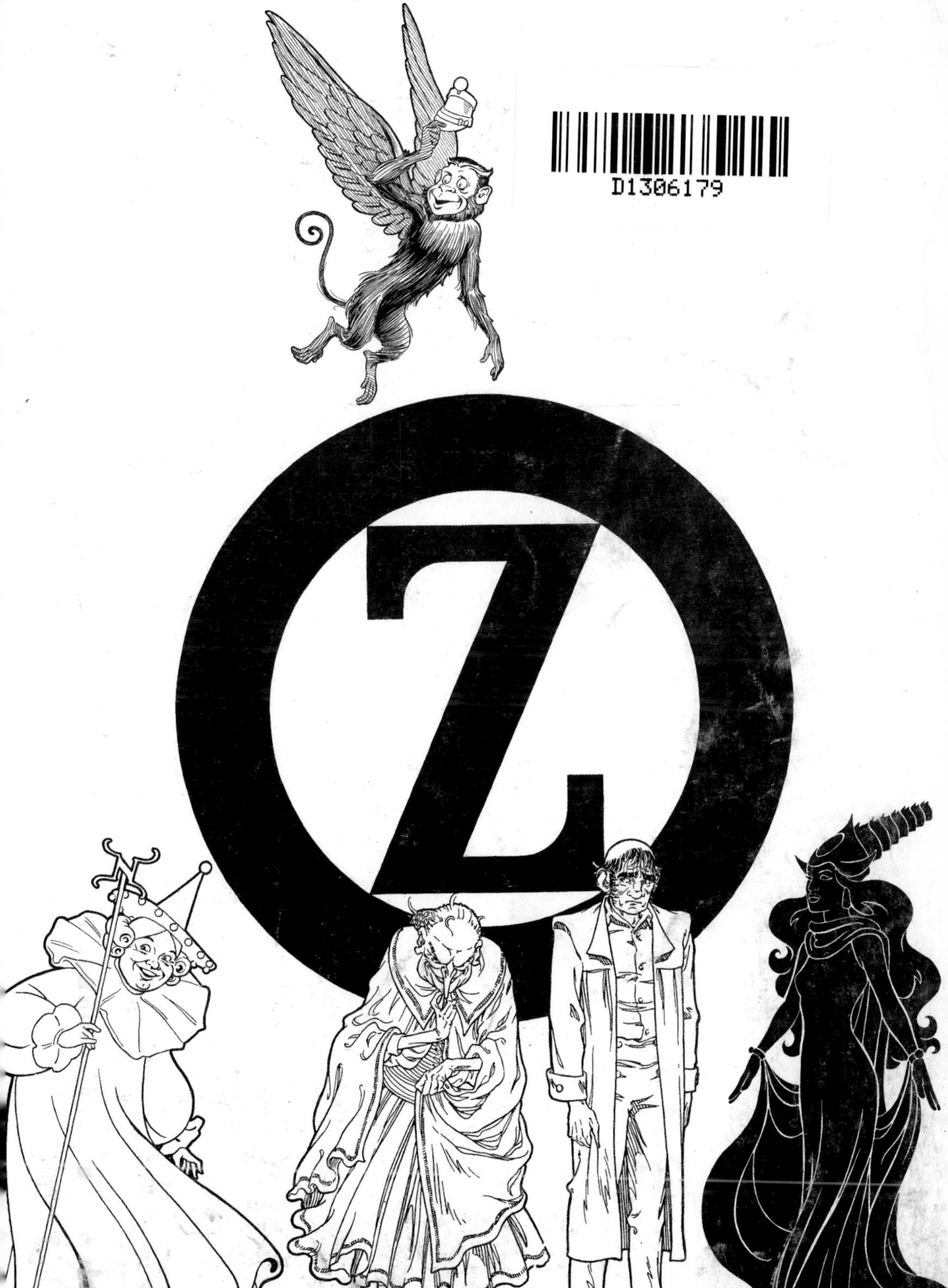
OZ

# Eric Shanower
Writer and Illustrator

## John Uhrich
Production Artist

## Neil Uyetake
Design Production Director

## Rick Oliver
Original editor for *The Enchanted Apples of Oz* and *The Ice King of Oz*

## Justin Eisinger & Mariah Huehner
Collection Editors

*Founded on and continuing the famous Oz stories by L. Frank Baum.*

www.IDWpublishing.com    ISBN: 978-1-60010-589-0    13 12 11 10    1 2 3 4

Operations: Ted Adams, Chief Executive Officer • Greg Goldstein, Chief Operating Officer • Matthew Ruzicka, CPA, Chief Financial Officer • Alan Payne, VP of Sales • Lorelei Bunjes, Dir. of Digital Services • AnnaMaria White, Marketing & PR Manager • Marci Hubbard, Executive Assistant • Alonzo Simon, Shipping Manager • Angela Loggins, Staff Accountant • Editorial: Chris Ryall, Publisher/Editor-in-Chief • Scott Dunbier, Editor, Special Projects • Andy Schmidt, Senior Editor • Bob Schreck, Senior Editor • Justin Eisinger, Editor • Kris Oprisko, Editor/Foreign Lic. • Denton J. Tipton, Editor • Tom Waltz, Editor • Mariah Huehner, Associate Editor • Carlos Guzman, Editorial Assistant • Design: Robbie Robbins, EVP/Sr. Graphic Artist • Neil Uyetake, Art Director • Chris Mowry, Graphic Artist • Amauri Osorio, Graphic Artist • Gilberto Lazcano, Production Assistant • Shawn Lee, Production Assistant

Originally published as ADVENTURES IN OZ: THE ENCHANTED APPLES OF OZ and ADVENTURES IN OZ: THE ICE KING OF OZ.

# LITTLE ADVENTURES IN OZ



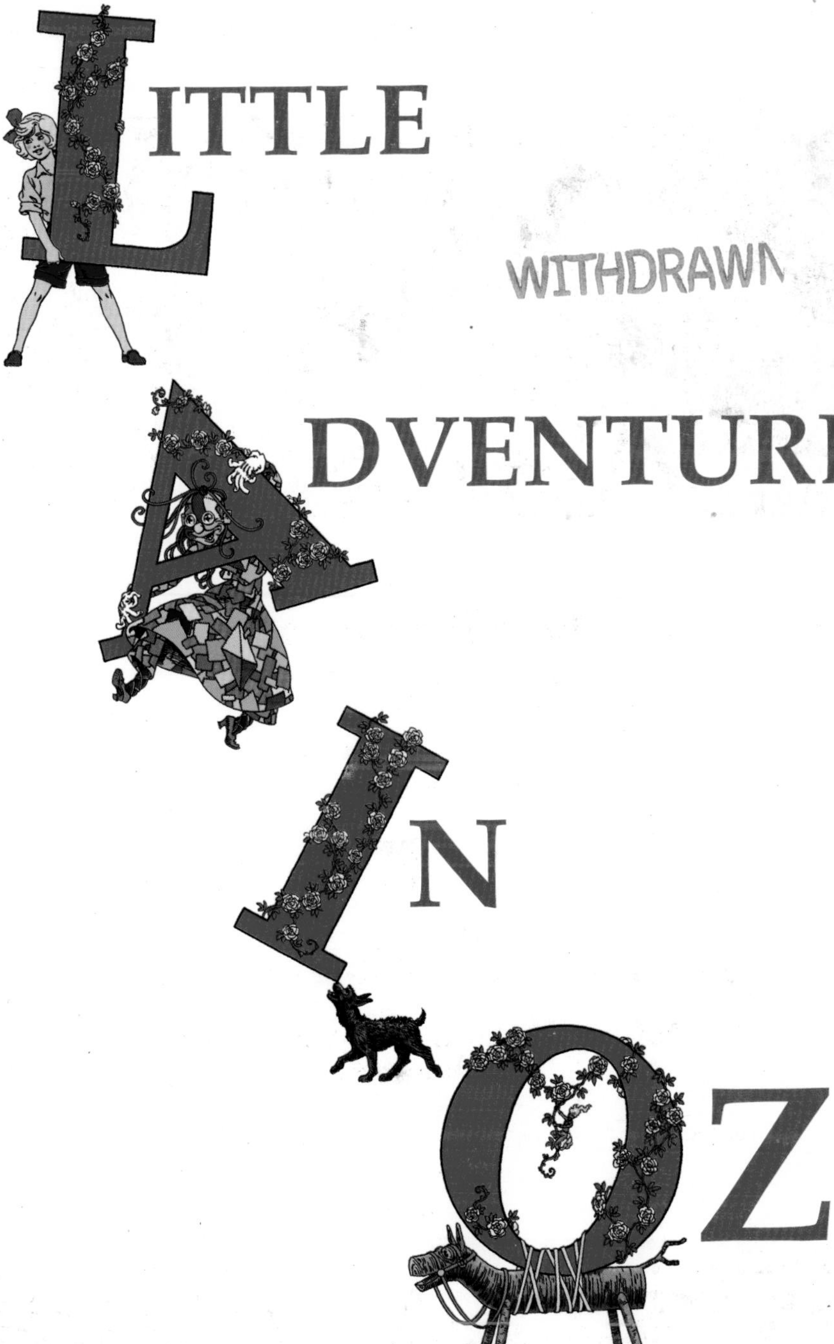

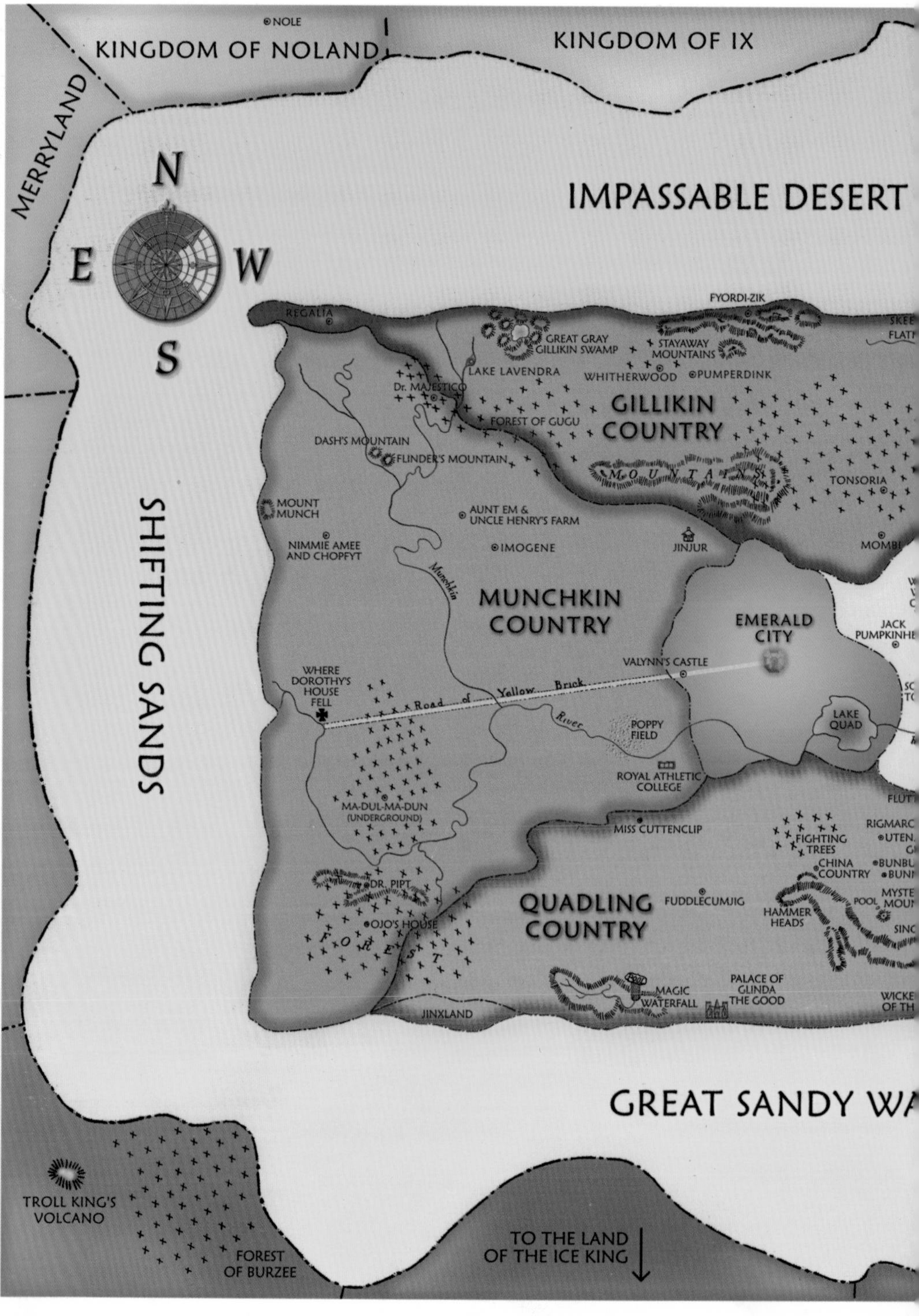
NOLE
KINGDOM OF NOLAND
KINGDOM OF IX
MERRYLAND
N
E
W
S
IMPASSABLE DESERT
SHIFTING SANDS
REGALIA
FYORDI-ZIK
GREAT GRAY GILLIKIN SWAMP
STAYAWAY MOUNTAINS
LAKE LAVENDRA
WHITHERWOOD
PUMPERDINK
Dr. MAJESTICO
FOREST OF GUGU
GILLIKIN COUNTRY
DASH'S MOUNTAIN
FLINDER'S MOUNTAIN
MOUNTAINS
TONSORIA
MOUNT MUNCH
AUNT EM & UNCLE HENRY'S FARM
NIMMIE AMEE AND CHOPFYT
IMOGENE
JINJUR
Munchkin
MUNCHKIN COUNTRY
EMERALD CITY
VALYNN'S CASTLE
WHERE DOROTHY'S HOUSE FELL
Road of Yellow Brick
River
POPPY FIELD
LAKE QUAD
ROYAL ATHLETIC COLLEGE
MA-DUL-MA-DUN (UNDERGROUND)
MISS CUTTENCLIP
FIGHTING TREES
CHINA COUNTRY
DR. PIPT
OJO'S HOUSE
FOREST
QUADLING COUNTRY
FUDDLECUMJIG
HAMMER HEADS
POOL
MAGIC WATERFALL
PALACE OF GLINDA THE GOOD
JINXLAND
TROLL KING'S VOLCANO
FOREST OF BURZEE
TO THE LAND OF THE ICE KING

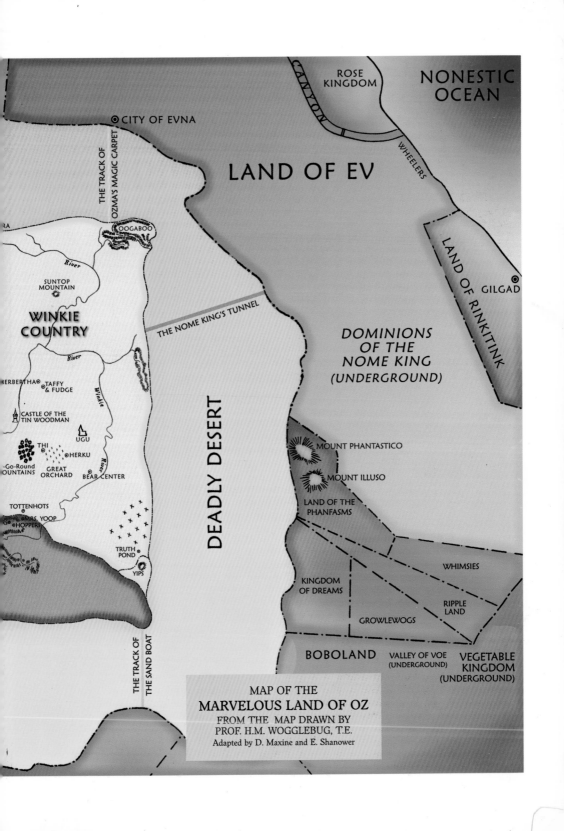

ROSE KINGDOM

NONESTIC OCEAN

CANYON

⊙ CITY OF EVNA

LAND OF EV

WHEELERS

THE TRACK OF OZMA'S MAGIC CARPET

OOGABOO

RA

River

SUNTOP MOUNTAIN

WINKIE COUNTRY

THE NOME KING'S TUNNEL

River

LAND OF RINKITINK

⊙ GILGAD

DOMINIONS OF THE NOME KING (UNDERGROUND)

Winkie

HERBERTHA ⊙  TAFFY & FUDGE

CASTLE OF THE TIN WOODMAN

UGU

THI  ⊙ HERKU

-Go-Round OUNTAINS  GREAT ORCHARD  BEAR CENTER

River

DEADLY DESERT

MOUNT PHANTASTICO

MOUNT ILLUSO

LAND OF THE PHANFASMS

TOTTENHOTS

MRS. YOOP

⊙ HOPPERS

TRUTH POND

YIPS

WHIMSIES

KINGDOM OF DREAMS

RIPPLE LAND

GROWLEWOGS

THE TRACK OF THE SAND BOAT

BOBOLAND

VALLEY OF VOE (UNDERGROUND)

VEGETABLE KINGDOM (UNDERGROUND)

MAP OF THE
**MARVELOUS LAND OF OZ**
FROM THE MAP DRAWN BY
PROF. H.M. WOGGLEBUG, T.E.
Adapted by D. Maxine and E. Shanower

# The Enchanted Apples of Oz

To Margaret and Chris
for enchantment created.

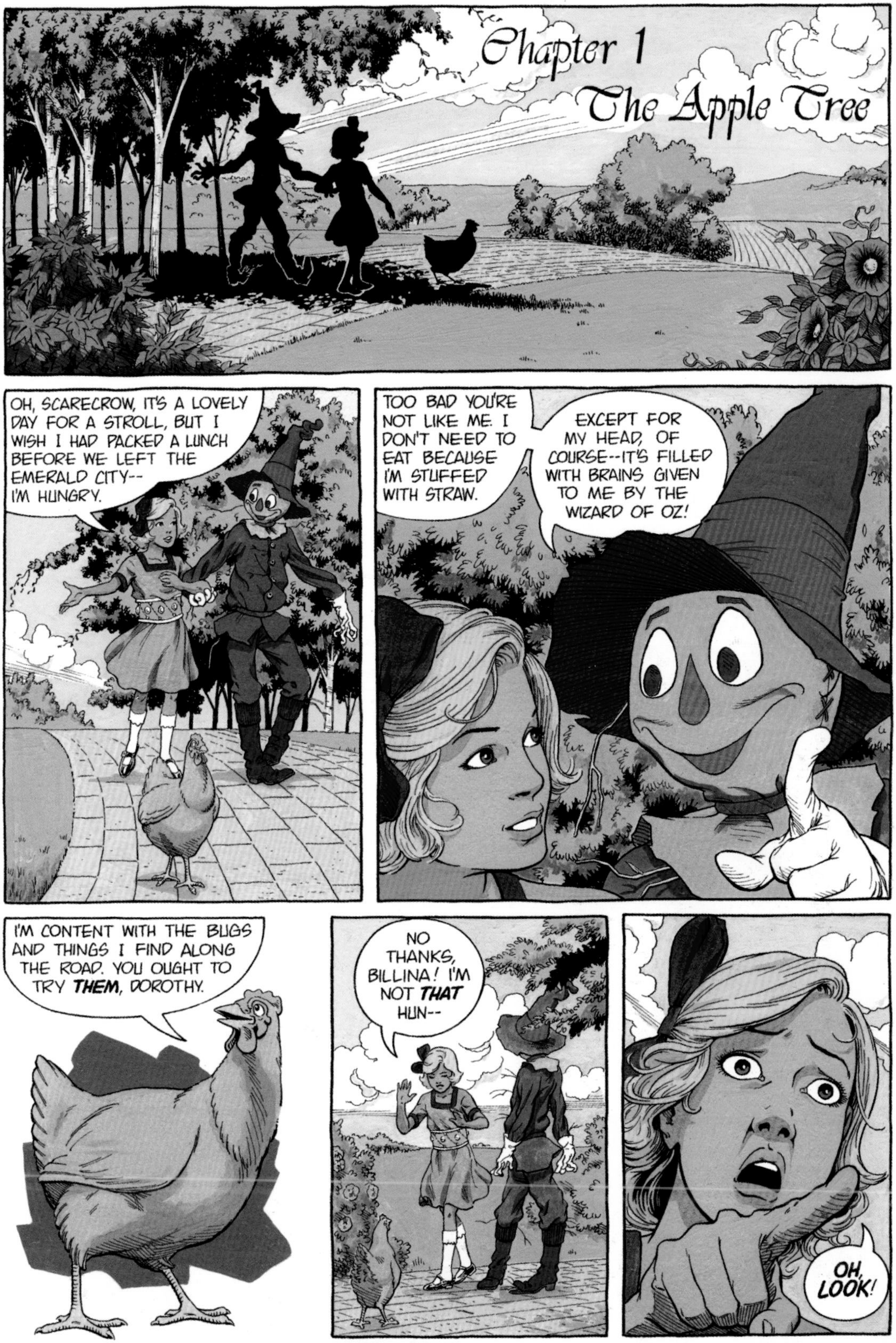
Chapter 1
The Apple Tree
OH, SCARECROW, IT'S A LOVELY DAY FOR A STROLL, BUT I WISH I HAD PACKED A LUNCH BEFORE WE LEFT THE EMERALD CITY-- I'M HUNGRY.
TOO BAD YOU'RE NOT LIKE ME. I DON'T NEED TO EAT BECAUSE I'M STUFFED WITH STRAW.
EXCEPT FOR MY HEAD, OF COURSE--IT'S FILLED WITH BRAINS GIVEN TO ME BY THE WIZARD OF OZ!
I'M CONTENT WITH THE BUGS AND THINGS I FIND ALONG THE ROAD. YOU OUGHT TO TRY **THEM**, DOROTHY.
NO THANKS, BILLINA! I'M NOT **THAT** HUN--
OH, LOOK!

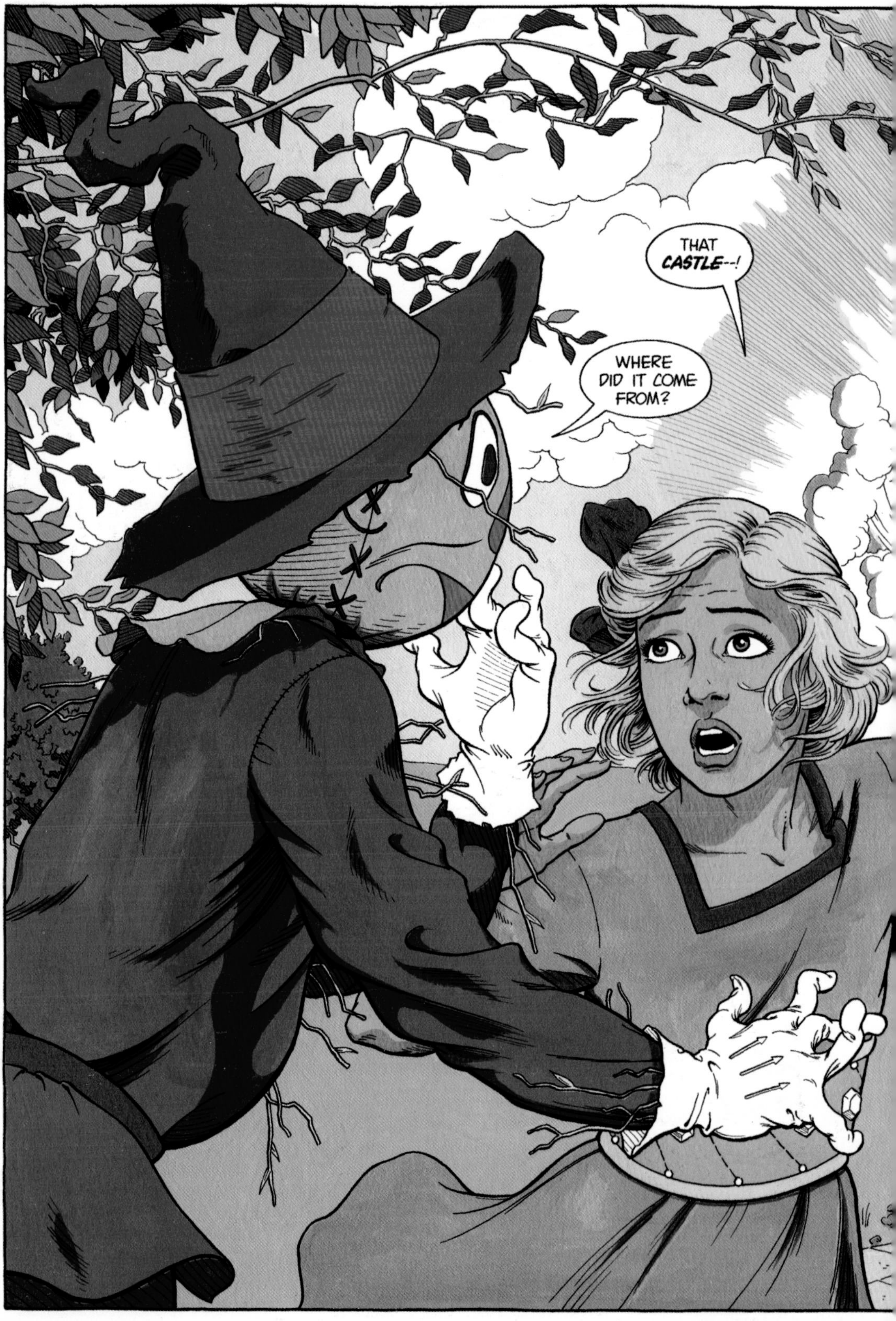
THAT CASTLE--!
WHERE DID IT COME FROM?

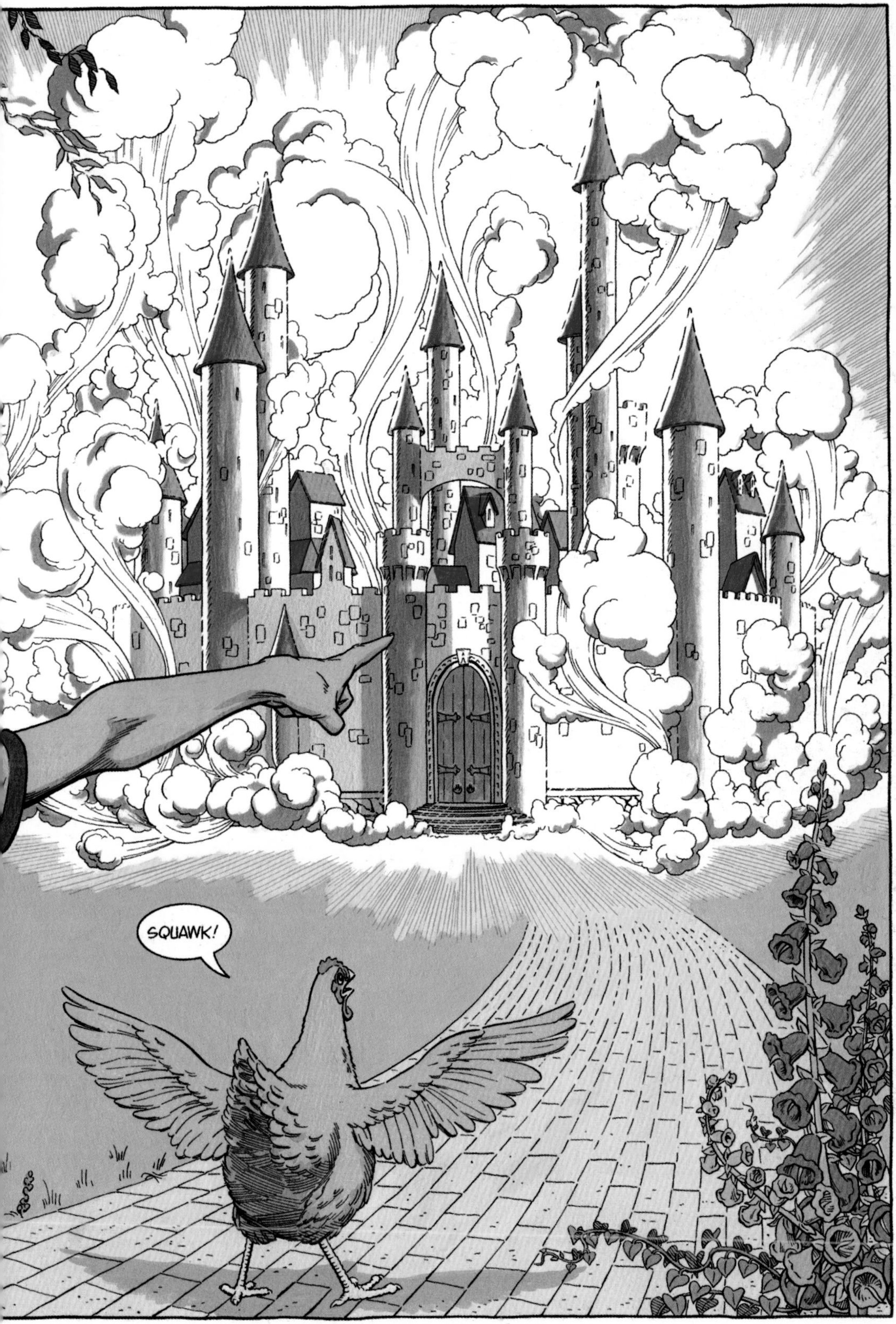
SQUAWK!

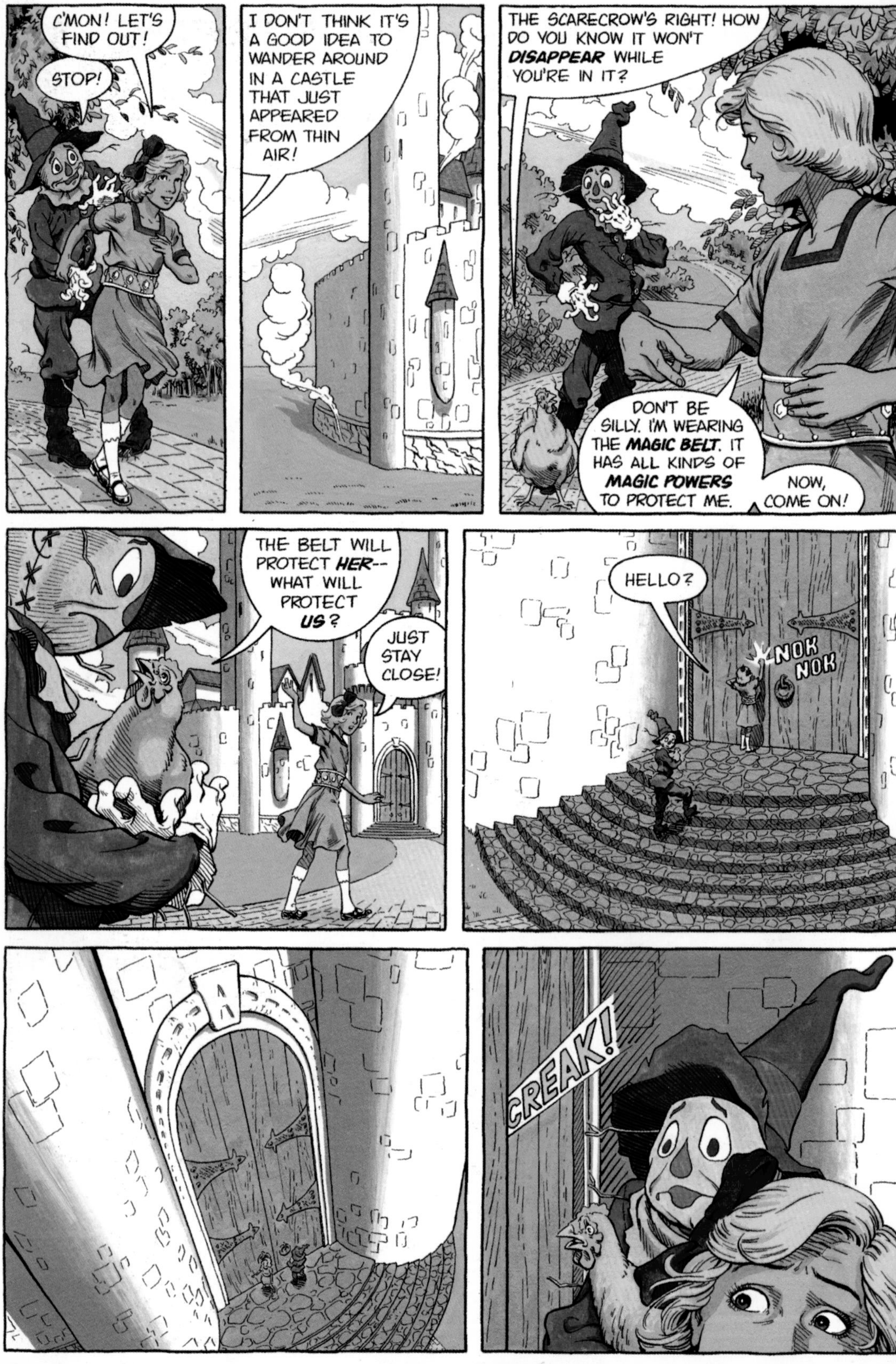
C'MON! LET'S FIND OUT!
STOP!
I DON'T THINK IT'S A GOOD IDEA TO WANDER AROUND IN A CASTLE THAT JUST APPEARED FROM THIN AIR!
THE SCARECROW'S RIGHT! HOW DO YOU KNOW IT WON'T **DISAPPEAR** WHILE YOU'RE IN IT?
DON'T BE SILLY. I'M WEARING THE **MAGIC BELT**. IT HAS ALL KINDS OF **MAGIC POWERS** TO PROTECT ME.
NOW, COME ON!
THE BELT WILL PROTECT **HER**-- WHAT WILL PROTECT **US**?
JUST STAY CLOSE!
HELLO?
NOK NOK
CREAK!

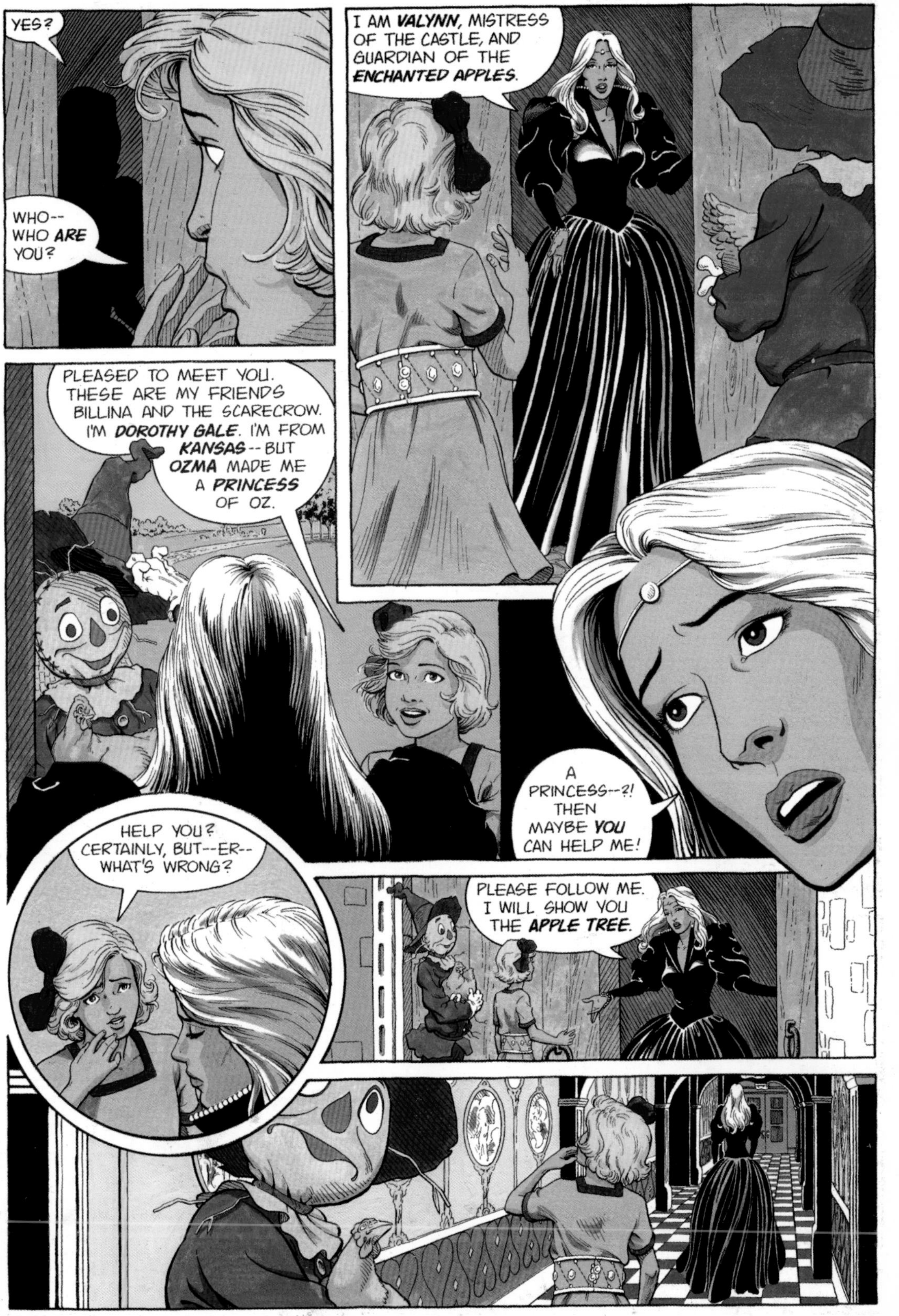
YES?
WHO-- WHO **ARE** YOU?
I AM **VALYNN**, MISTRESS OF THE CASTLE, AND GUARDIAN OF THE **ENCHANTED APPLES**.
PLEASED TO MEET YOU. THESE ARE MY FRIENDS BILLINA AND THE SCARECROW. I'M **DOROTHY GALE**. I'M FROM **KANSAS**--BUT **OZMA** MADE ME A **PRINCESS** OF OZ.
A PRINCESS--?! THEN MAYBE **YOU** CAN HELP ME!
HELP YOU? CERTAINLY, BUT--ER-- WHAT'S WRONG?
PLEASE FOLLOW ME. I WILL SHOW YOU THE **APPLE TREE**.

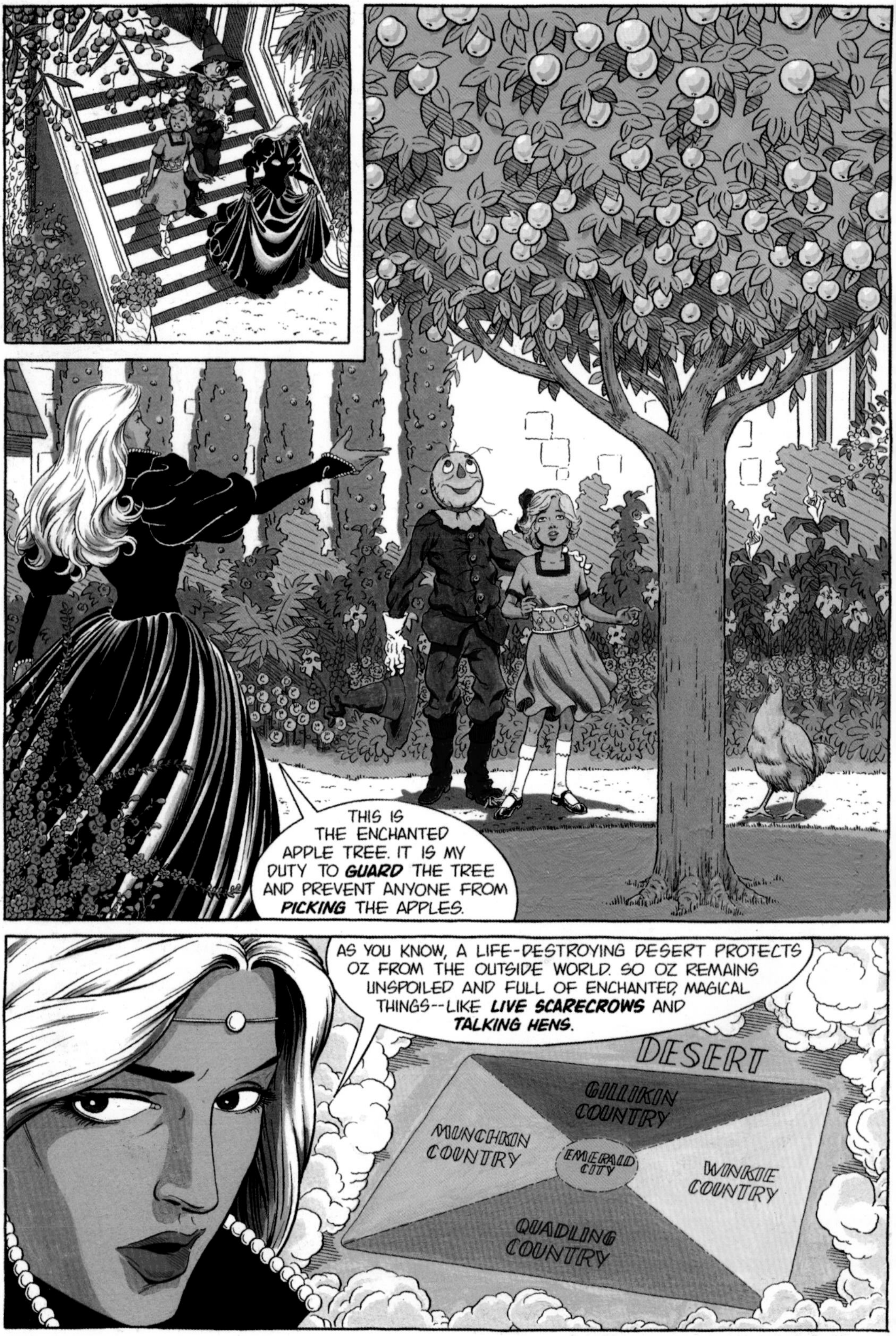
THIS IS THE ENCHANTED APPLE TREE. IT IS MY DUTY TO GUARD THE TREE AND PREVENT ANYONE FROM PICKING THE APPLES.
AS YOU KNOW, A LIFE-DESTROYING DESERT PROTECTS OZ FROM THE OUTSIDE WORLD. SO OZ REMAINS UNSPOILED AND FULL OF ENCHANTED, MAGICAL THINGS--LIKE LIVE SCARECROWS AND TALKING HENS.
DESERT
GILLIKIN COUNTRY
MUNCHKIN COUNTRY
EMERALD CITY
WINKIE COUNTRY
QUADLING COUNTRY

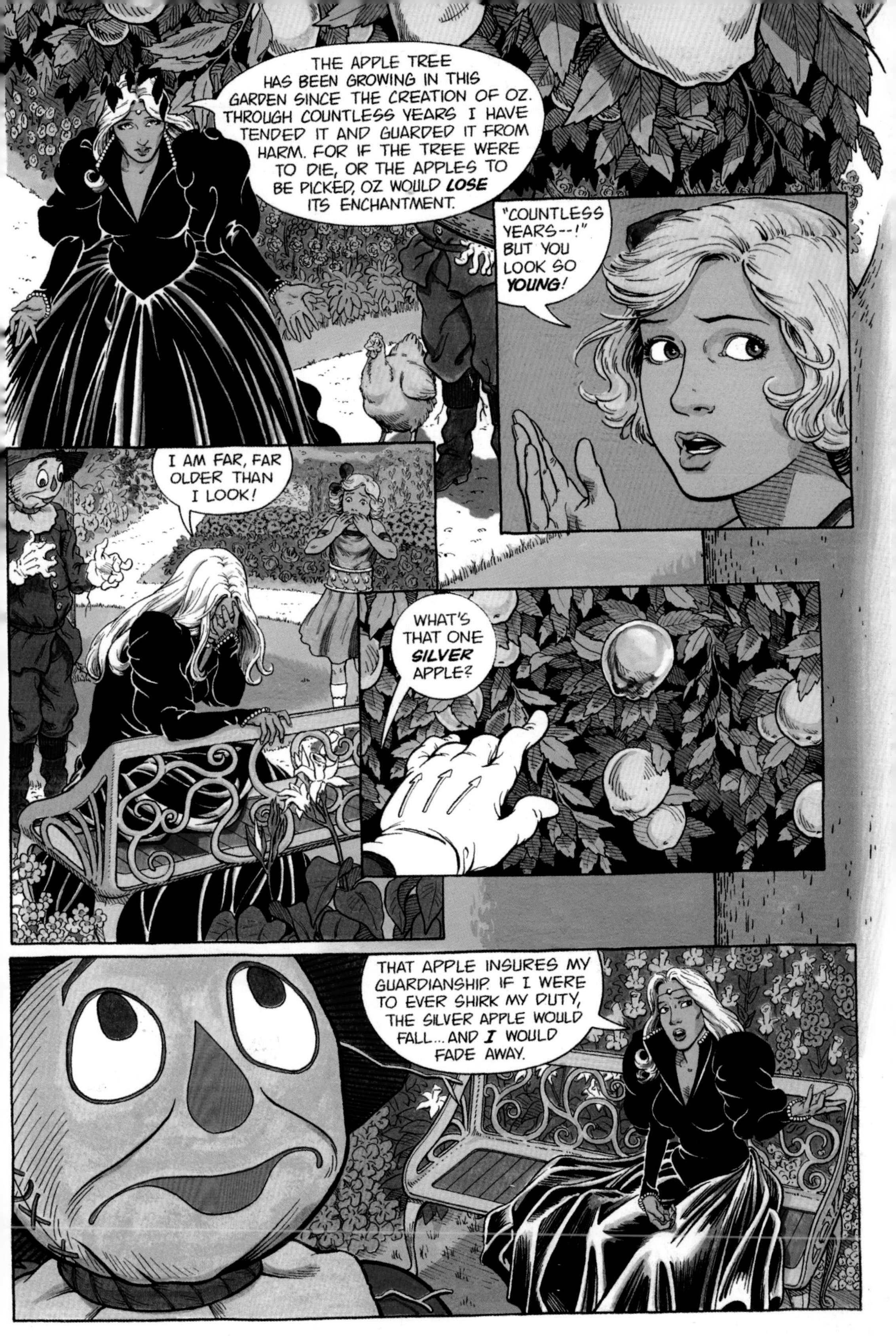
THE APPLE TREE HAS BEEN GROWING IN THIS GARDEN SINCE THE CREATION OF OZ. THROUGH COUNTLESS YEARS I HAVE TENDED IT AND GUARDED IT FROM HARM. FOR IF THE TREE WERE TO DIE, OR THE APPLES TO BE PICKED, OZ WOULD **LOSE** ITS ENCHANTMENT.
"COUNTLESS YEARS--!" BUT YOU LOOK SO **YOUNG**!
I AM FAR, FAR OLDER THAN I LOOK!
WHAT'S THAT ONE **SILVER** APPLE?
THAT APPLE INSURES MY GUARDIANSHIP. IF I WERE TO EVER SHIRK MY DUTY, THE SILVER APPLE WOULD FALL... AND **I** WOULD FADE AWAY.

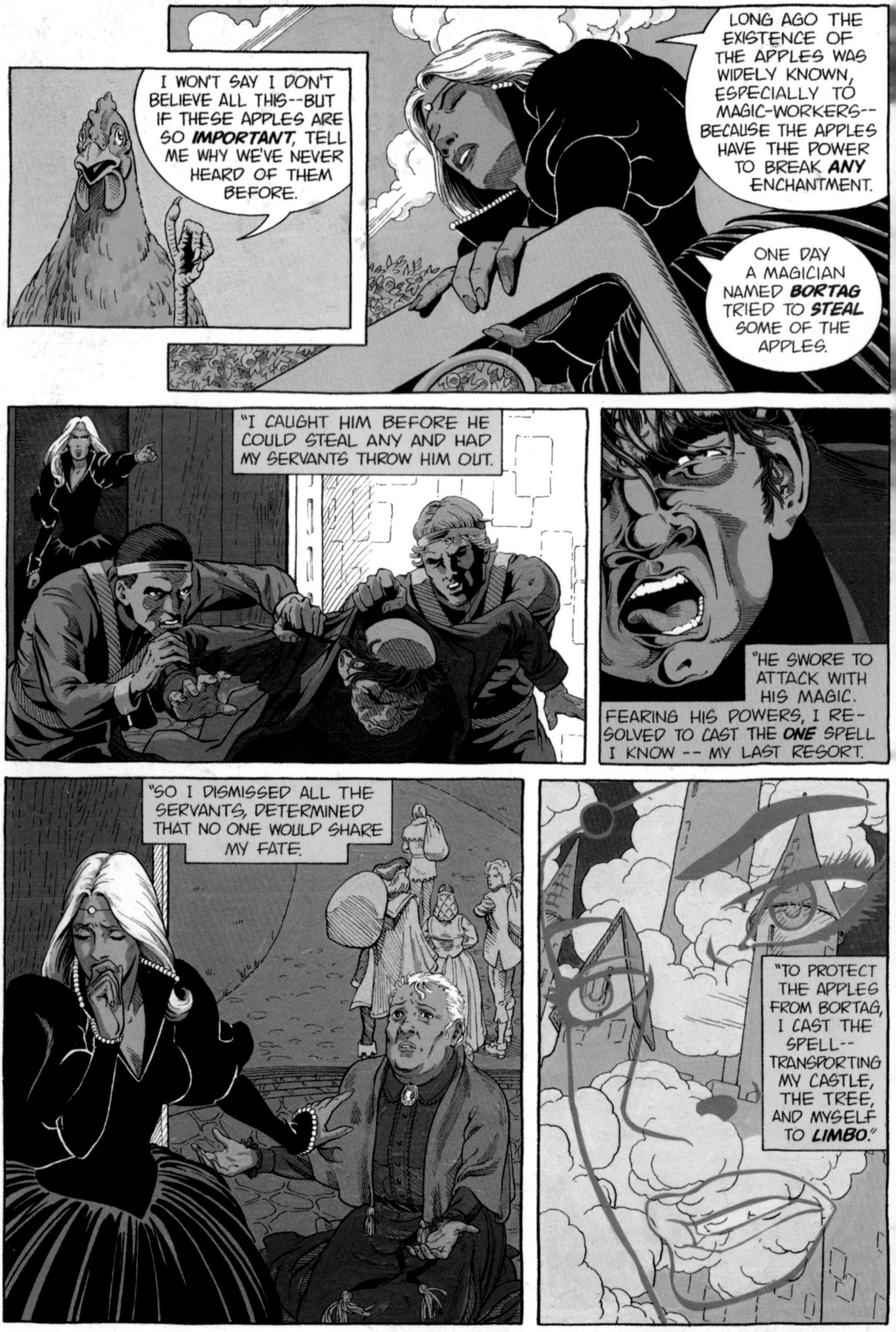
I WON'T SAY I DON'T BELIEVE ALL THIS--BUT IF THESE APPLES ARE SO IMPORTANT, TELL ME WHY WE'VE NEVER HEARD OF THEM BEFORE.
LONG AGO THE EXISTENCE OF THE APPLES WAS WIDELY KNOWN, ESPECIALLY TO MAGIC-WORKERS-- BECAUSE THE APPLES HAVE THE POWER TO BREAK ANY ENCHANTMENT.
ONE DAY A MAGICIAN NAMED BORTAG TRIED TO STEAL SOME OF THE APPLES.
"I CAUGHT HIM BEFORE HE COULD STEAL ANY AND HAD MY SERVANTS THROW HIM OUT.
"HE SWORE TO ATTACK WITH HIS MAGIC. FEARING HIS POWERS, I RESOLVED TO CAST THE ONE SPELL I KNOW -- MY LAST RESORT.
"SO I DISMISSED ALL THE SERVANTS, DETERMINED THAT NO ONE WOULD SHARE MY FATE.
"TO PROTECT THE APPLES FROM BORTAG, I CAST THE SPELL-- TRANSPORTING MY CASTLE, THE TREE, AND MYSELF TO LIMBO."

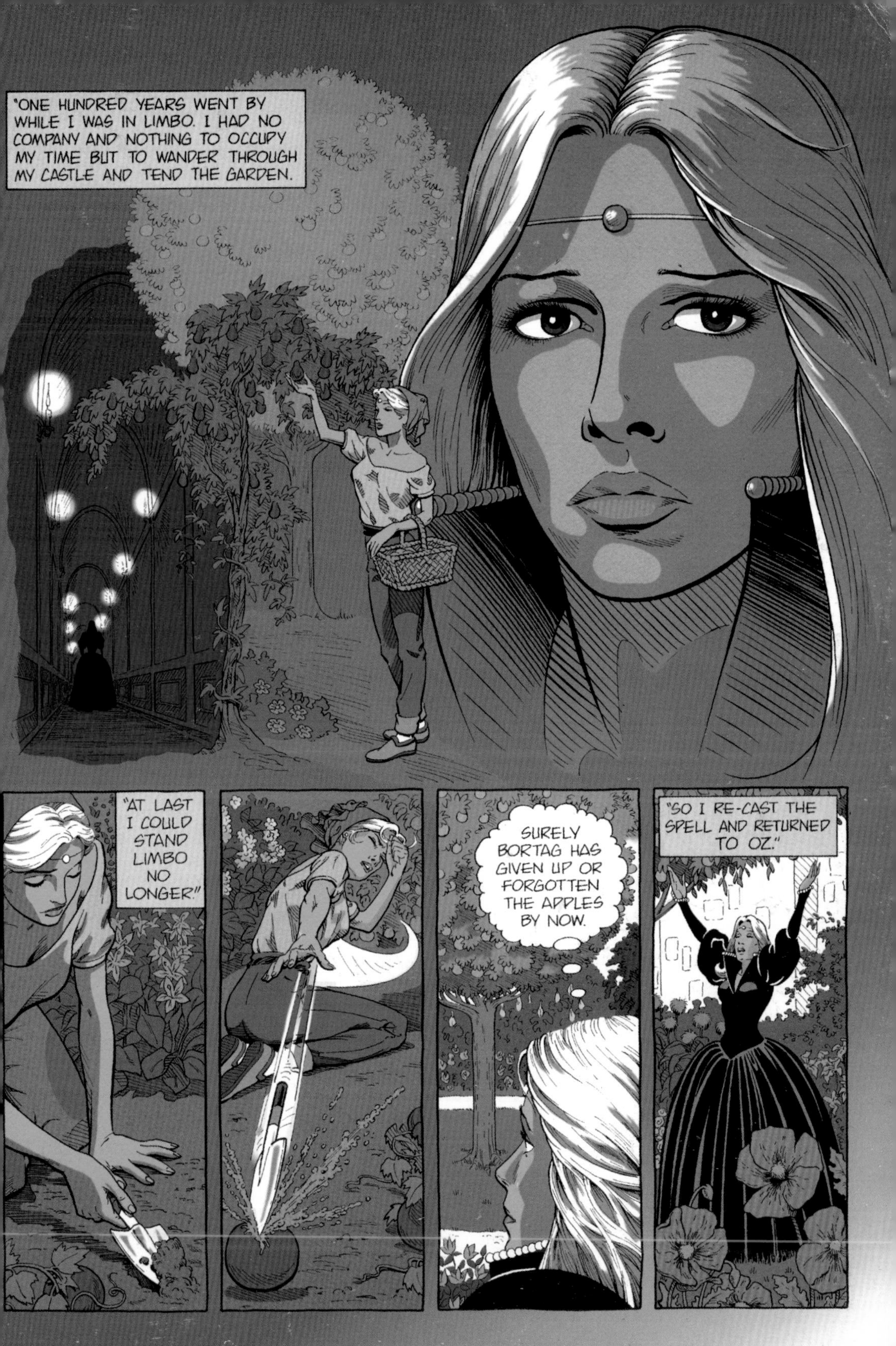
"ONE HUNDRED YEARS WENT BY WHILE I WAS IN LIMBO. I HAD NO COMPANY AND NOTHING TO OCCUPY MY TIME BUT TO WANDER THROUGH MY CASTLE AND TEND THE GARDEN.
"AT LAST I COULD STAND LIMBO NO LONGER."
SURELY BORTAG HAS GIVEN UP OR FORGOTTEN THE APPLES BY NOW.
"SO I RE-CAST THE SPELL AND RETURNED TO OZ."

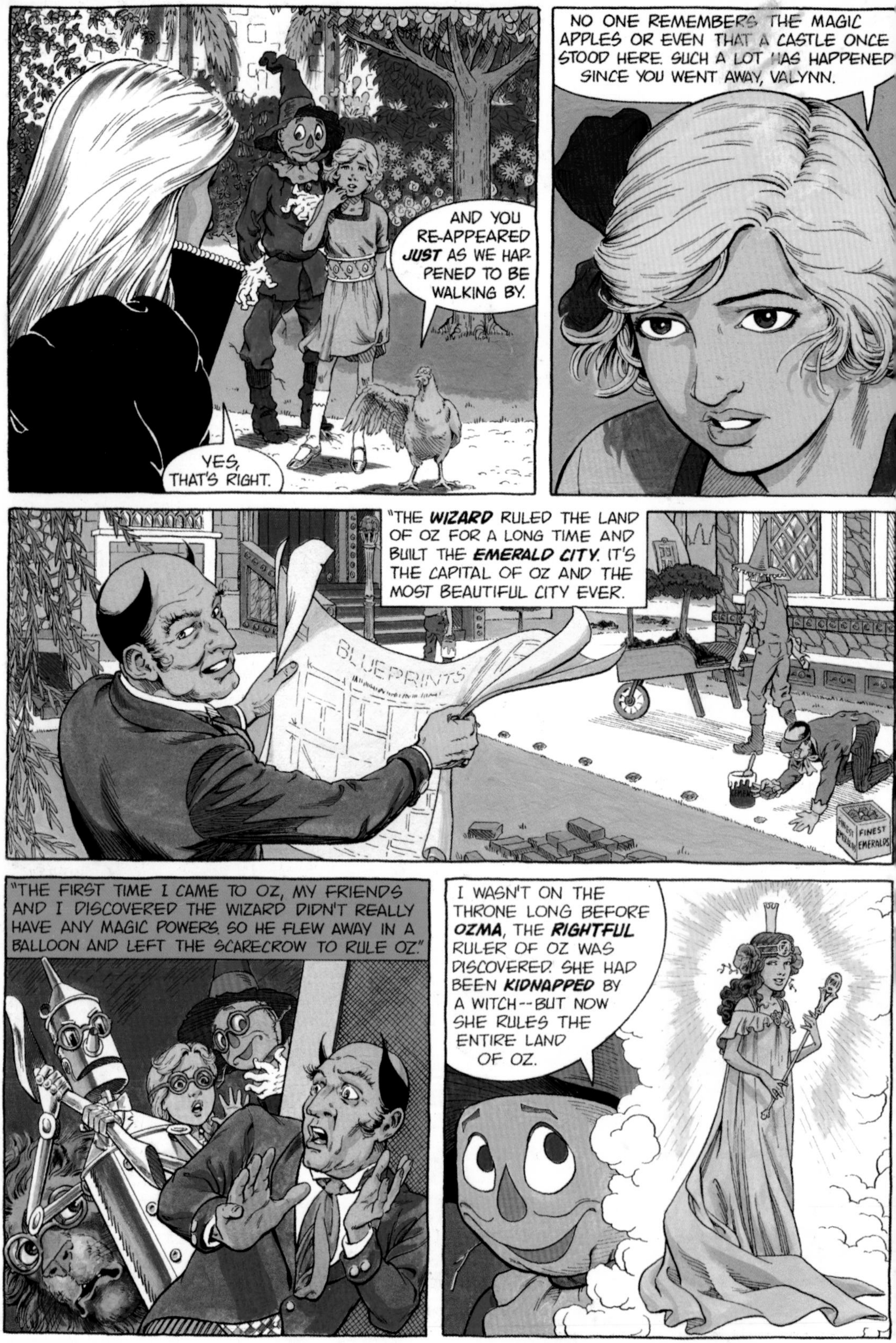
AND YOU RE-APPEARED ***JUST*** AS WE HAPPENED TO BE WALKING BY.
YES, THAT'S RIGHT.
NO ONE REMEMBERS THE MAGIC APPLES OR EVEN THAT A CASTLE ONCE STOOD HERE. SUCH A LOT HAS HAPPENED SINCE YOU WENT AWAY, VALYNN.
"THE ***WIZARD*** RULED THE LAND OF OZ FOR A LONG TIME AND BUILT THE ***EMERALD CITY***. IT'S THE CAPITAL OF OZ AND THE MOST BEAUTIFUL CITY EVER.
BLUEPRINTS
FINEST EMERALDS
FINEST EMERALDS
"THE FIRST TIME I CAME TO OZ, MY FRIENDS AND I DISCOVERED THE WIZARD DIDN'T REALLY HAVE ANY MAGIC POWERS. SO HE FLEW AWAY IN A BALLOON AND LEFT THE SCARECROW TO RULE OZ."
I WASN'T ON THE THRONE LONG BEFORE ***OZMA***, THE ***RIGHTFUL*** RULER OF OZ WAS DISCOVERED. SHE HAD BEEN ***KIDNAPPED*** BY A WITCH--BUT NOW SHE RULES THE ENTIRE LAND OF OZ.

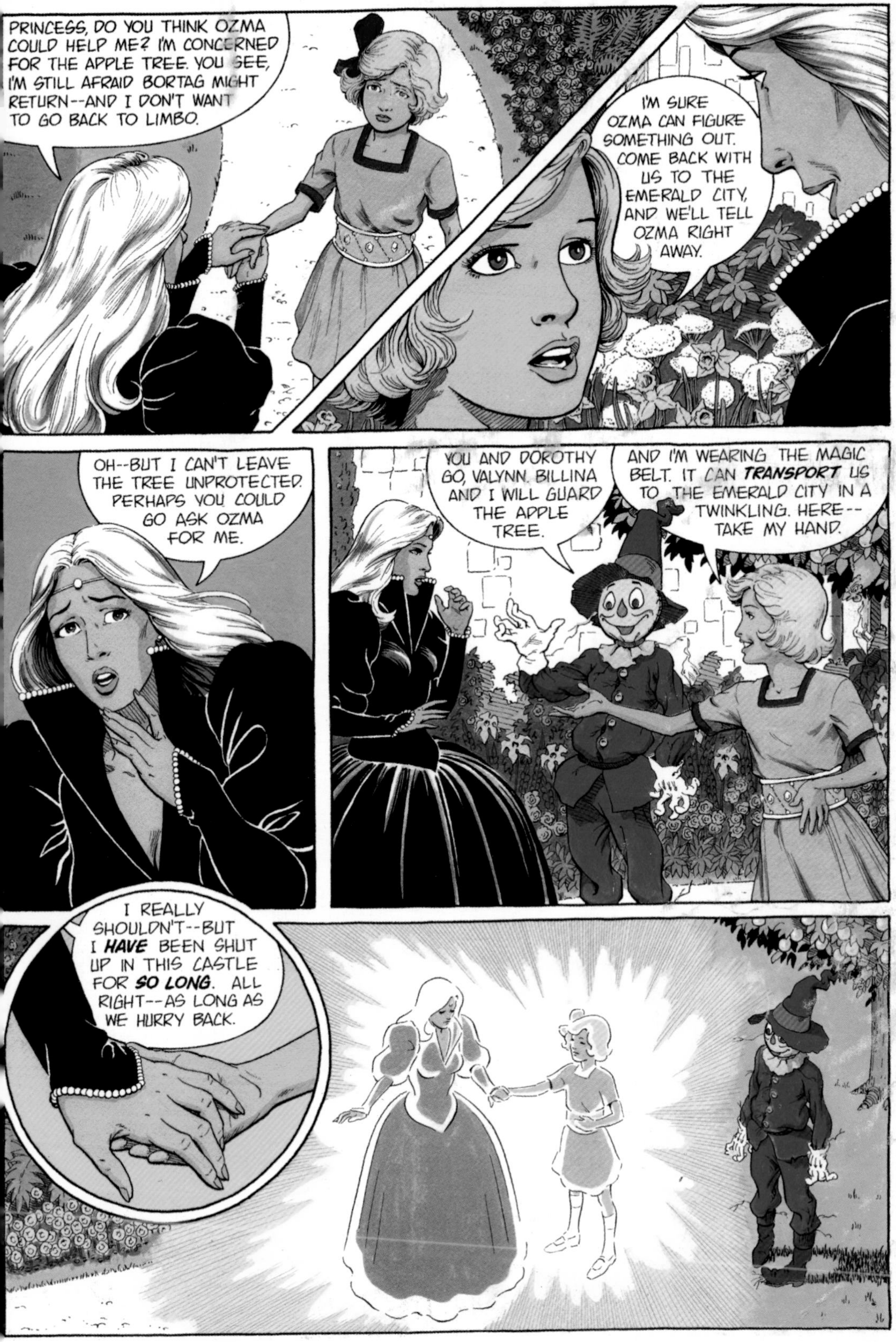
PRINCESS, DO YOU THINK OZMA COULD HELP ME? I'M CONCERNED FOR THE APPLE TREE. YOU SEE, I'M STILL AFRAID BORTAG MIGHT RETURN--AND I DON'T WANT TO GO BACK TO LIMBO.
I'M SURE OZMA CAN FIGURE SOMETHING OUT. COME BACK WITH US TO THE EMERALD CITY, AND WE'LL TELL OZMA RIGHT AWAY.
OH--BUT I CAN'T LEAVE THE TREE UNPROTECTED. PERHAPS YOU COULD GO ASK OZMA FOR ME.
YOU AND DOROTHY GO, VALYNN. BILLINA AND I WILL GUARD THE APPLE TREE.
AND I'M WEARING THE MAGIC BELT. IT CAN TRANSPORT US TO THE EMERALD CITY IN A TWINKLING. HERE-- TAKE MY HAND.
I REALLY SHOULDN'T--BUT I HAVE BEEN SHUT UP IN THIS CASTLE FOR SO LONG. ALL RIGHT--AS LONG AS WE HURRY BACK.

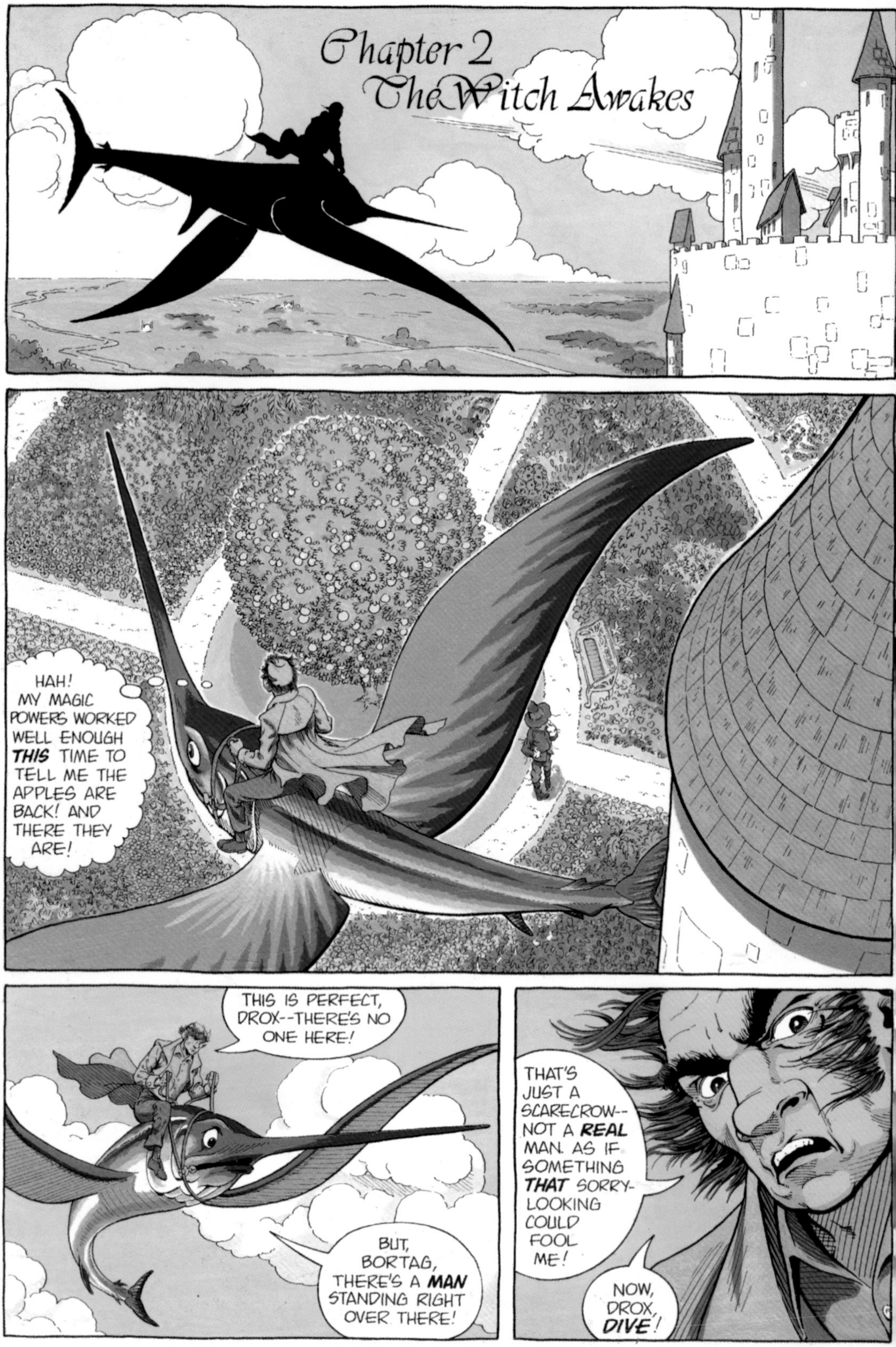
Chapter 2
The Witch Awakes
HAH! MY MAGIC POWERS WORKED WELL ENOUGH THIS TIME TO TELL ME THE APPLES ARE BACK! AND THERE THEY ARE!
THIS IS PERFECT, DROX--THERE'S NO ONE HERE!
BUT, BORTAG, THERE'S A MAN STANDING RIGHT OVER THERE!
THAT'S JUST A SCARECROW--NOT A REAL MAN. AS IF SOMETHING THAT SORRY-LOOKING COULD FOOL ME!
NOW, DROX, DIVE!

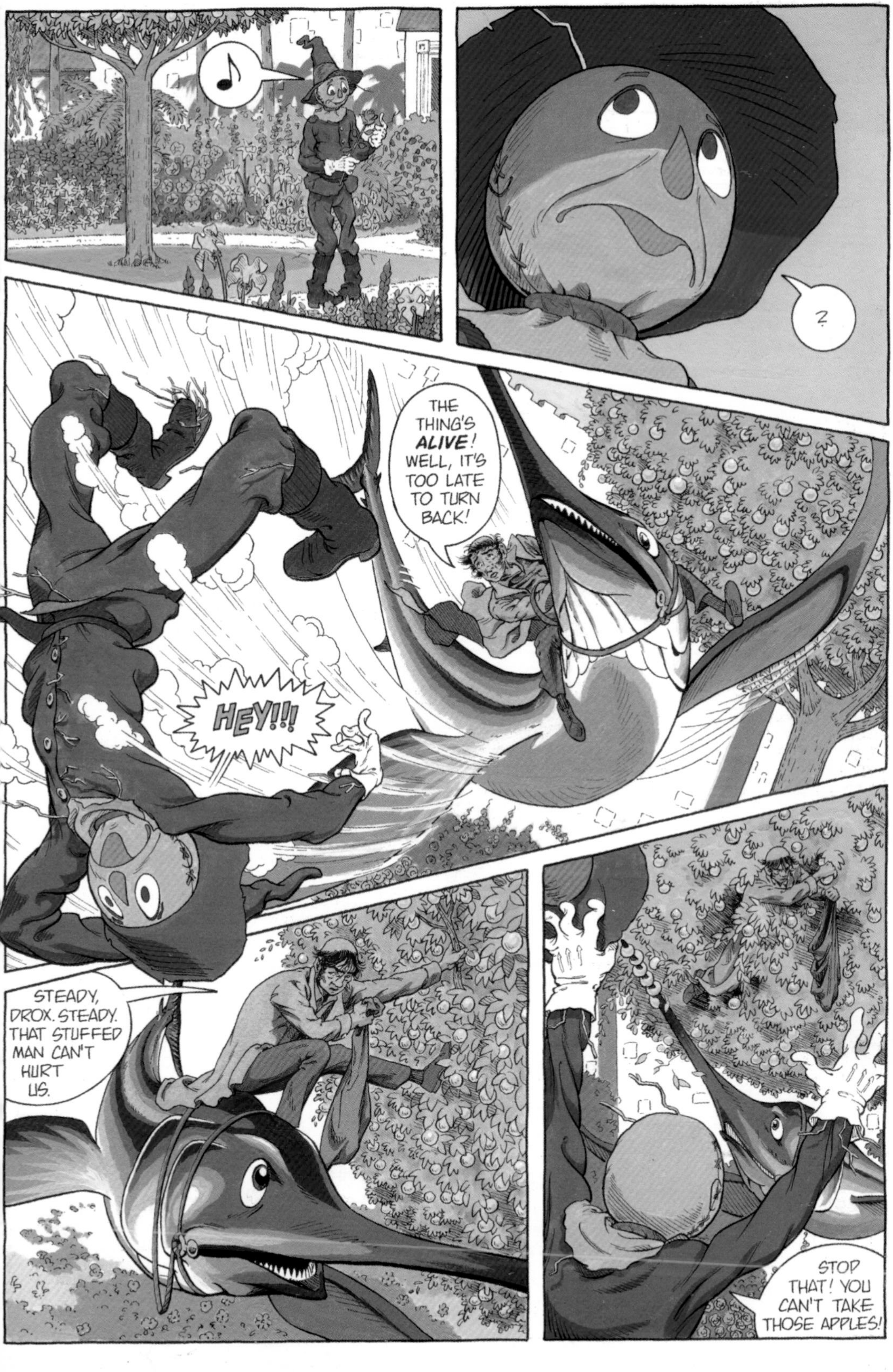
♪
?
THE THING'S **ALIVE**! WELL, IT'S TOO LATE TO TURN BACK!
HEY!!!
STEADY, DROX. STEADY. THAT STUFFED MAN CAN'T HURT US.
STOP THAT! YOU CAN'T TAKE THOSE APPLES!

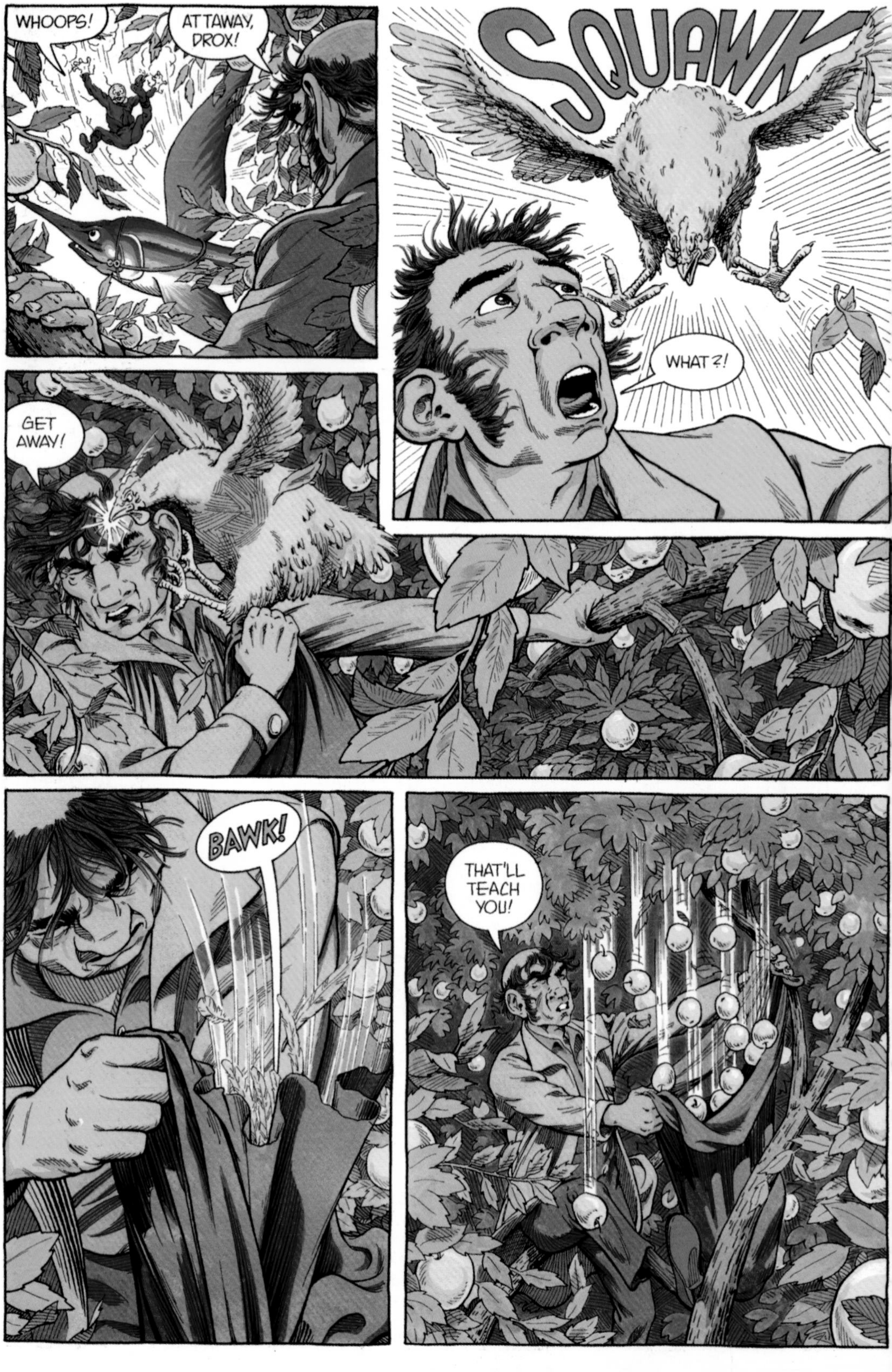
WHOOPS!
ATTAWAY, DROX!
SQUAWK
WHAT?!
GET AWAY!
BAWK!
THAT'LL TEACH YOU!

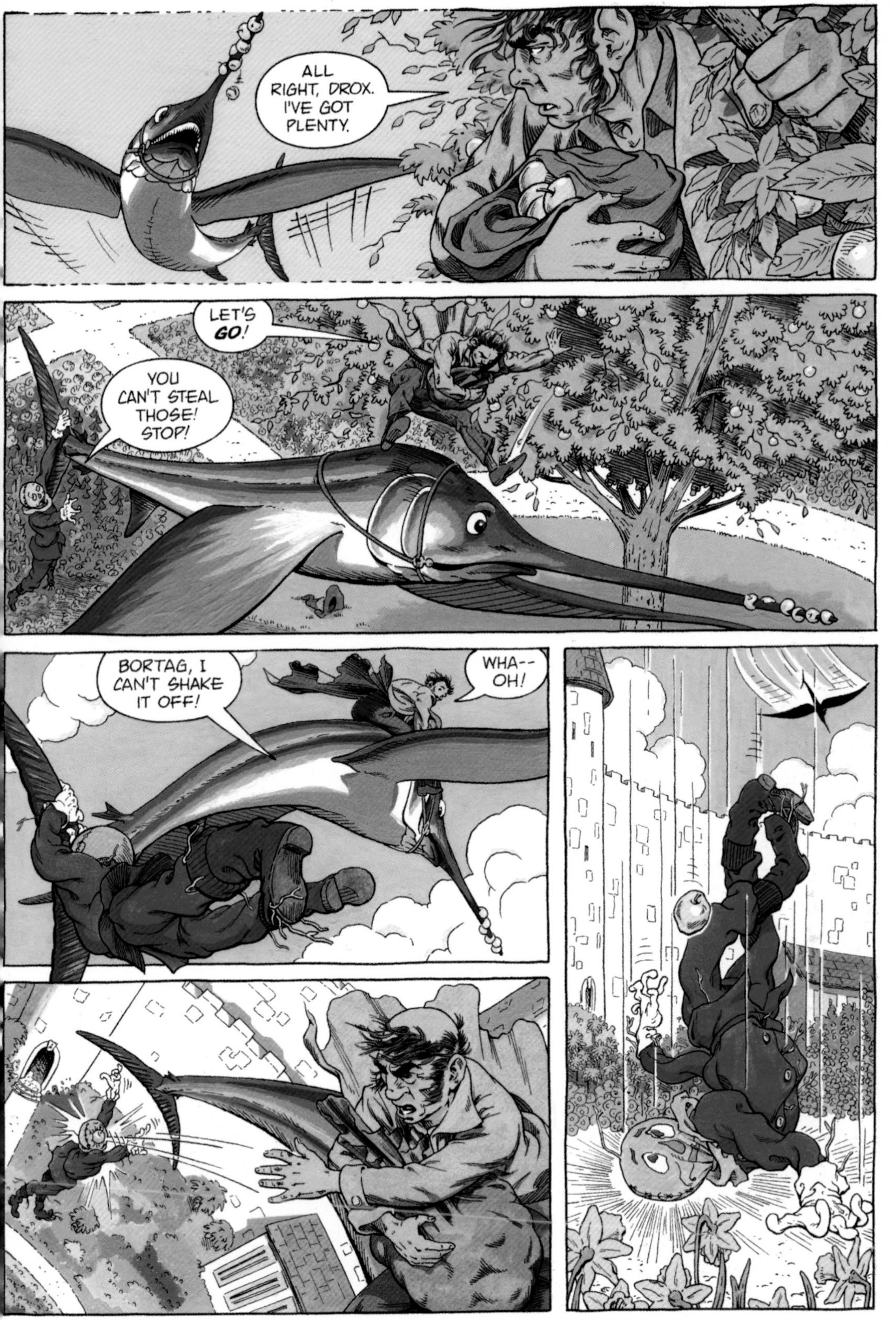
ALL RIGHT, DROX. I'VE GOT PLENTY.
LET'S GO!
YOU CAN'T STEAL THOSE! STOP!
BORTAG, I CAN'T SHAKE IT OFF!
WHA--OH!

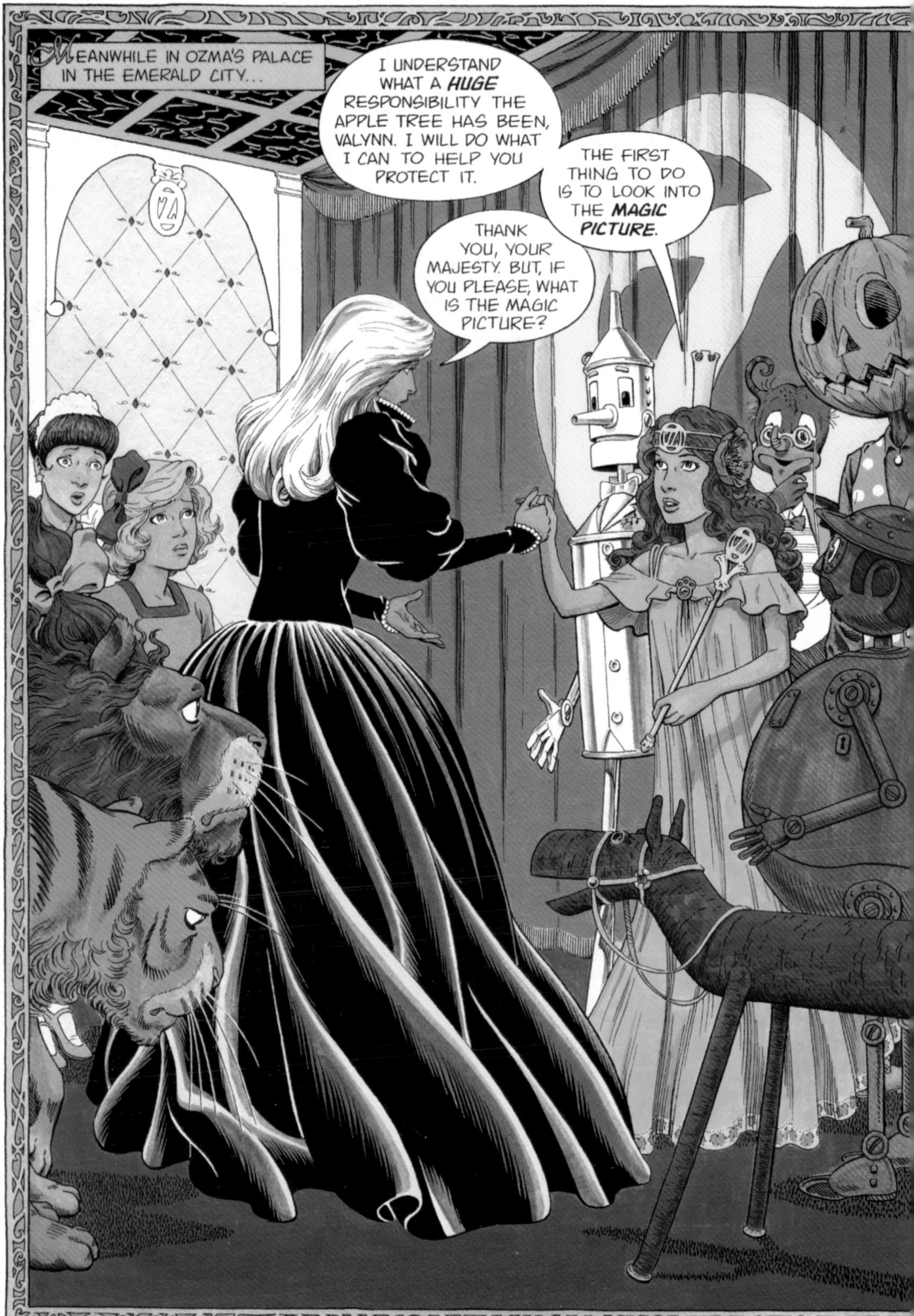
MEANWHILE IN OZMA'S PALACE IN THE EMERALD CITY...
I UNDERSTAND WHAT A HUGE RESPONSIBILITY THE APPLE TREE HAS BEEN, VALYNN. I WILL DO WHAT I CAN TO HELP YOU PROTECT IT.
THE FIRST THING TO DO IS TO LOOK INTO THE MAGIC PICTURE.
THANK YOU, YOUR MAJESTY. BUT, IF YOU PLEASE, WHAT IS THE MAGIC PICTURE?

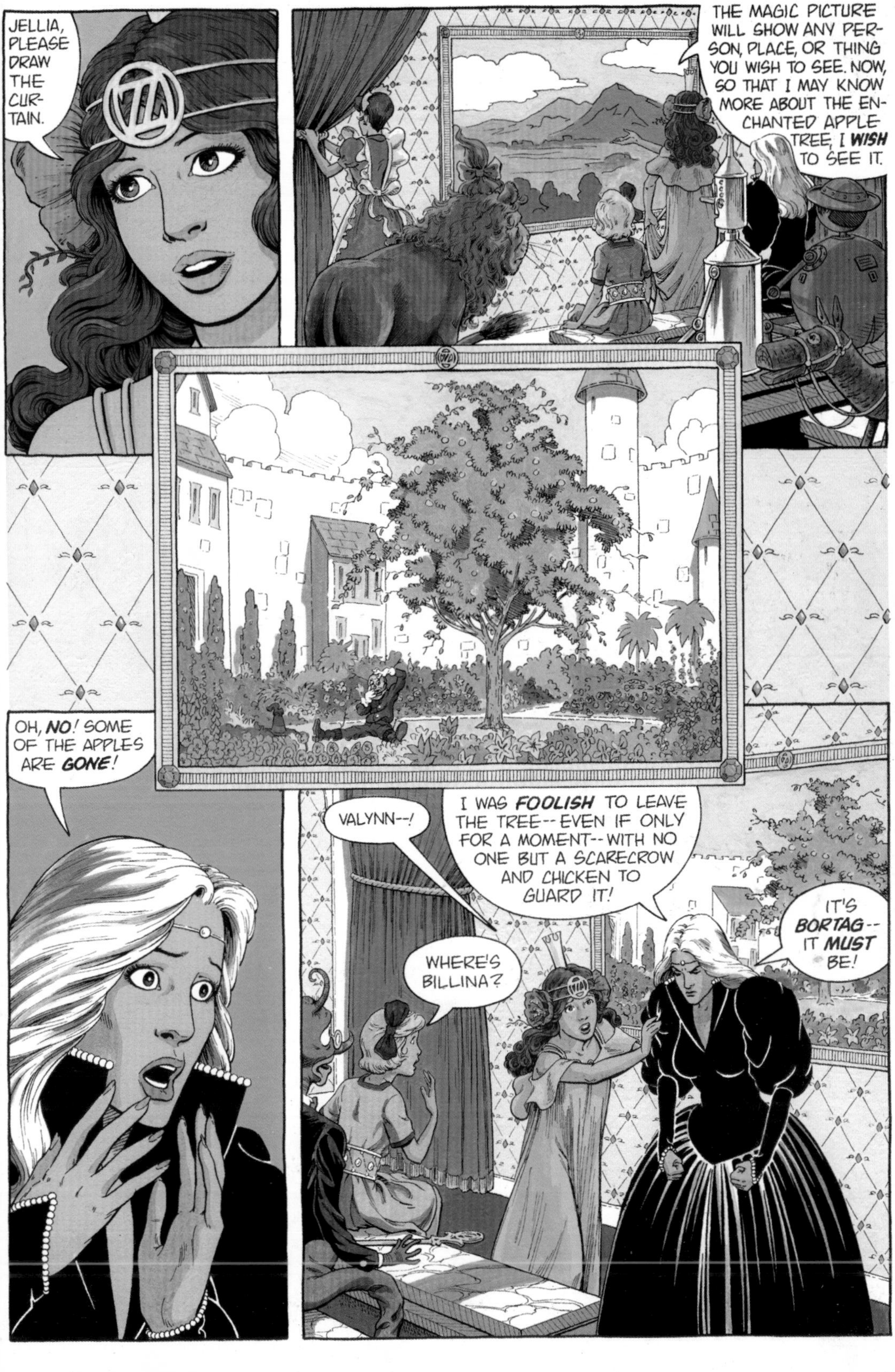
JELLIA, PLEASE DRAW THE CUR-TAIN.
THE MAGIC PICTURE WILL SHOW ANY PER-SON, PLACE, OR THING YOU WISH TO SEE. NOW, SO THAT I MAY KNOW MORE ABOUT THE EN-CHANTED APPLE TREE, I **WISH** TO SEE IT.
OH, **NO**! SOME OF THE APPLES ARE **GONE**!
VALYNN--!
I WAS **FOOLISH** TO LEAVE THE TREE-- EVEN IF ONLY FOR A MOMENT-- WITH NO ONE BUT A SCARECROW AND CHICKEN TO GUARD IT!
WHERE'S BILLINA?
IT'S **BORTAG**-- IT **MUST** BE!

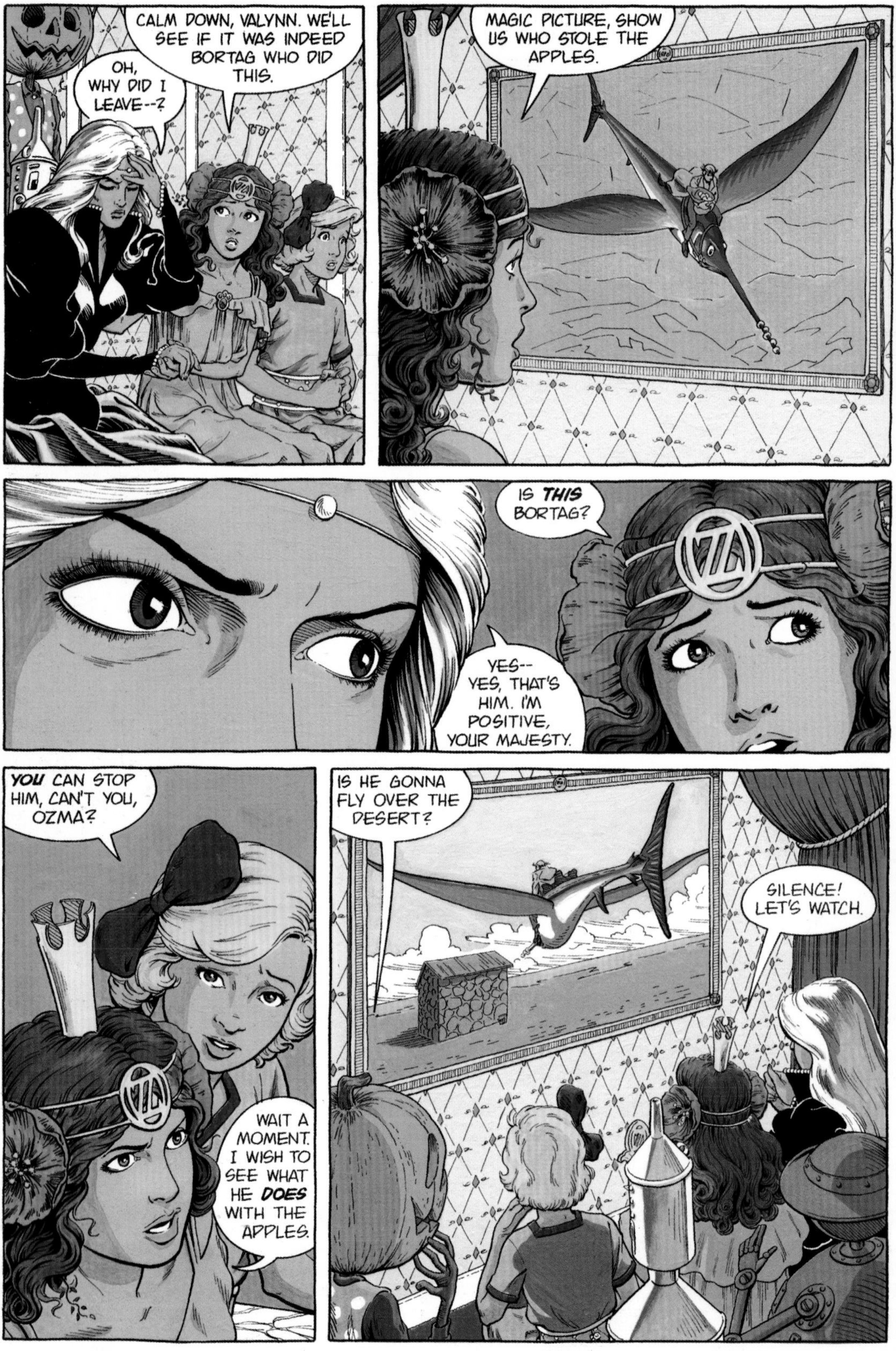
CALM DOWN, VALYNN. WE'LL SEE IF IT WAS INDEED BORTAG WHO DID THIS.
OH, WHY DID I LEAVE--?
MAGIC PICTURE, SHOW US WHO STOLE THE APPLES.
IS **THIS** BORTAG?
YES-- YES, THAT'S HIM. I'M POSITIVE, YOUR MAJESTY.
**YOU** CAN STOP HIM, CAN'T YOU, OZMA?
WAIT A MOMENT. I WISH TO SEE WHAT HE **DOES** WITH THE APPLES.
IS HE GONNA FLY OVER THE DESERT?
SILENCE! LET'S WATCH.

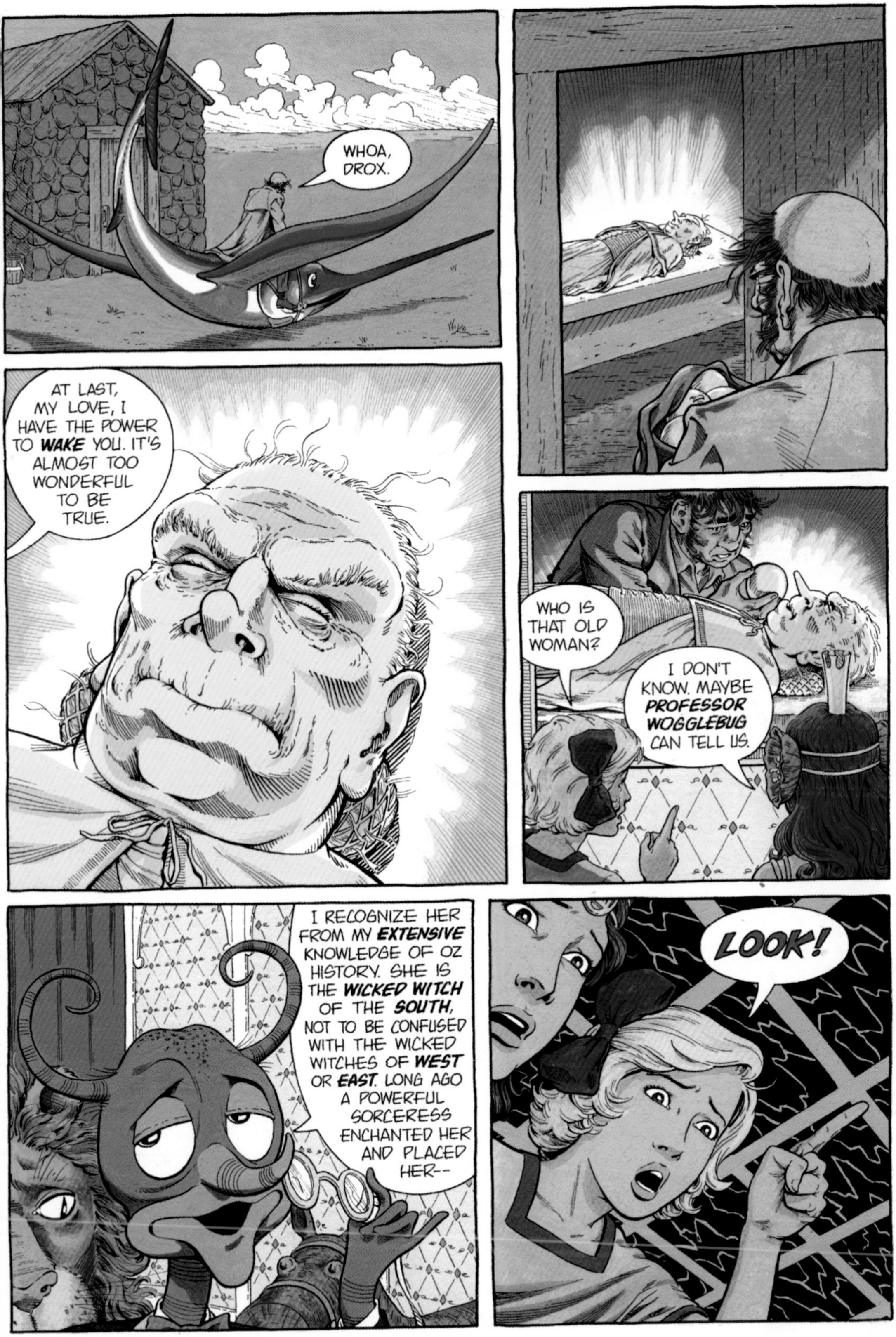
WHOA, DROX.
AT LAST, MY LOVE, I HAVE THE POWER TO WAKE YOU. IT'S ALMOST TOO WONDERFUL TO BE TRUE.
WHO IS THAT OLD WOMAN?
I DON'T KNOW. MAYBE PROFESSOR WOGGLEBUG CAN TELL US.
I RECOGNIZE HER FROM MY EXTENSIVE KNOWLEDGE OF OZ HISTORY. SHE IS THE WICKED WITCH OF THE SOUTH, NOT TO BE CONFUSED WITH THE WICKED WITCHES OF WEST OR EAST. LONG AGO A POWERFUL SORCERESS ENCHANTED HER AND PLACED HER--
LOOK!

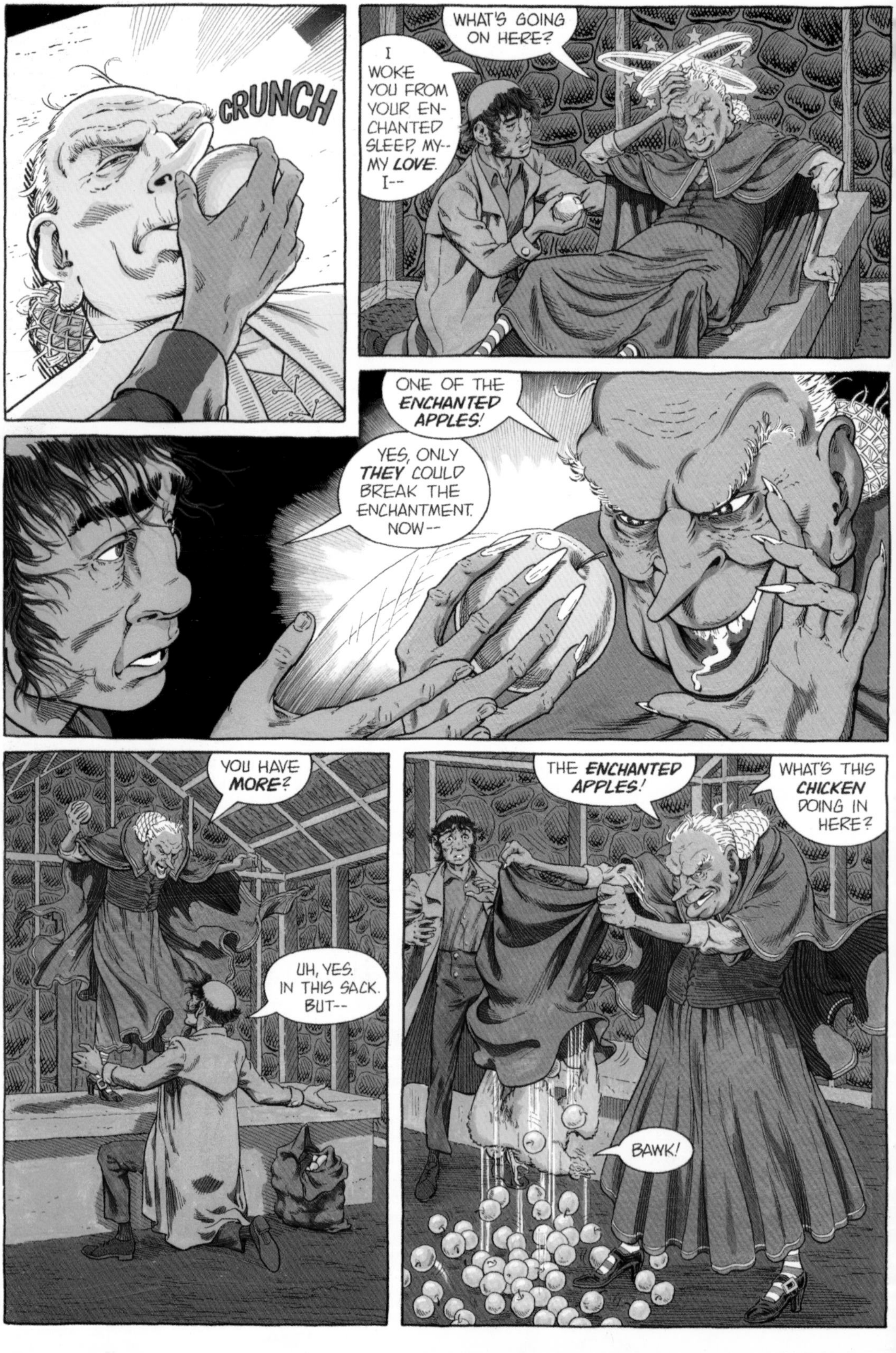
CRUNCH
WHAT'S GOING ON HERE?
I WOKE YOU FROM YOUR ENCHANTED SLEEP, MY-- MY LOVE. I--
ONE OF THE ENCHANTED APPLES!
YES, ONLY THEY COULD BREAK THE ENCHANTMENT. NOW--
YOU HAVE MORE?
UH, YES. IN THIS SACK. BUT--
THE ENCHANTED APPLES!
WHAT'S THIS CHICKEN DOING IN HERE?
BAWK!

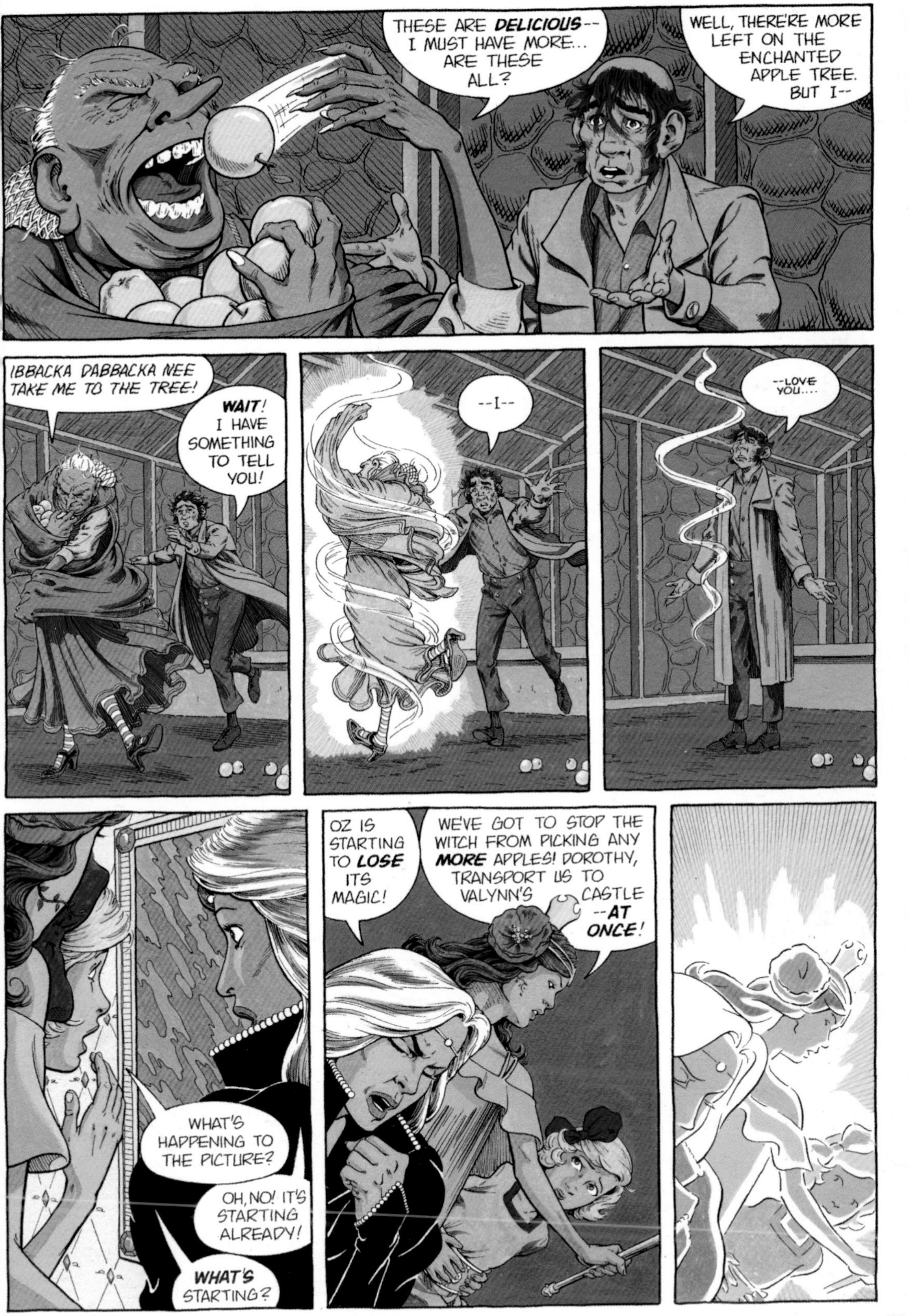
THESE ARE **DELICIOUS**-- I MUST HAVE MORE... ARE THESE ALL?
WELL, THERE'RE MORE LEFT ON THE ENCHANTED APPLE TREE. BUT I--
IBBACKA DABBACKA NEE TAKE ME TO THE TREE!
**WAIT**! I HAVE SOMETHING TO TELL YOU!
--I--
--LOVE YOU....
WHAT'S HAPPENING TO THE PICTURE?
OH, NO! IT'S STARTING ALREADY!
**WHAT'S** STARTING?
OZ IS STARTING TO **LOSE** ITS MAGIC!
WE'VE GOT TO STOP THE WITCH FROM PICKING ANY **MORE** APPLES! DOROTHY, TRANSPORT US TO VALYNN'S CASTLE --**AT ONCE**!

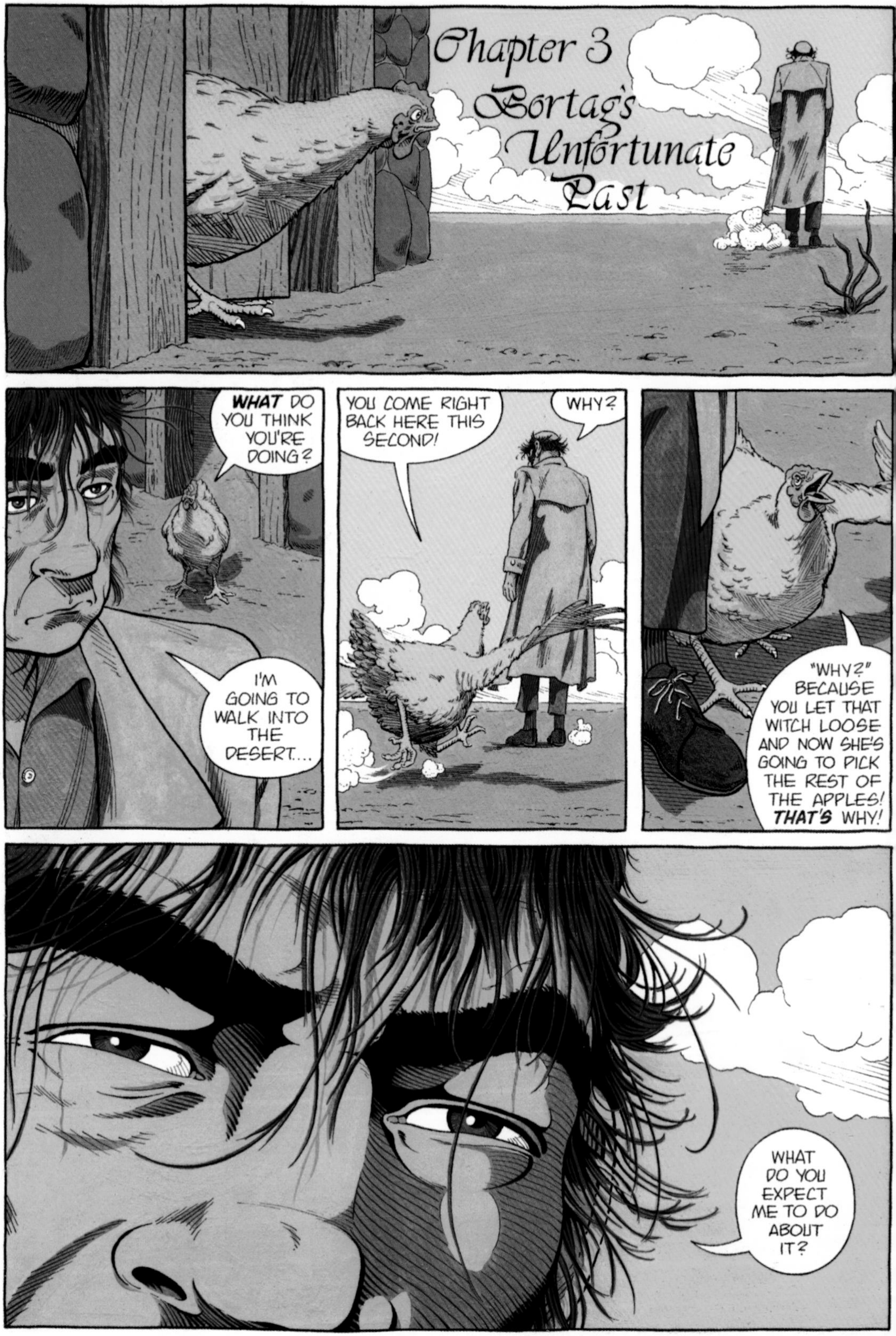
Chapter 3
Bortag's Unfortunate Past
WHAT DO YOU THINK YOU'RE DOING?
I'M GOING TO WALK INTO THE DESERT....
YOU COME RIGHT BACK HERE THIS SECOND!
WHY?
"WHY?" BECAUSE YOU LET THAT WITCH LOOSE AND NOW SHE'S GOING TO PICK THE REST OF THE APPLES! THAT'S WHY!
WHAT DO YOU EXPECT ME TO DO ABOUT IT?

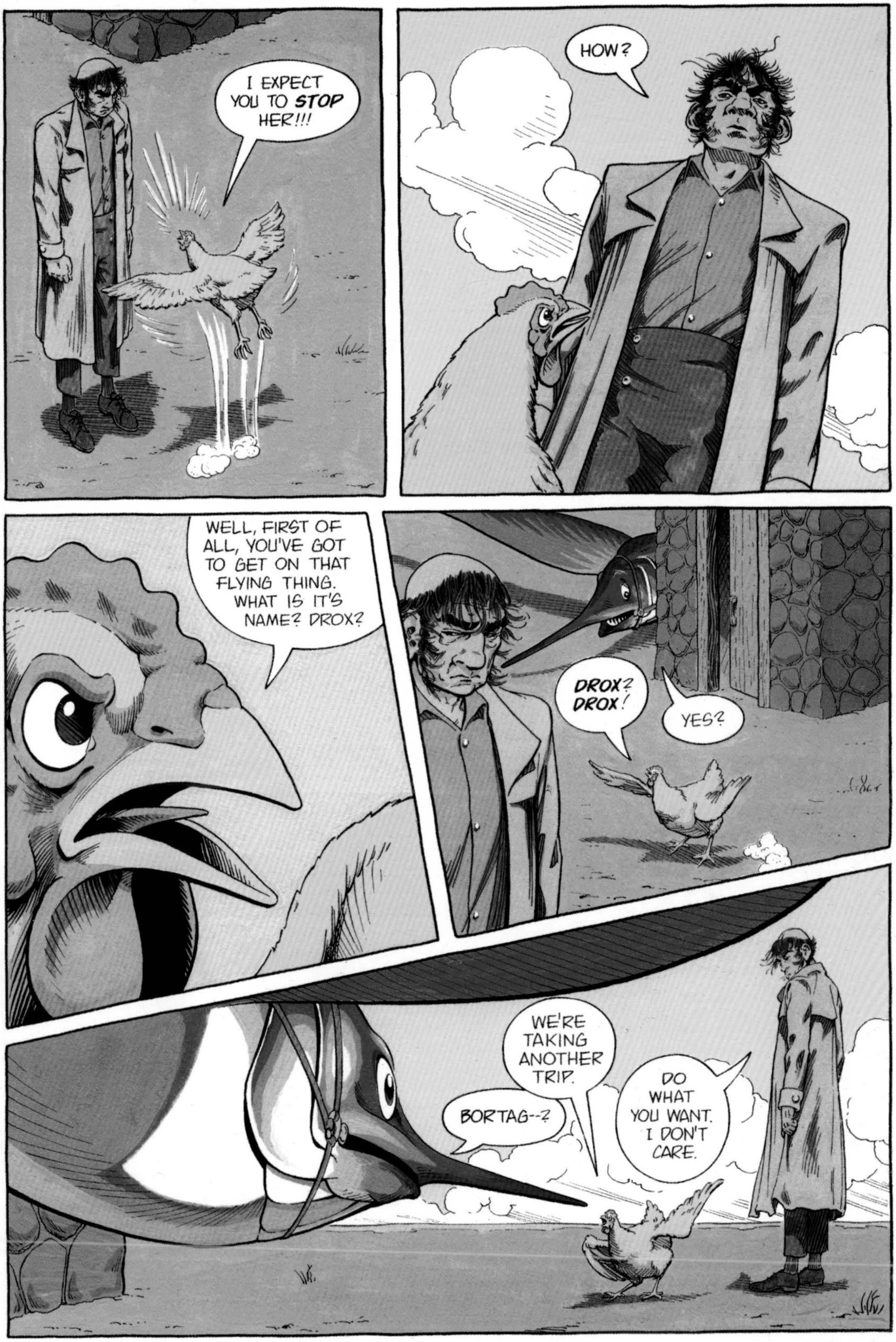
I EXPECT YOU TO **STOP** HER!!!
HOW?
WELL, FIRST OF ALL, YOU'VE GOT TO GET ON THAT FLYING THING. WHAT IS IT'S NAME? DROX?
**DROX? DROX!**
YES?
BORTAG--?
WE'RE TAKING ANOTHER TRIP.
DO WHAT YOU WANT. I DON'T CARE.

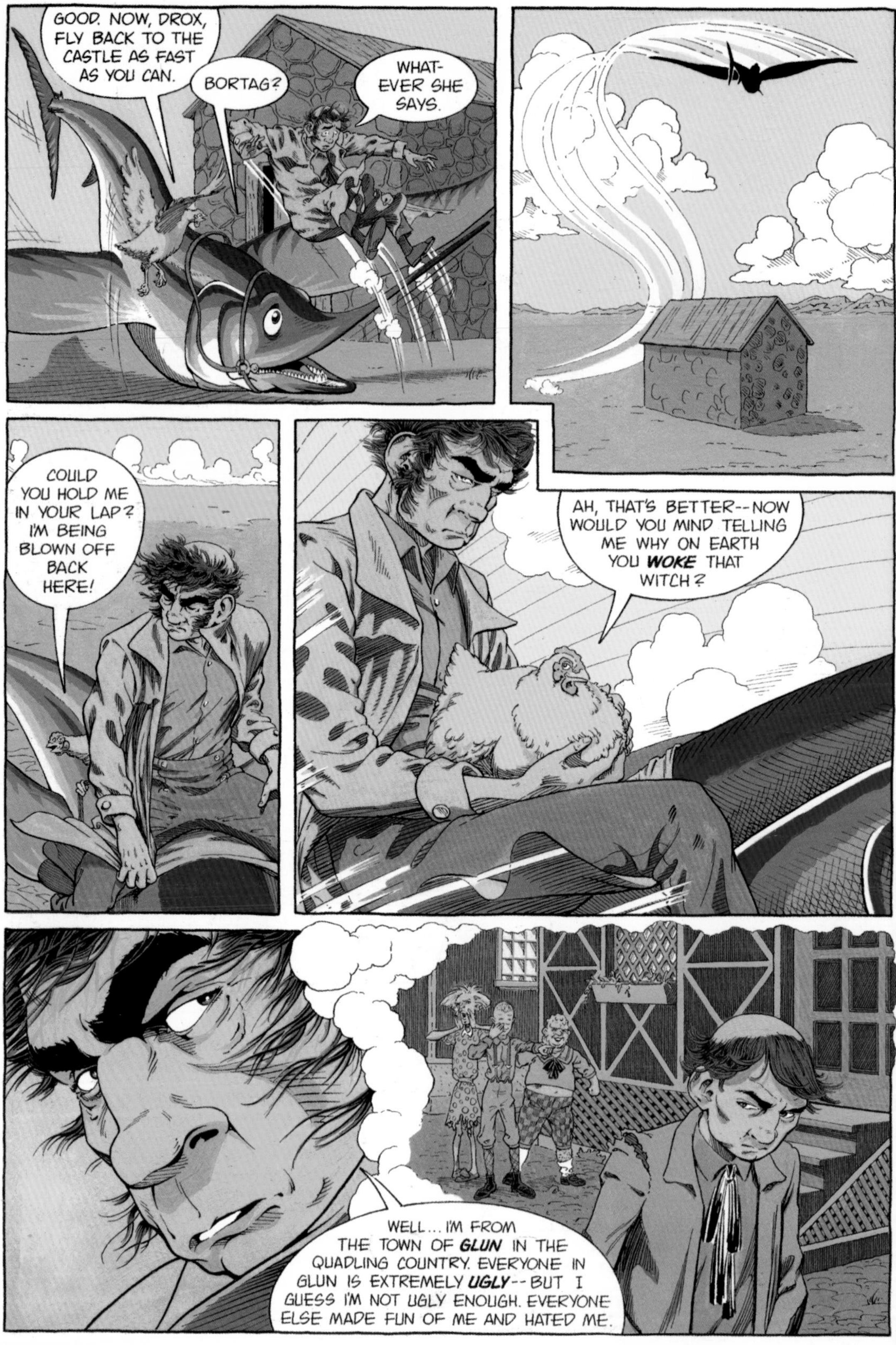
GOOD. NOW, DROX, FLY BACK TO THE CASTLE AS FAST AS YOU CAN.
BORTAG?
WHAT-EVER SHE SAYS.
COULD YOU HOLD ME IN YOUR LAP? I'M BEING BLOWN OFF BACK HERE!
AH, THAT'S BETTER--NOW WOULD YOU MIND TELLING ME WHY ON EARTH YOU **WOKE** THAT WITCH?
WELL... I'M FROM THE TOWN OF **GLUN** IN THE QUADLING COUNTRY. EVERYONE IN GLUN IS EXTREMELY ***UGLY***--BUT I GUESS I'M NOT UGLY ENOUGH. EVERYONE ELSE MADE FUN OF ME AND HATED ME.

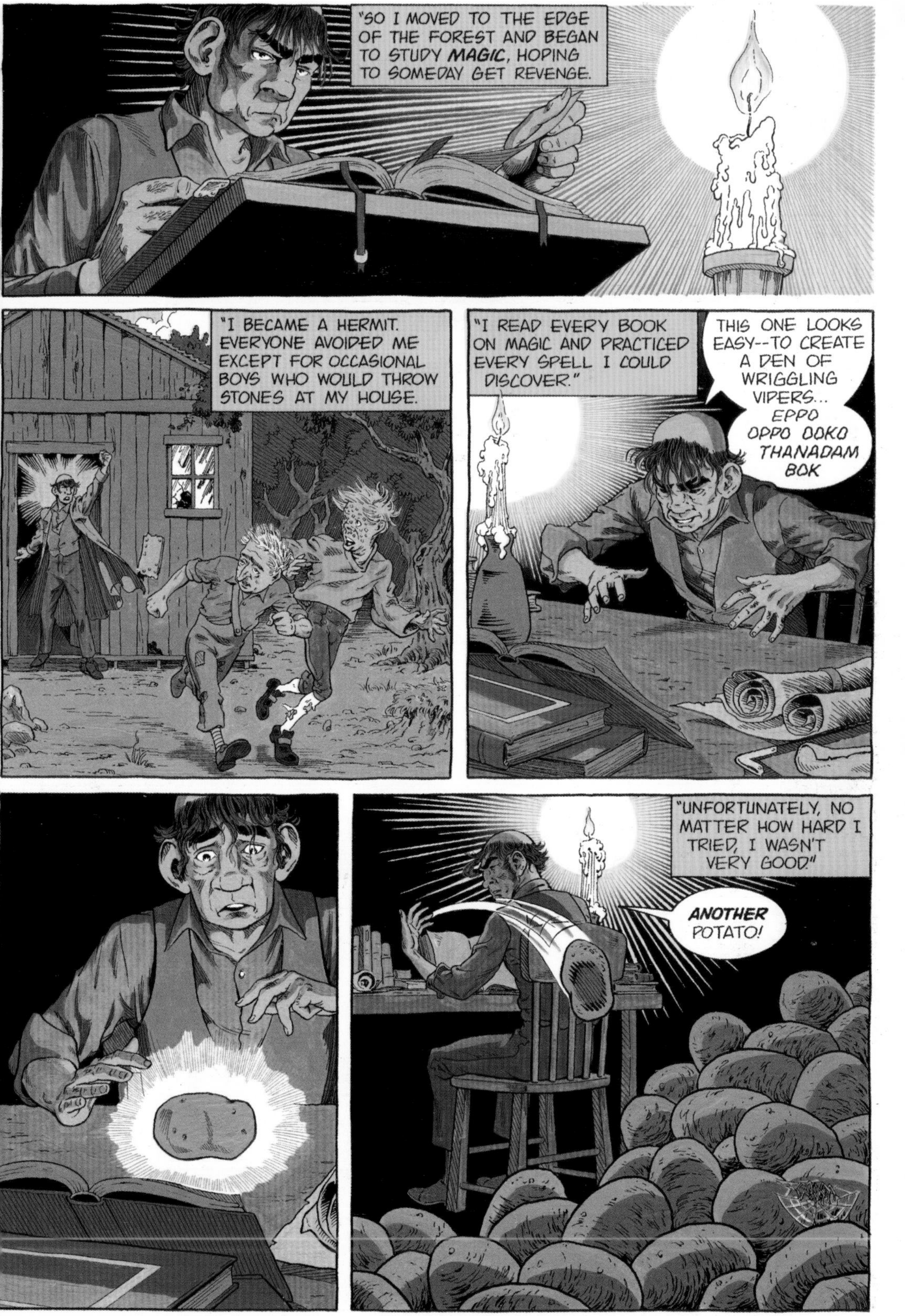
"SO I MOVED TO THE EDGE OF THE FOREST AND BEGAN TO STUDY *MAGIC*, HOPING TO SOMEDAY GET REVENGE.
"I BECAME A HERMIT. EVERYONE AVOIDED ME EXCEPT FOR OCCASIONAL BOYS WHO WOULD THROW STONES AT MY HOUSE.
"I READ EVERY BOOK ON MAGIC AND PRACTICED EVERY SPELL I COULD DISCOVER."
THIS ONE LOOKS EASY--TO CREATE A DEN OF WRIGGLING VIPERS... *EPPO OPPO OOKO THANADAM BOK*
"UNFORTUNATELY, NO MATTER HOW HARD I TRIED, I WASN'T VERY GOOD."
***ANOTHER*** POTATO!

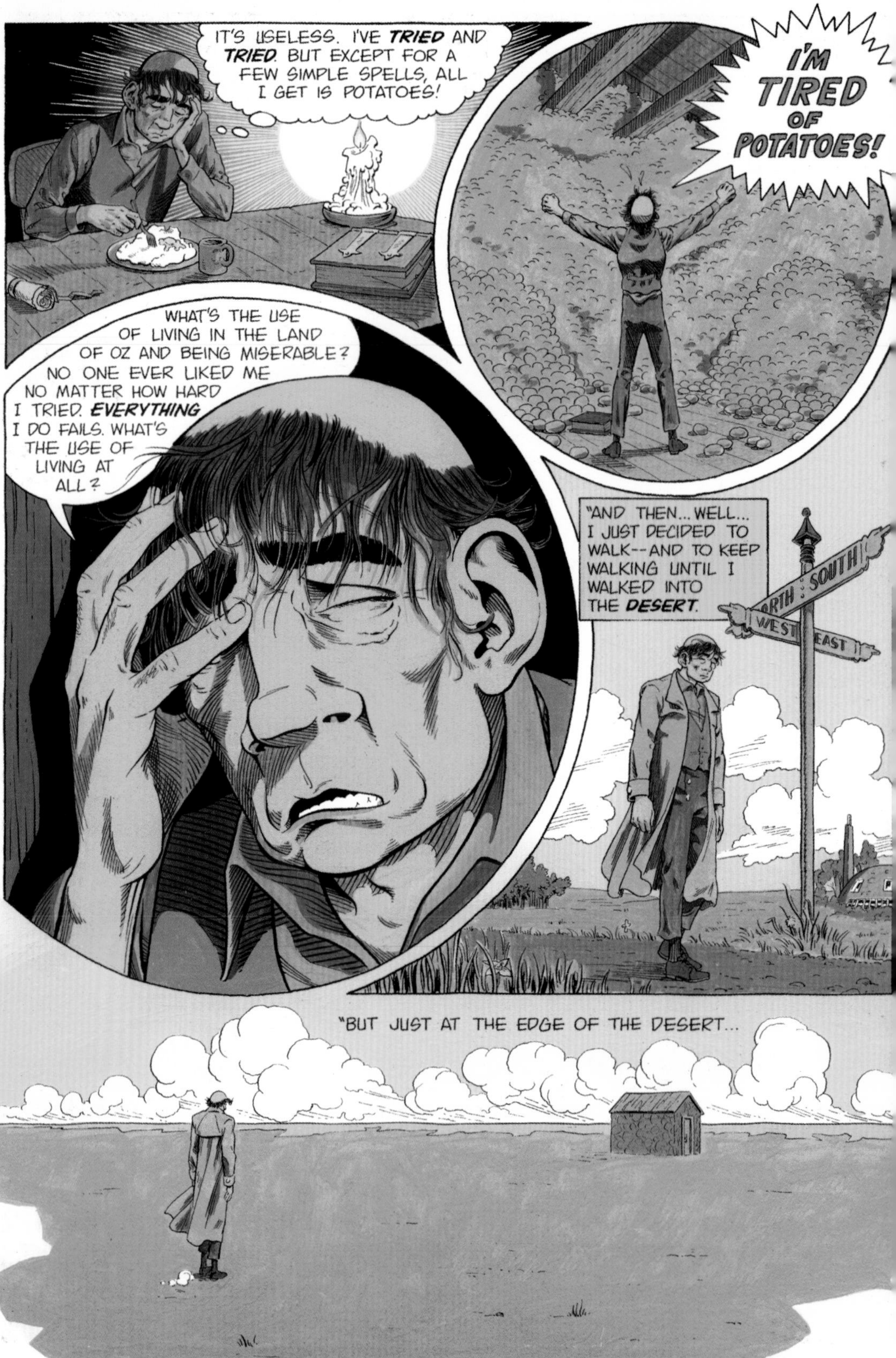
IT'S USELESS. I'VE **TRIED** AND **TRIED**. BUT EXCEPT FOR A FEW SIMPLE SPELLS, ALL I GET IS POTATOES!
I'M TIRED OF POTATOES!
WHAT'S THE USE OF LIVING IN THE LAND OF OZ AND BEING MISERABLE? NO ONE EVER LIKED ME NO MATTER HOW HARD I TRIED. **EVERYTHING** I DO FAILS. WHAT'S THE USE OF LIVING AT ALL?
"AND THEN... WELL... I JUST DECIDED TO WALK--AND TO KEEP WALKING UNTIL I WALKED INTO THE **DESERT**.
SOUTH
WEST
EAST
"BUT JUST AT THE EDGE OF THE DESERT...

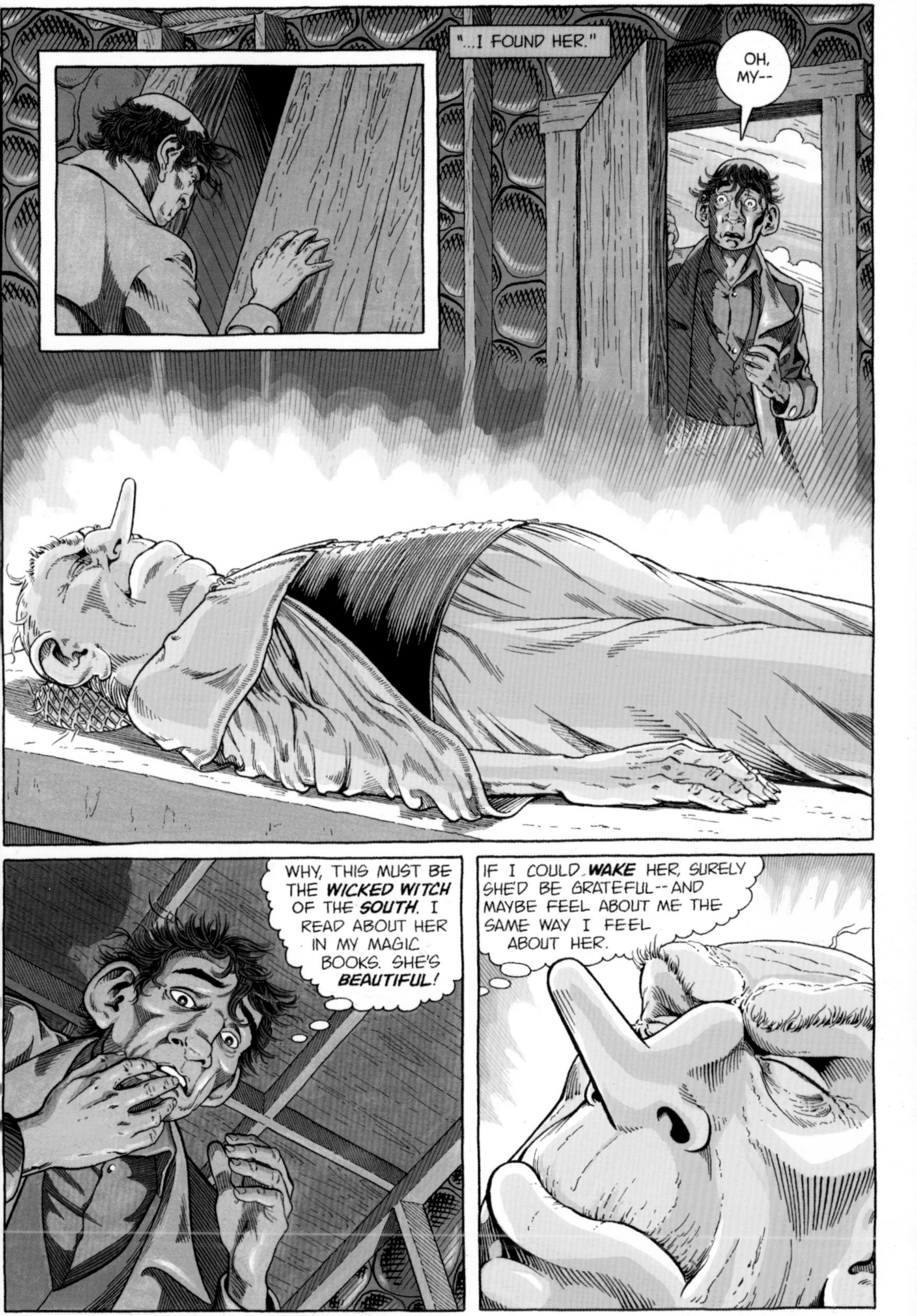
"...I FOUND HER."
OH, MY--
WHY, THIS MUST BE THE WICKED WITCH OF THE SOUTH. I READ ABOUT HER IN MY MAGIC BOOKS. SHE'S BEAUTIFUL!
IF I COULD WAKE HER, SURELY SHE'D BE GRATEFUL--AND MAYBE FEEL ABOUT ME THE SAME WAY I FEEL ABOUT HER.

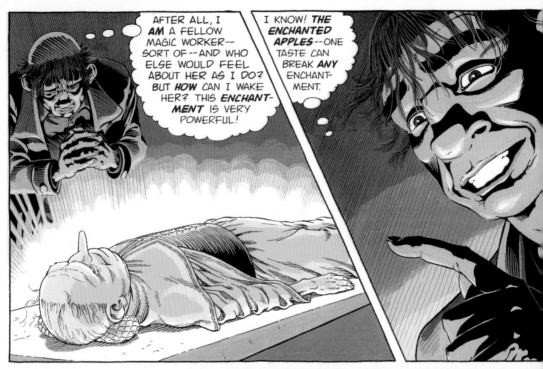

AFTER ALL, I *AM* A FELLOW MAGIC WORKER-- SORT OF -- AND WHO ELSE WOULD FEEL ABOUT HER AS I DO? BUT *HOW* CAN I WAKE HER? THIS *ENCHANTMENT* IS VERY POWERFUL!

I KNOW! *THE ENCHANTED APPLES*--ONE TASTE CAN BREAK *ANY* ENCHANTMENT.

"SO AGAIN I SET OUT, BUT THIS TIME I WAS *DETERMINED* NOT TO FAIL. I HAD TO GET AN APPLE, THOUGH I KNEW THEY WERE FORBIDDEN.

"I GOT INTO THE CASTLE WITHOUT MUCH TROUBLE...

"...BUT I DIDN'T GET AN APPLE.

"HOPING TO **SCARE** THEM INTO GIVING ME AN APPLE, I THREATENED TO USE MY MAGIC AGAINST THEM. I DIDN'T HAVE MUCH HOPE--A MAGICAL ATTACK WAS BEYOND MY FEW ABILITIES. WHAT COULD I DO, THROW **POTATOES** AT THEM?"

"I SCARED THEM, ALL RIGHT, BUT NOT AS I HAD INTENDED."

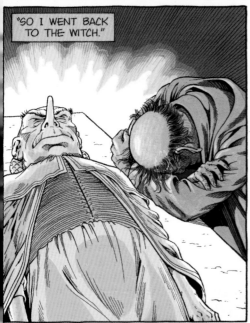

"SO I WENT BACK TO THE WITCH."

SOMEDAY THE APPLES WILL COME BACK. I DON'T KNOW WHEN, BUT I'LL WAIT--AND WHEN THEY DO, **NOTHING** WILL STOP ME FROM TAKING ONE.

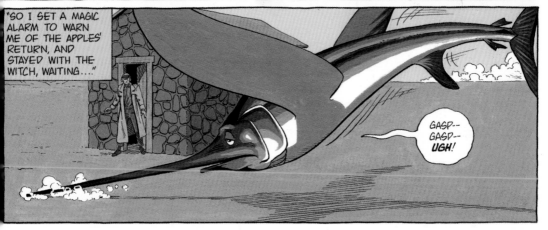

"SO I SET A MAGIC ALARM TO WARN ME OF THE APPLES' RETURN, AND STAYED WITH THE WITCH, WAITING...."

GASP-- GASP-- **UGH!**

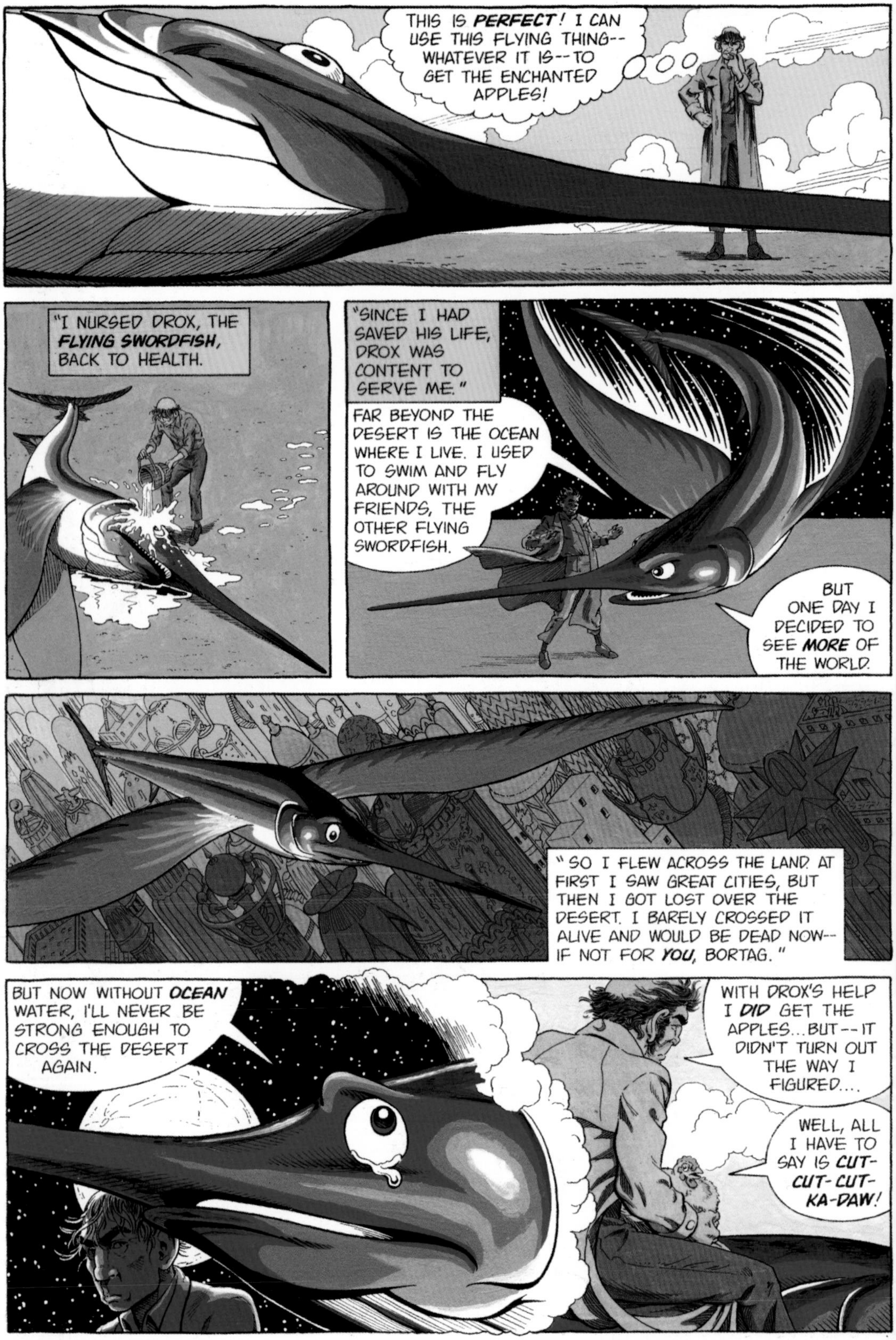

THIS IS PERFECT! I CAN USE THIS FLYING THING-- WHATEVER IT IS--TO GET THE ENCHANTED APPLES!
"I NURSED DROX, THE FLYING SWORDFISH, BACK TO HEALTH.
"SINCE I HAD SAVED HIS LIFE, DROX WAS CONTENT TO SERVE ME."
FAR BEYOND THE DESERT IS THE OCEAN WHERE I LIVE. I USED TO SWIM AND FLY AROUND WITH MY FRIENDS, THE OTHER FLYING SWORDFISH.
BUT ONE DAY I DECIDED TO SEE MORE OF THE WORLD.
"SO I FLEW ACROSS THE LAND. AT FIRST I SAW GREAT CITIES, BUT THEN I GOT LOST OVER THE DESERT. I BARELY CROSSED IT ALIVE AND WOULD BE DEAD NOW-- IF NOT FOR YOU, BORTAG."
BUT NOW WITHOUT OCEAN WATER, I'LL NEVER BE STRONG ENOUGH TO CROSS THE DESERT AGAIN.
WITH DROX'S HELP I DID GET THE APPLES...BUT--IT DIDN'T TURN OUT THE WAY I FIGURED....
WELL, ALL I HAVE TO SAY IS CUT-CUT-CUT-KA-DAW!

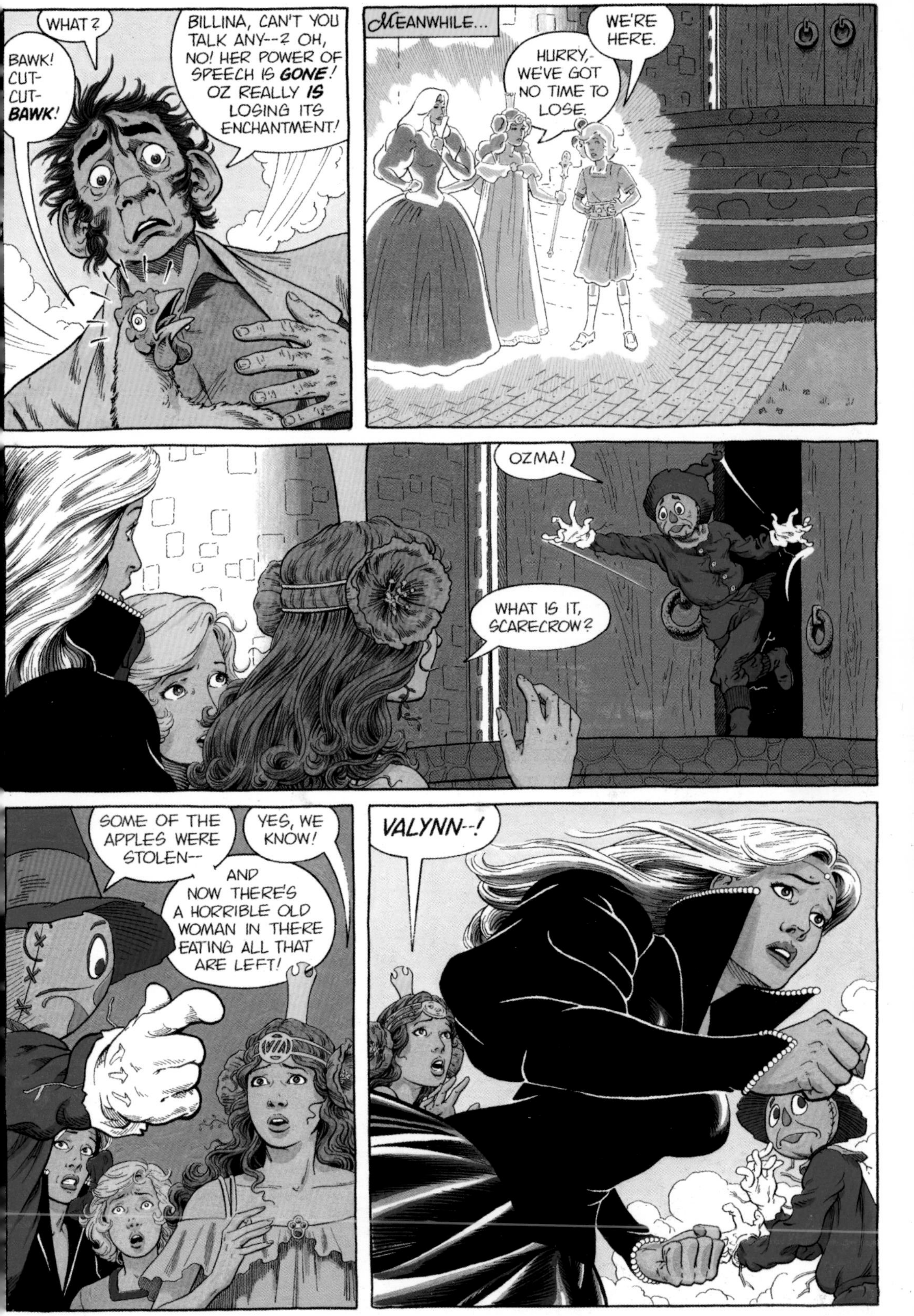
WHAT?
BAWK! CUT-CUT-BAWK!
BILLINA, CAN'T YOU TALK ANY--? OH, NO! HER POWER OF SPEECH IS **GONE**! OZ REALLY **IS** LOSING ITS ENCHANTMENT!
MEANWHILE...
HURRY, WE'VE GOT NO TIME TO LOSE.
WE'RE HERE.
OZMA!
WHAT IS IT, SCARECROW?
SOME OF THE APPLES WERE STOLEN--
YES, WE KNOW!
AND NOW THERE'S A HORRIBLE OLD WOMAN IN THERE EATING ALL THAT ARE LEFT!
VALYNN--!

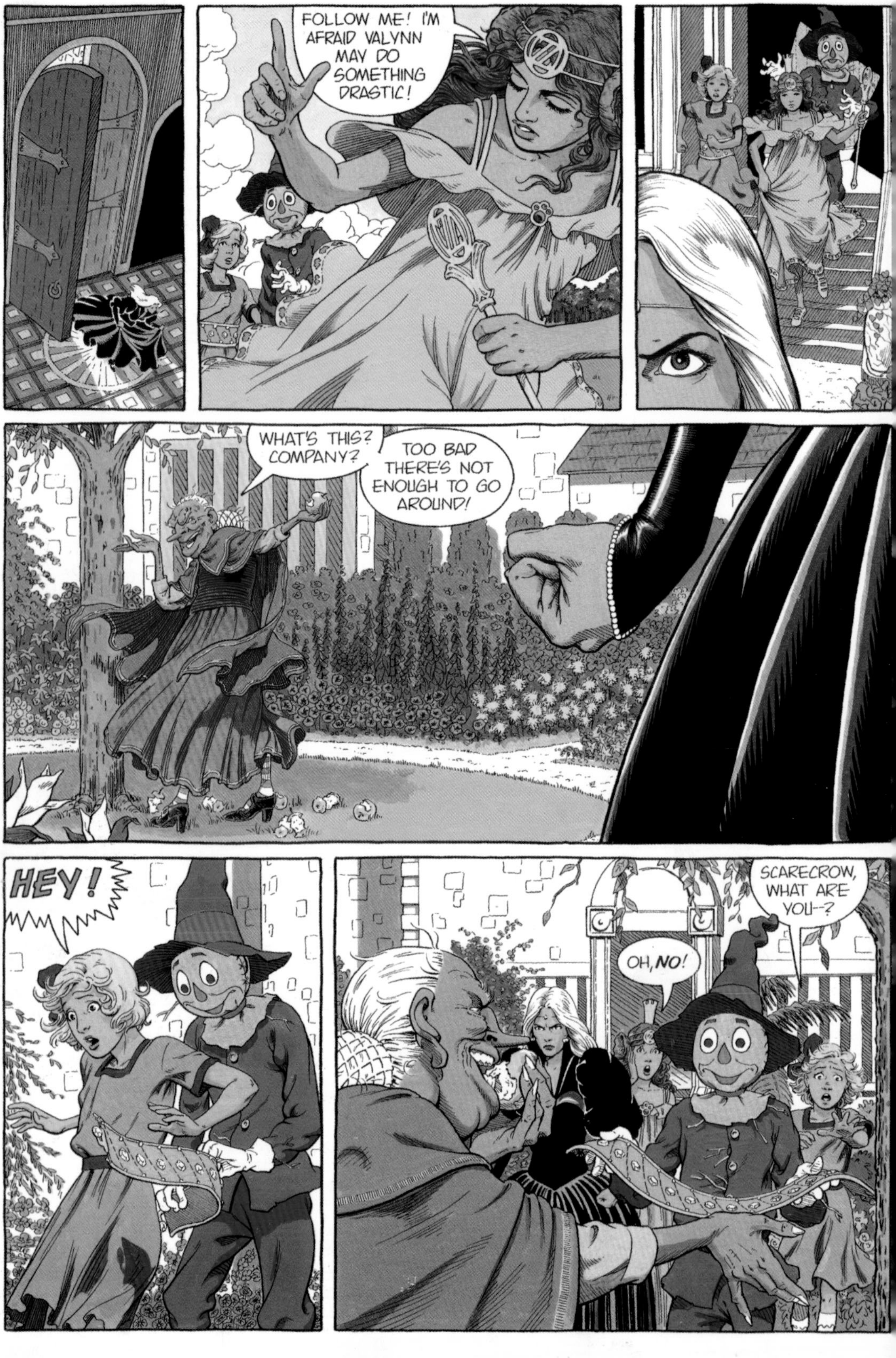
FOLLOW ME! I'M AFRAID VALYNN MAY DO SOMETHING DRASTIC!
WHAT'S THIS? COMPANY?
TOO BAD THERE'S NOT ENOUGH TO GO AROUND!
HEY!
SCARECROW, WHAT ARE YOU--?
OH, NO!

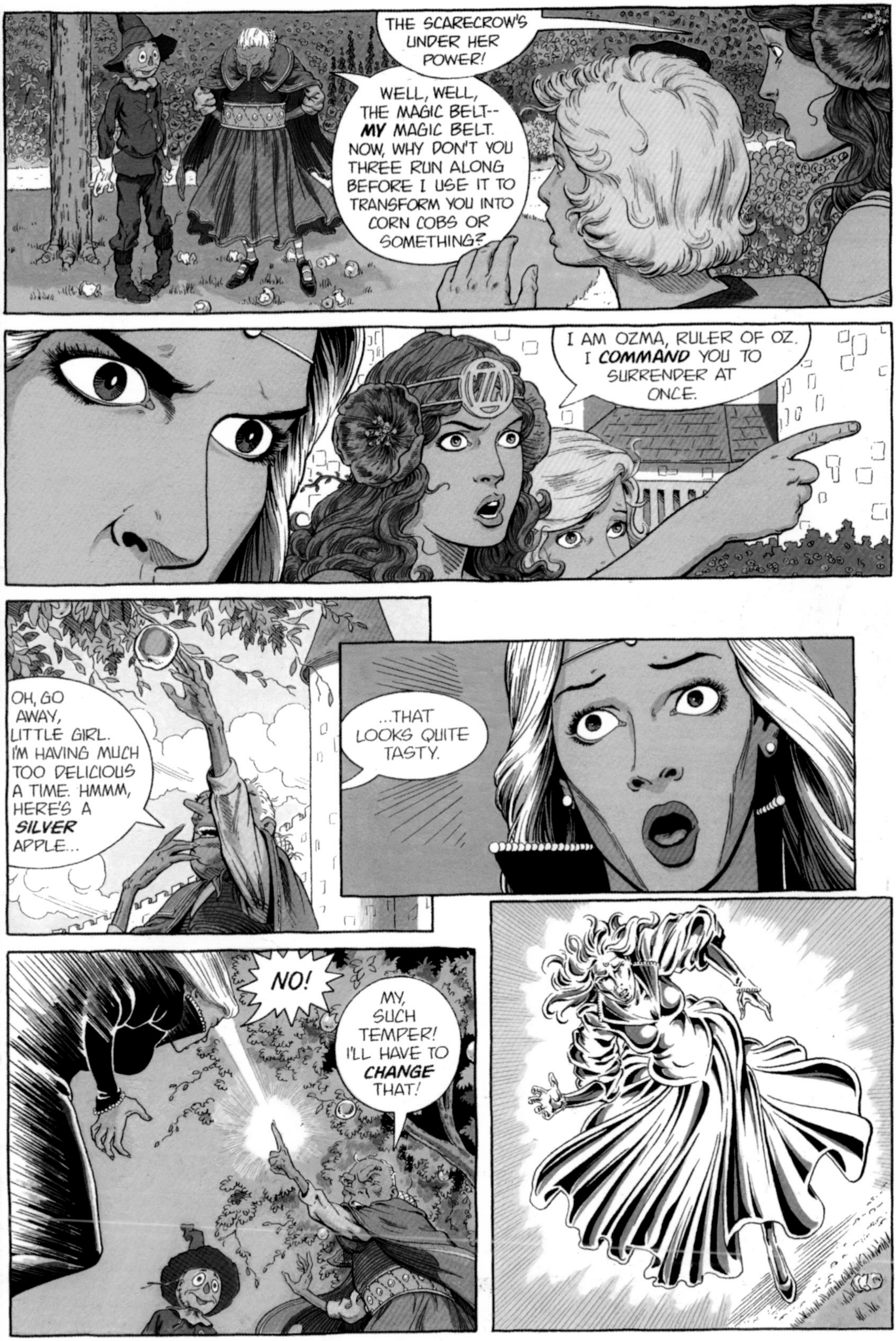
THE SCARECROW'S UNDER HER POWER!
WELL, WELL, THE MAGIC BELT-- **MY** MAGIC BELT. NOW, WHY DON'T YOU THREE RUN ALONG BEFORE I USE IT TO TRANSFORM YOU INTO CORN COBS OR SOMETHING?
I AM OZMA, RULER OF OZ. I **COMMAND** YOU TO SURRENDER AT ONCE.
OH, GO AWAY, LITTLE GIRL. I'M HAVING MUCH TOO DELICIOUS A TIME. HMMM, HERE'S A ***SILVER*** APPLE...
...THAT LOOKS QUITE TASTY.
NO!
MY, SUCH TEMPER! I'LL HAVE TO ***CHANGE*** THAT!

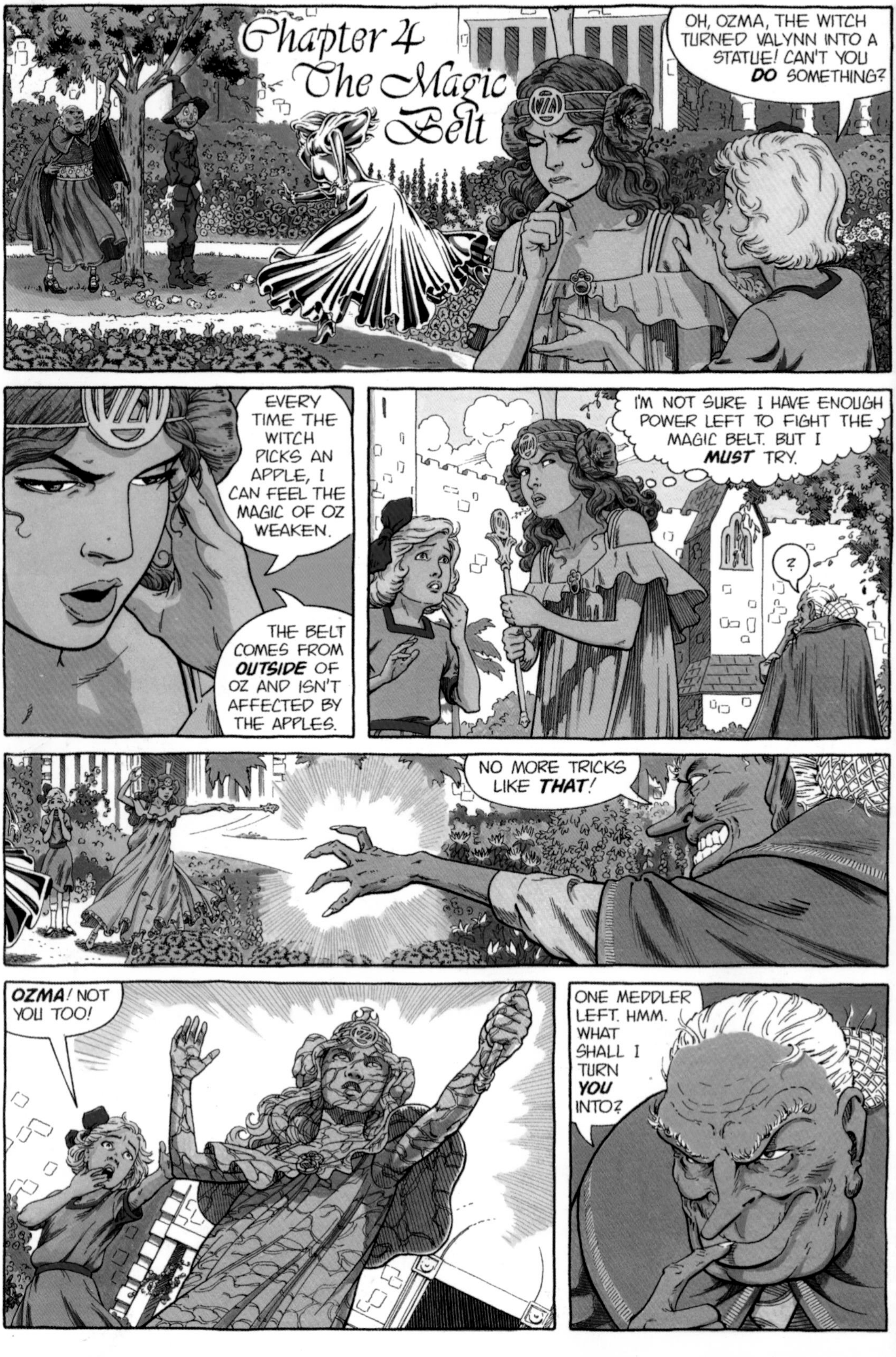
Chapter 4
The Magic Belt
OH, OZMA, THE WITCH TURNED VALYNN INTO A STATUE! CAN'T YOU DO SOMETHING?
EVERY TIME THE WITCH PICKS AN APPLE, I CAN FEEL THE MAGIC OF OZ WEAKEN.
THE BELT COMES FROM OUTSIDE OF OZ AND ISN'T AFFECTED BY THE APPLES.
I'M NOT SURE I HAVE ENOUGH POWER LEFT TO FIGHT THE MAGIC BELT. BUT I MUST TRY.
?
NO MORE TRICKS LIKE THAT!
OZMA! NOT YOU TOO!
ONE MEDDLER LEFT. HMM. WHAT SHALL I TURN YOU INTO?

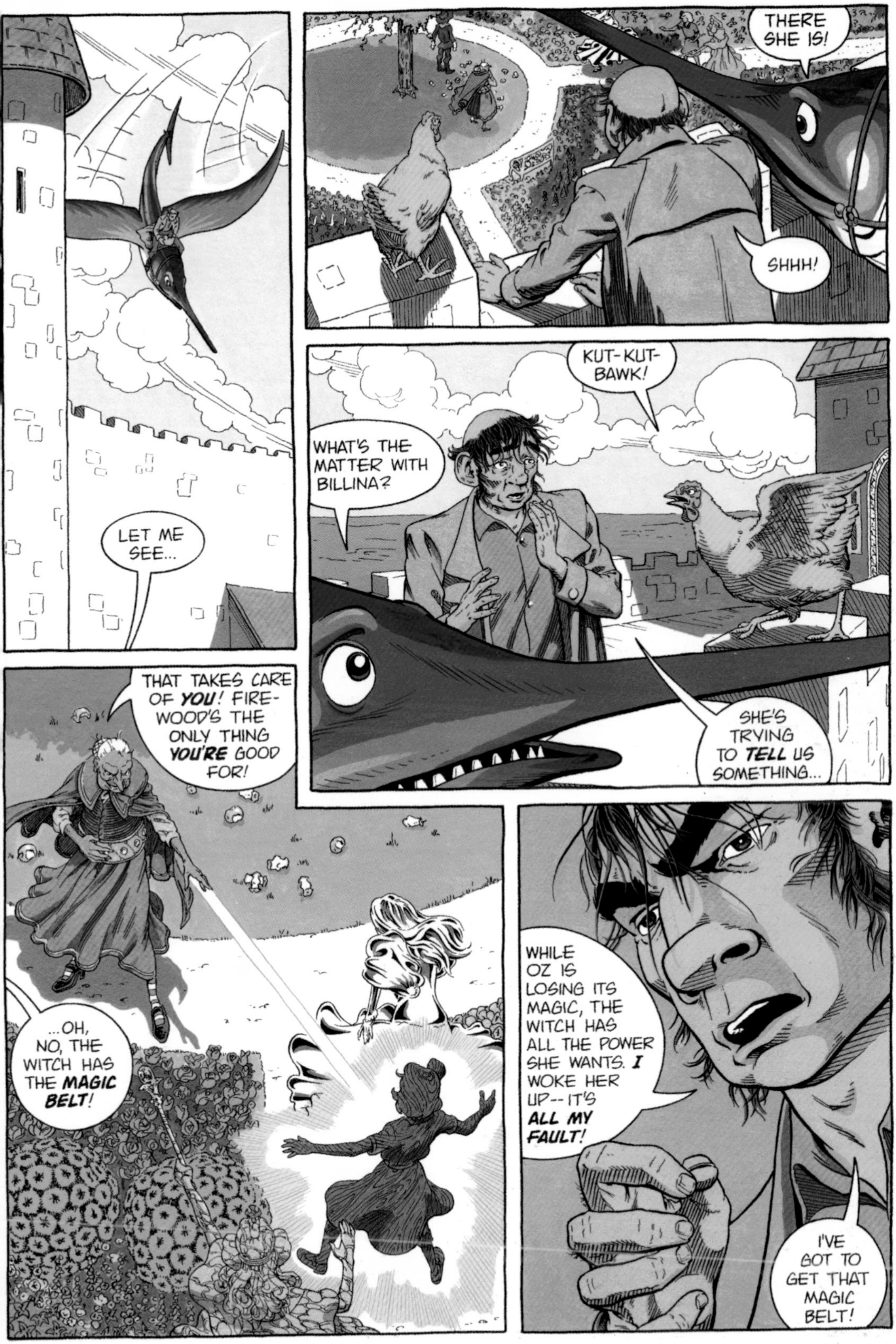
LET ME SEE...
THERE SHE IS!
SHHH!
KUT-KUT-BAWK!
WHAT'S THE MATTER WITH BILLINA?
SHE'S TRYING TO **TELL** US SOMETHING...
THAT TAKES CARE OF ***YOU***! FIRE-WOOD'S THE ONLY THING ***YOU'RE*** GOOD FOR!
...OH, NO, THE WITCH HAS THE ***MAGIC BELT***!
WHILE OZ IS LOSING ITS MAGIC, THE WITCH HAS ALL THE POWER SHE WANTS. ***I*** WOKE HER UP-- IT'S ***ALL MY FAULT***!
I'VE GOT TO GET THAT MAGIC BELT!

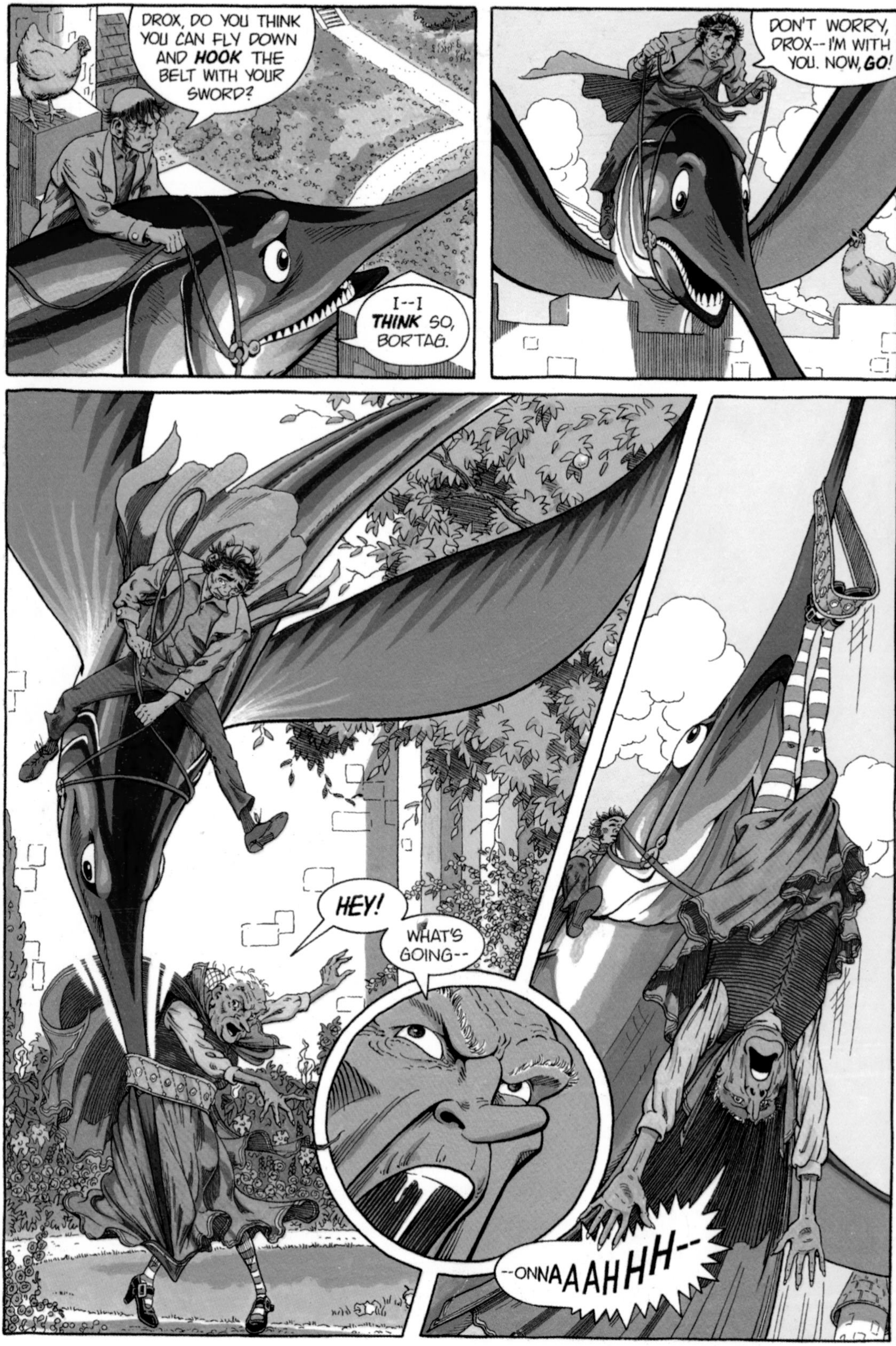
DROX, DO YOU THINK YOU CAN FLY DOWN AND HOOK THE BELT WITH YOUR SWORD?
I--I THINK SO, BORTAG.
DON'T WORRY, DROX--I'M WITH YOU. NOW, GO!
HEY!
WHAT'S GOING--
--ONNAAAHHH--

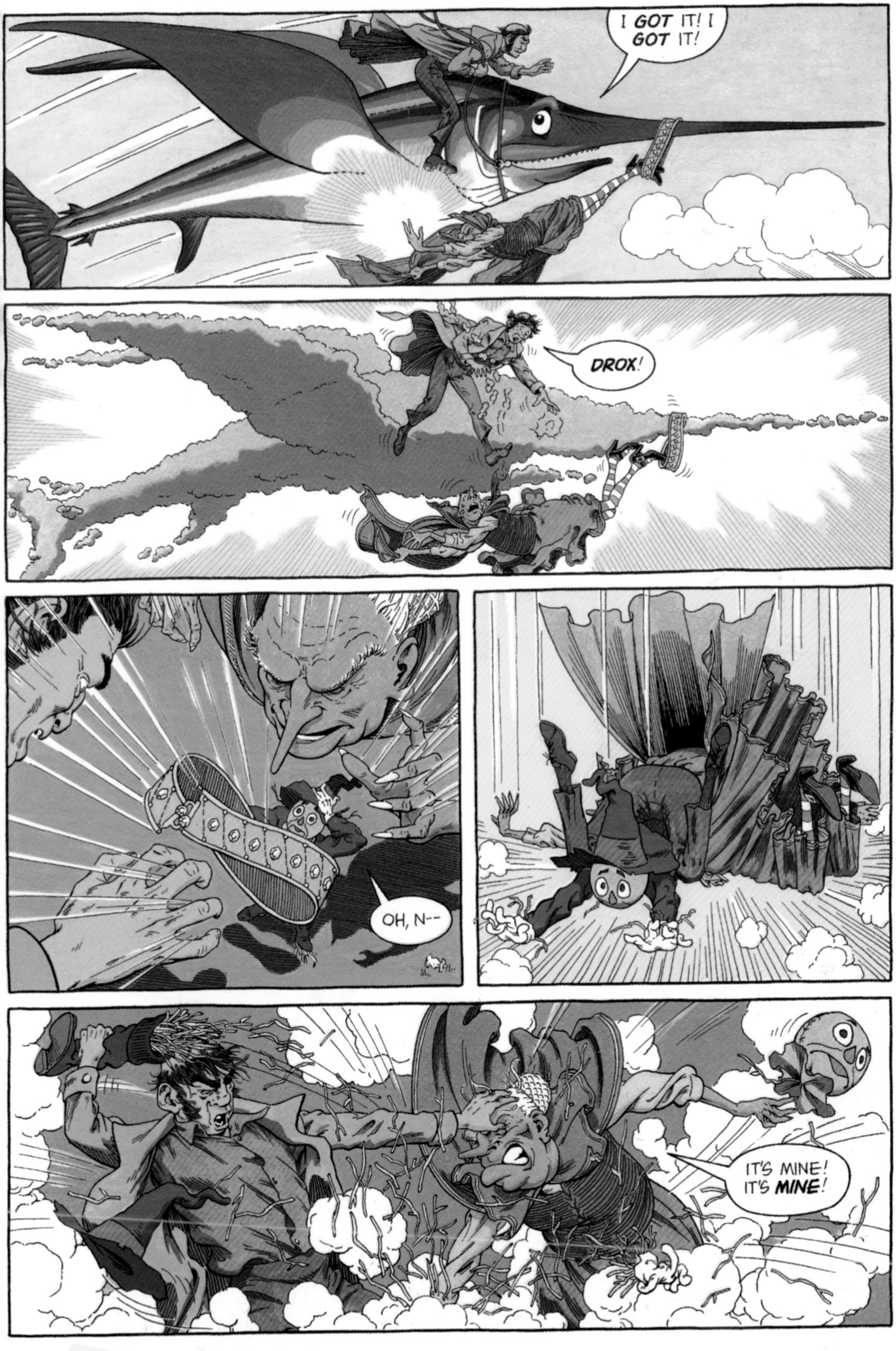
I **GOT** IT! I **GOT** IT!
***DROX***!
OH, N--
IT'S MINE! IT'S ***MINE***!

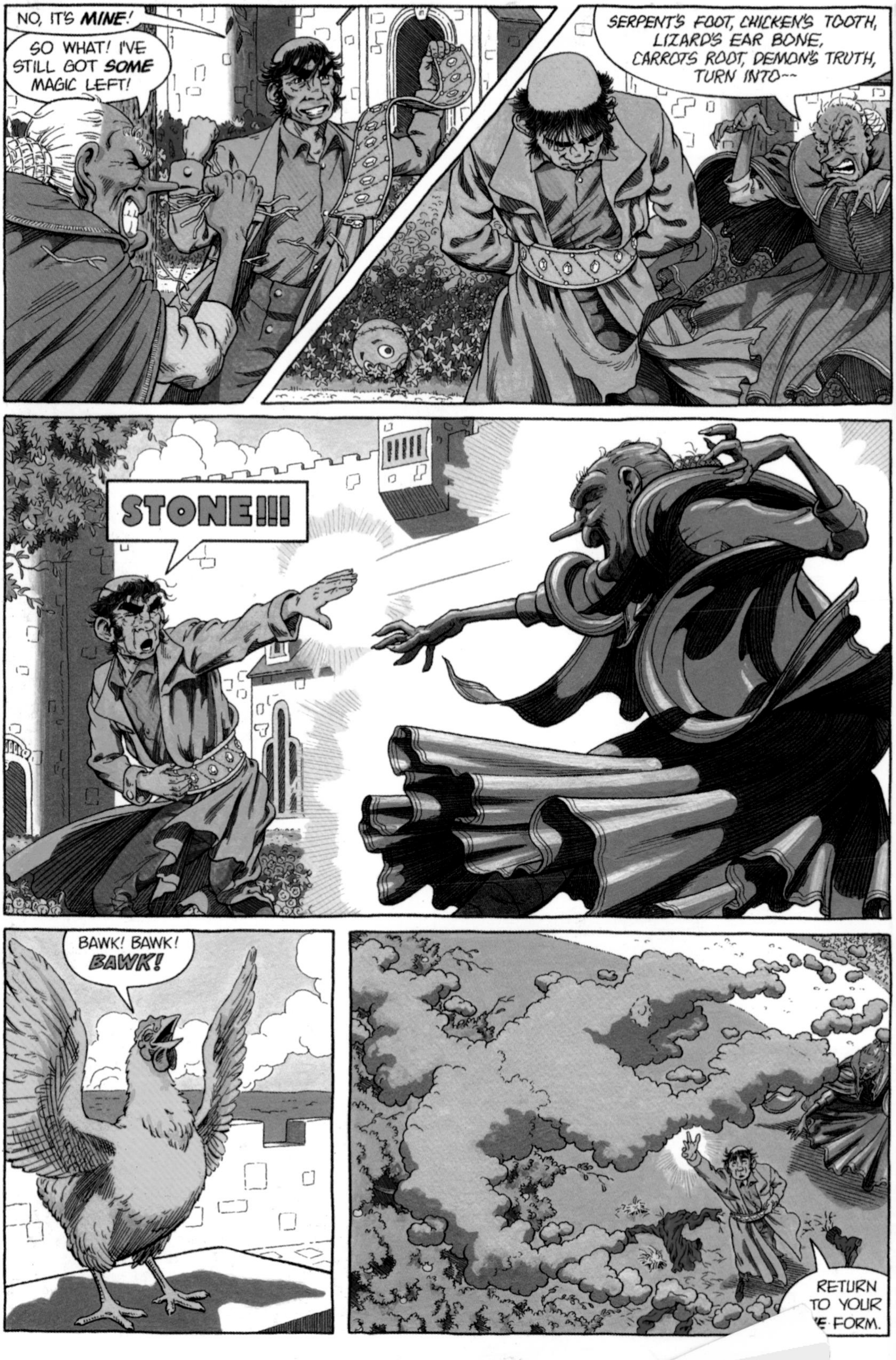
NO, IT'S **MINE**!
SO WHAT! I'VE STILL GOT **SOME** MAGIC LEFT!
SERPENT'S FOOT, CHICKEN'S TOOTH, LIZARD'S EAR BONE, CARROTS ROOT, DEMON'S TRUTH, TURN INTO~~
STONE!!!
BAWK! BAWK! **BAWK!**
RETURN TO YOUR E FORM.

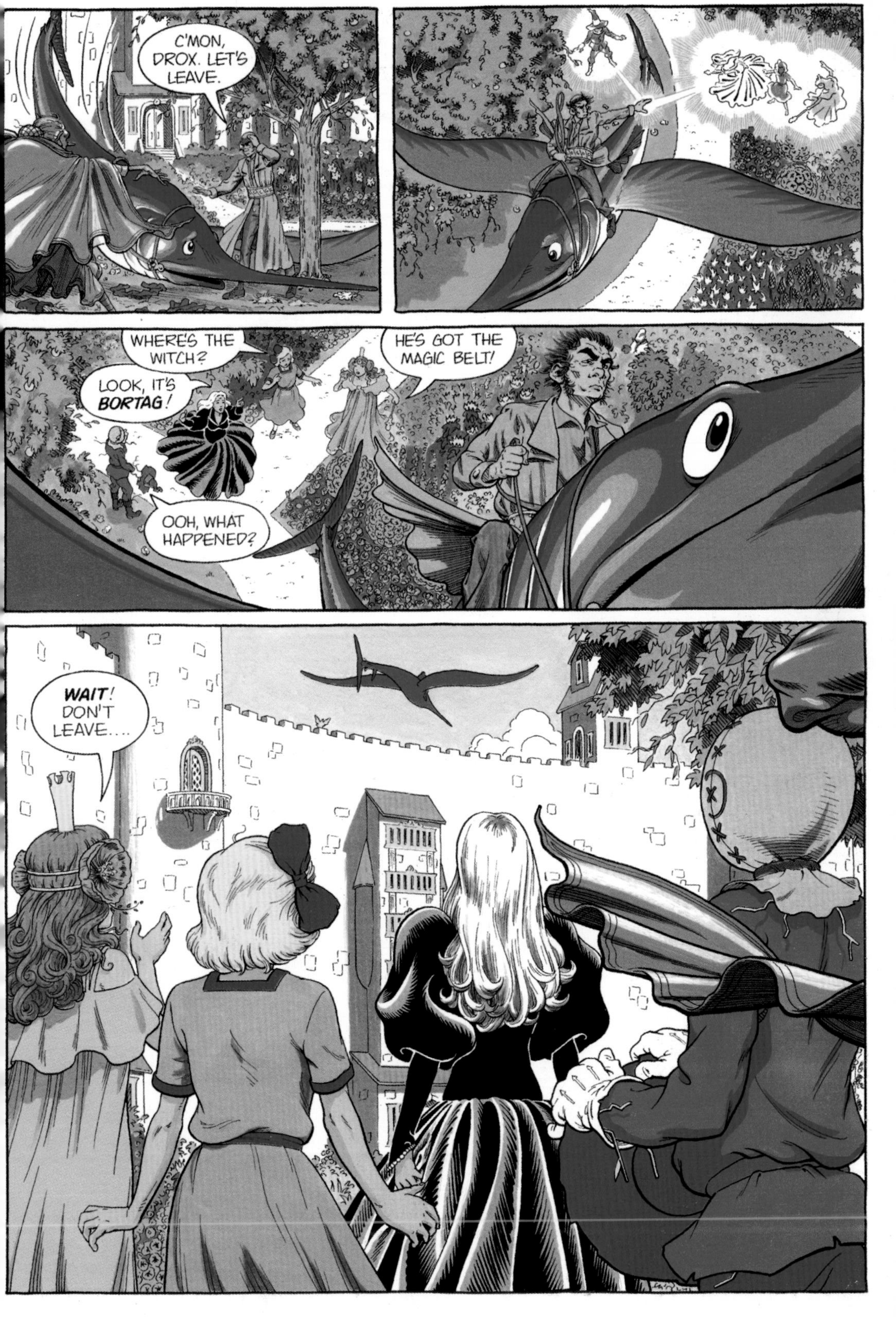
C'MON, DROX. LET'S LEAVE.
WHERE'S THE WITCH?
LOOK, IT'S **BORTAG**!
HE'S GOT THE MAGIC BELT!
OOH, WHAT HAPPENED?
**WAIT**! DON'T LEAVE....

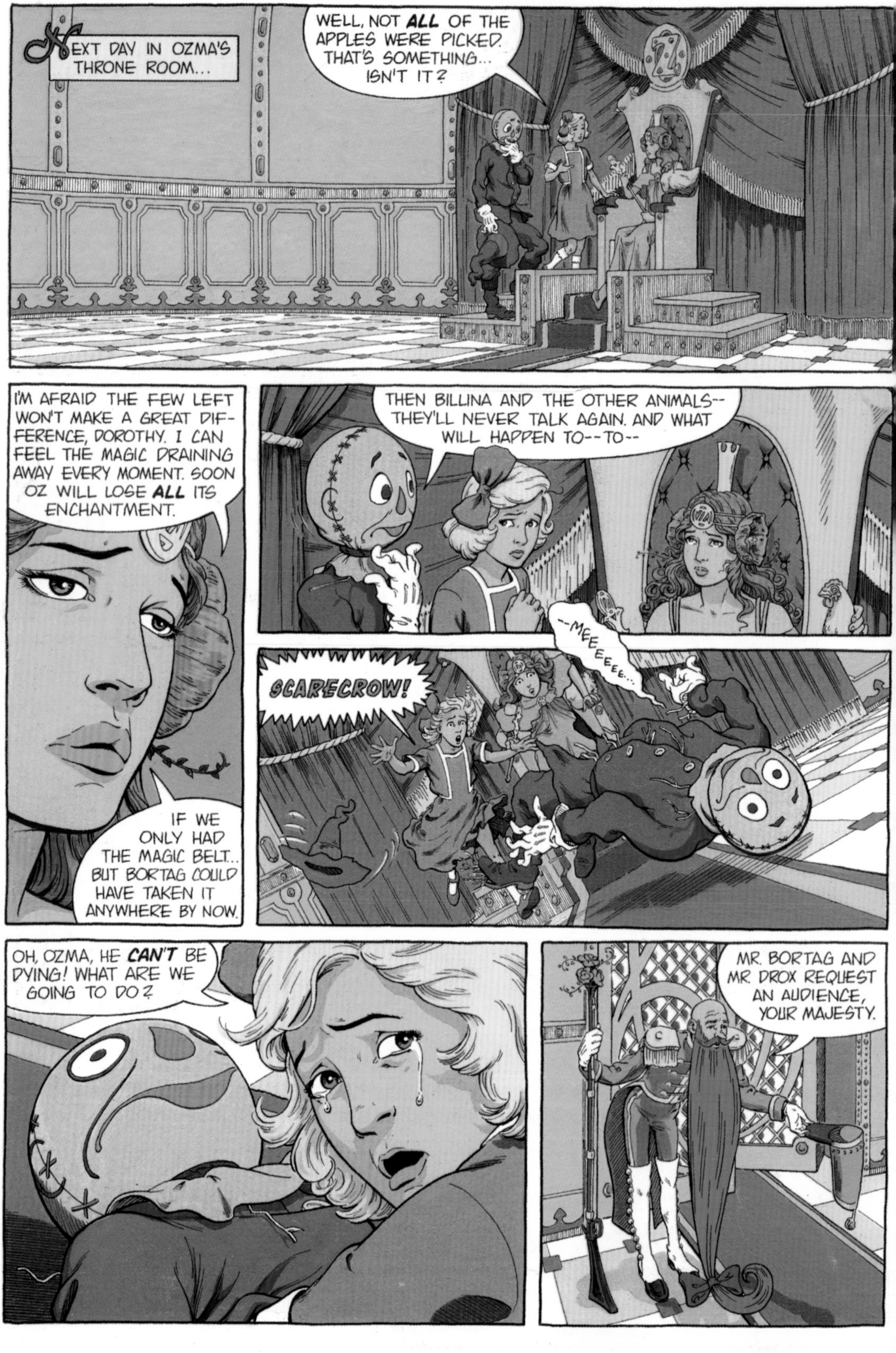
NEXT DAY IN OZMA'S THRONE ROOM...
WELL, NOT ALL OF THE APPLES WERE PICKED. THAT'S SOMETHING... ISN'T IT?
I'M AFRAID THE FEW LEFT WON'T MAKE A GREAT DIFFERENCE, DOROTHY. I CAN FEEL THE MAGIC DRAINING AWAY EVERY MOMENT. SOON OZ WILL LOSE ALL ITS ENCHANTMENT.
IF WE ONLY HAD THE MAGIC BELT... BUT BORTAG COULD HAVE TAKEN IT ANYWHERE BY NOW.
THEN BILLINA AND THE OTHER ANIMALS-- THEY'LL NEVER TALK AGAIN. AND WHAT WILL HAPPEN TO--TO--
--MEEEEEEE...
SCARECROW!
OH, OZMA, HE CAN'T BE DYING! WHAT ARE WE GOING TO DO?
MR. BORTAG AND MR. DROX REQUEST AN AUDIENCE, YOUR MAJESTY.

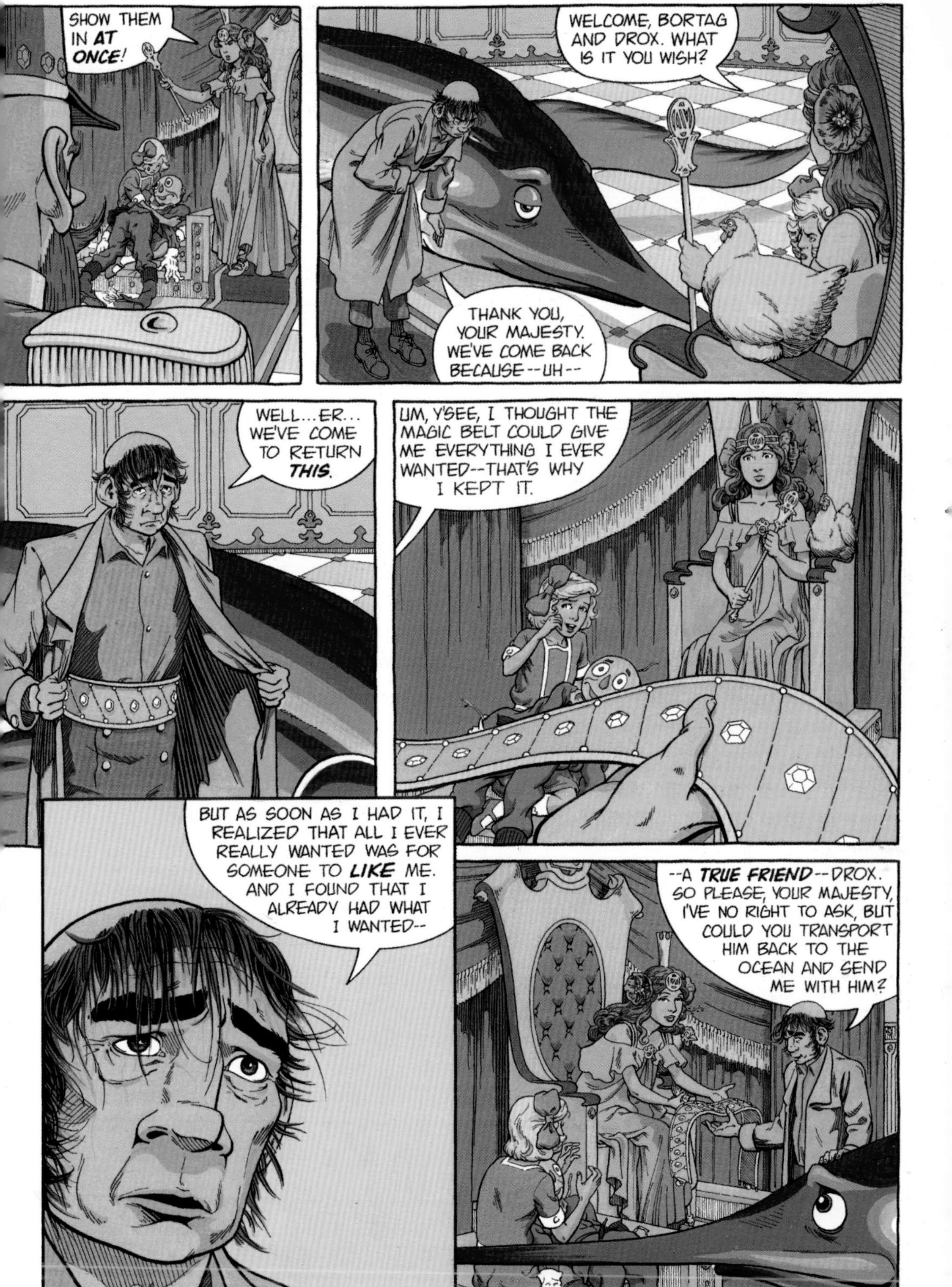
SHOW THEM IN **AT ONCE**!
WELCOME, BORTAG AND DROX. WHAT IS IT YOU WISH?
THANK YOU, YOUR MAJESTY. WE'VE COME BACK BECAUSE--UH--
WELL...ER... WE'VE COME TO RETURN **THIS**.
UM, Y'SEE, I THOUGHT THE MAGIC BELT COULD GIVE ME EVERYTHING I EVER WANTED--THAT'S WHY I KEPT IT.
BUT AS SOON AS I HAD IT, I REALIZED THAT ALL I EVER REALLY WANTED WAS FOR SOMEONE TO **LIKE** ME. AND I FOUND THAT I ALREADY HAD WHAT I WANTED--
--A **TRUE FRIEND**--DROX. SO PLEASE, YOUR MAJESTY, I'VE NO RIGHT TO ASK, BUT COULD YOU TRANSPORT HIM BACK TO THE OCEAN AND SEND ME WITH HIM?

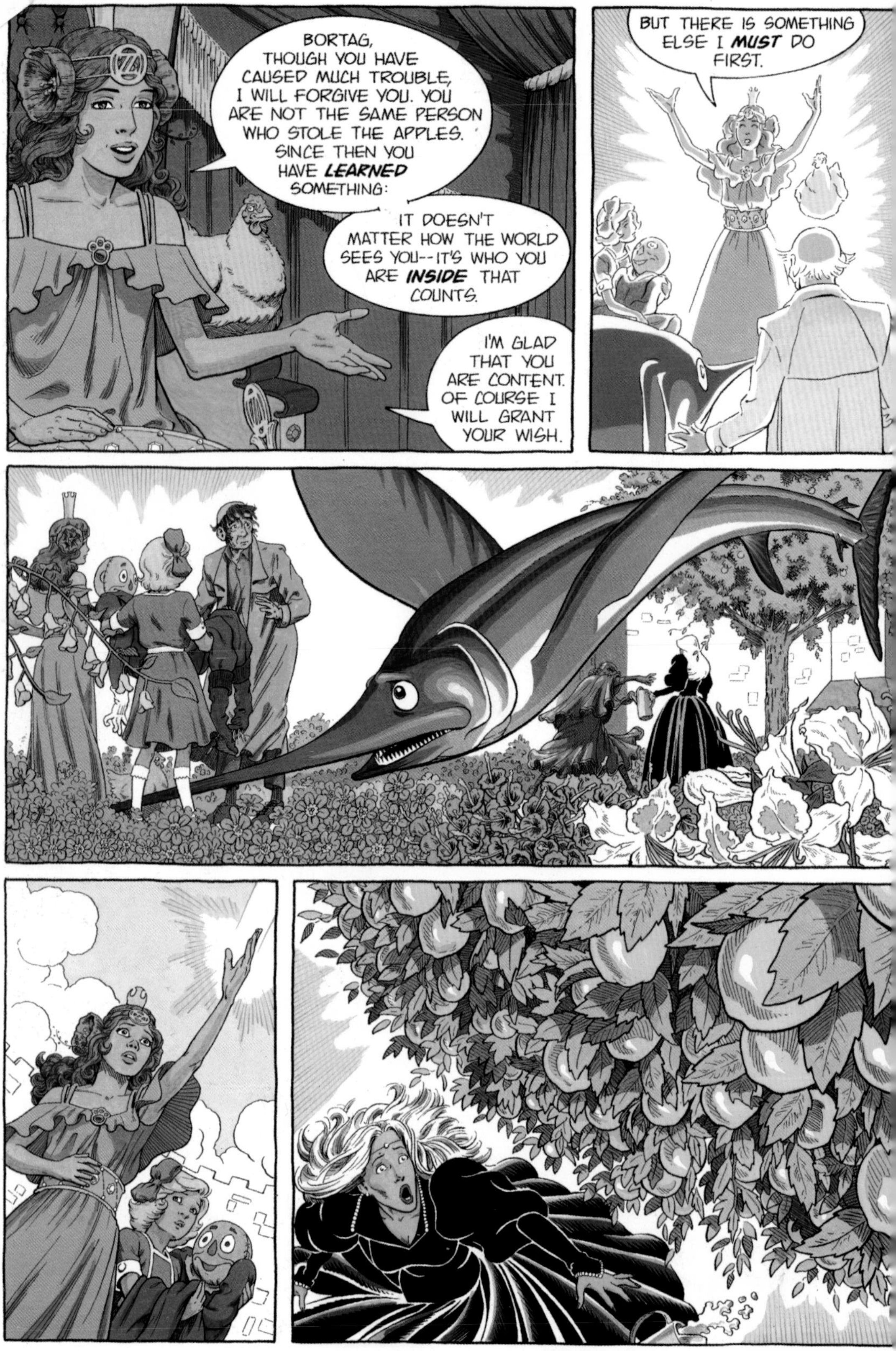
BORTAG, THOUGH YOU HAVE CAUSED MUCH TROUBLE, I WILL FORGIVE YOU. YOU ARE NOT THE SAME PERSON WHO STOLE THE APPLES. SINCE THEN YOU HAVE **LEARNED** SOMETHING:
IT DOESN'T MATTER HOW THE WORLD SEES YOU--IT'S WHO YOU ARE **INSIDE** THAT COUNTS.
I'M GLAD THAT YOU ARE CONTENT. OF COURSE I WILL GRANT YOUR WISH.
BUT THERE IS SOMETHING ELSE I **MUST** DO FIRST.

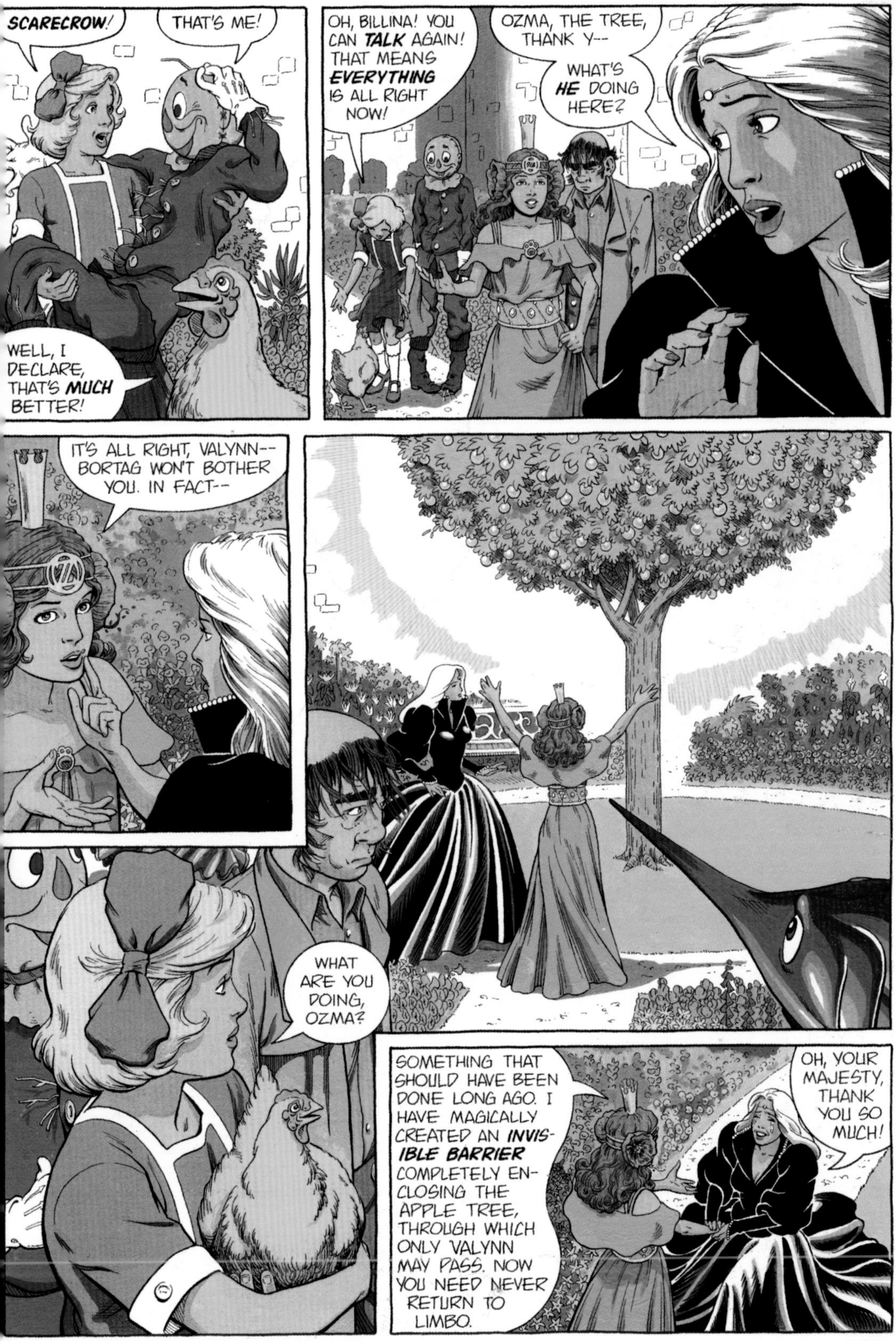
SCARECROW!
THAT'S ME!
WELL, I DECLARE, THAT'S MUCH BETTER!
OH, BILLINA! YOU CAN TALK AGAIN! THAT MEANS EVERYTHING IS ALL RIGHT NOW!
OZMA, THE TREE, THANK Y--
WHAT'S HE DOING HERE?
IT'S ALL RIGHT, VALYNN-- BORTAG WON'T BOTHER YOU. IN FACT--
WHAT ARE YOU DOING, OZMA?
SOMETHING THAT SHOULD HAVE BEEN DONE LONG AGO. I HAVE MAGICALLY CREATED AN INVISIBLE BARRIER COMPLETELY ENCLOSING THE APPLE TREE, THROUGH WHICH ONLY VALYNN MAY PASS. NOW YOU NEED NEVER RETURN TO LIMBO.
OH, YOUR MAJESTY, THANK YOU SO MUCH!

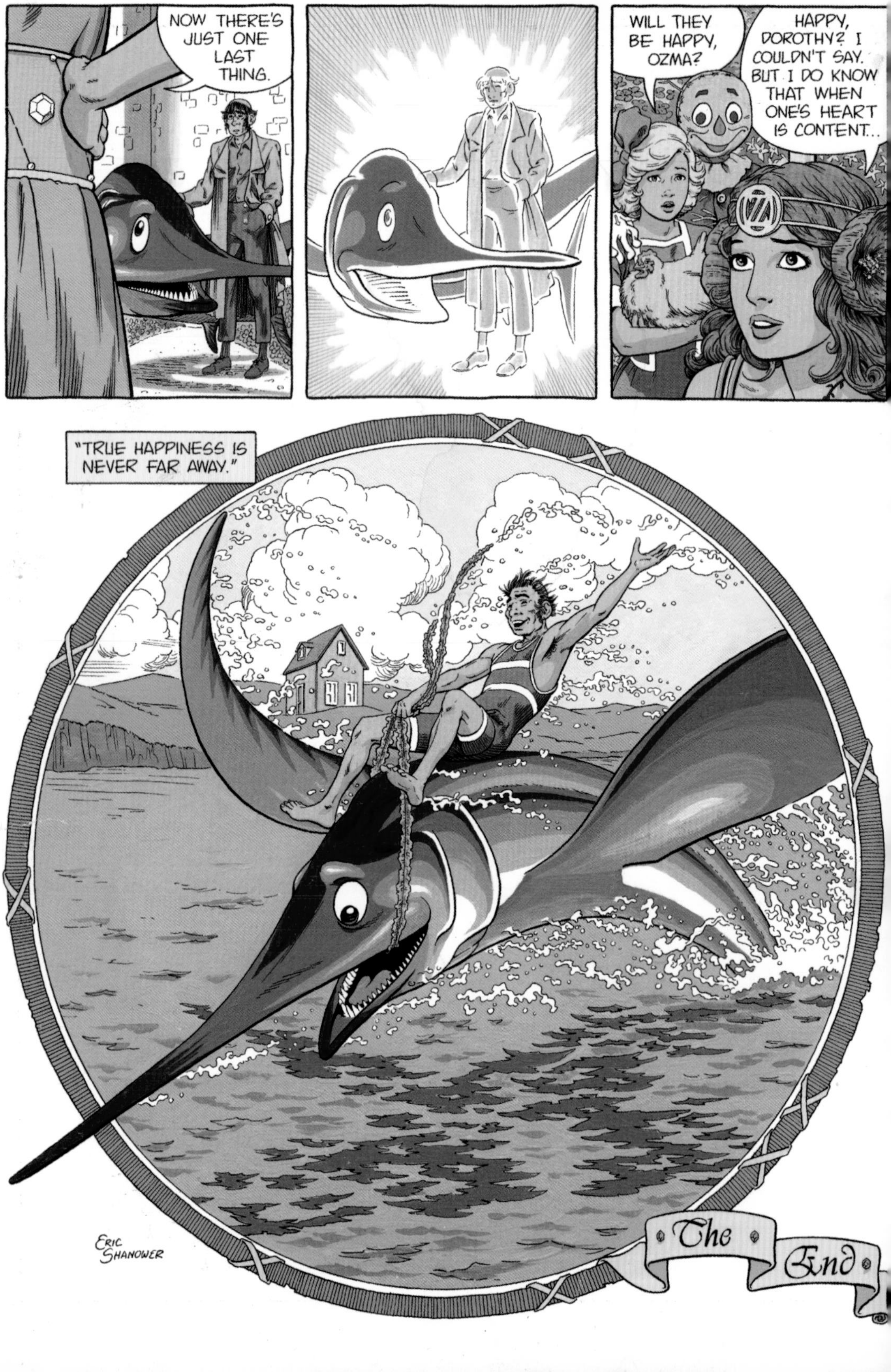
NOW THERE'S JUST ONE LAST THING.
WILL THEY BE HAPPY, OZMA?
HAPPY, DOROTHY? I COULDN'T SAY. BUT I DO KNOW THAT WHEN ONE'S HEART IS CONTENT...
"TRUE HAPPINESS IS NEVER FAR AWAY."
ERIC SHANOWER
The End

Oz

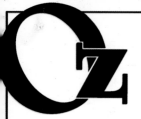

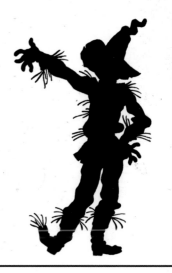

# Oz

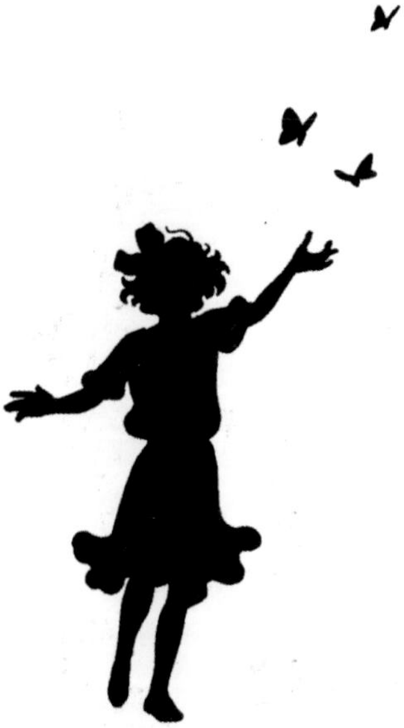

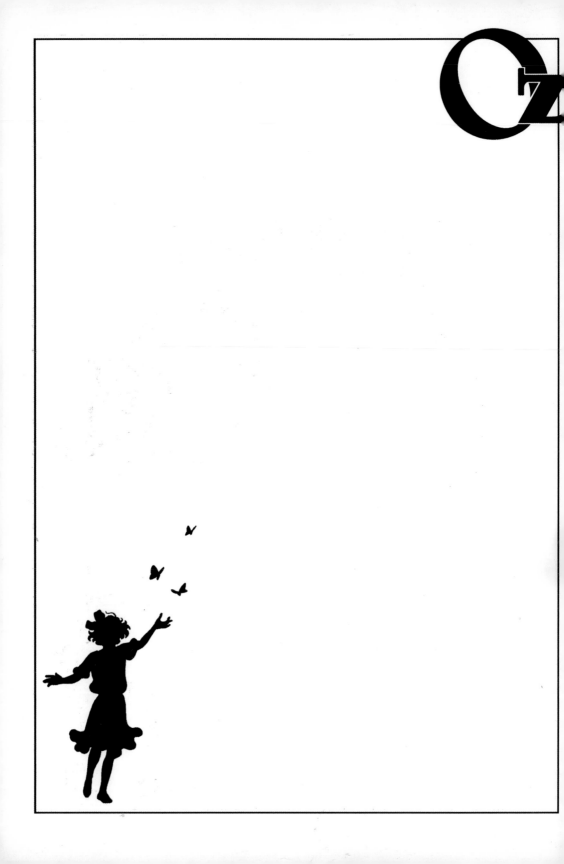

# The ICE KING of OZ

To the Olsons
Mary, Rick, Jimmy and Amy
with gratitude

# Chapter One The Proposal

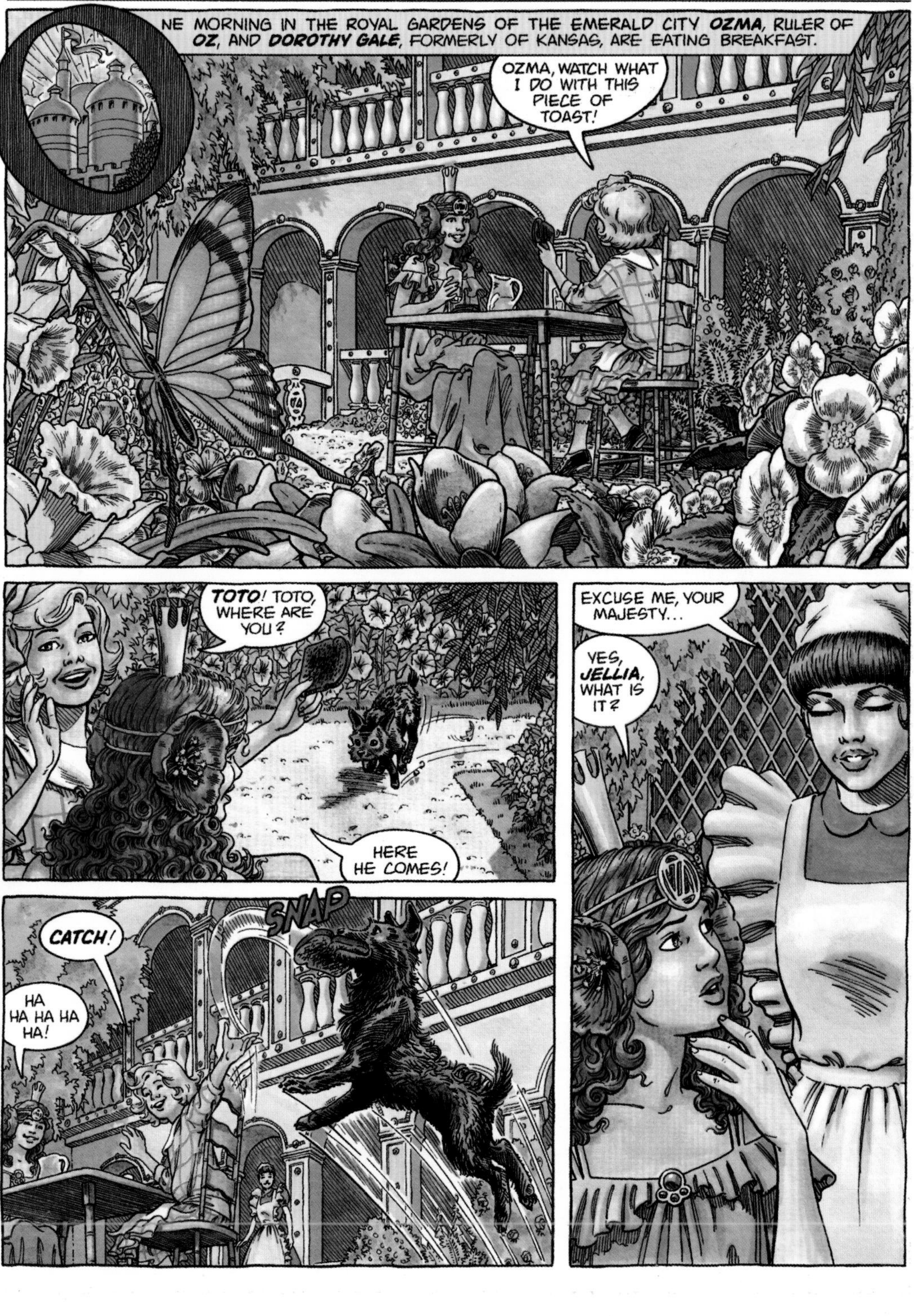

ONE MORNING IN THE ROYAL GARDENS OF THE EMERALD CITY *OZMA*, RULER OF *OZ*, AND *DOROTHY GALE*, FORMERLY OF KANSAS, ARE EATING BREAKFAST.
OZMA, WATCH WHAT I DO WITH THIS PIECE OF TOAST!
*TOTO*! TOTO, WHERE ARE YOU?
HERE HE COMES!
*CATCH*!
SNAP
HA HA HA HA HA!
EXCUSE ME, YOUR MAJESTY...
YES, *JELLIA*, WHAT IS IT?

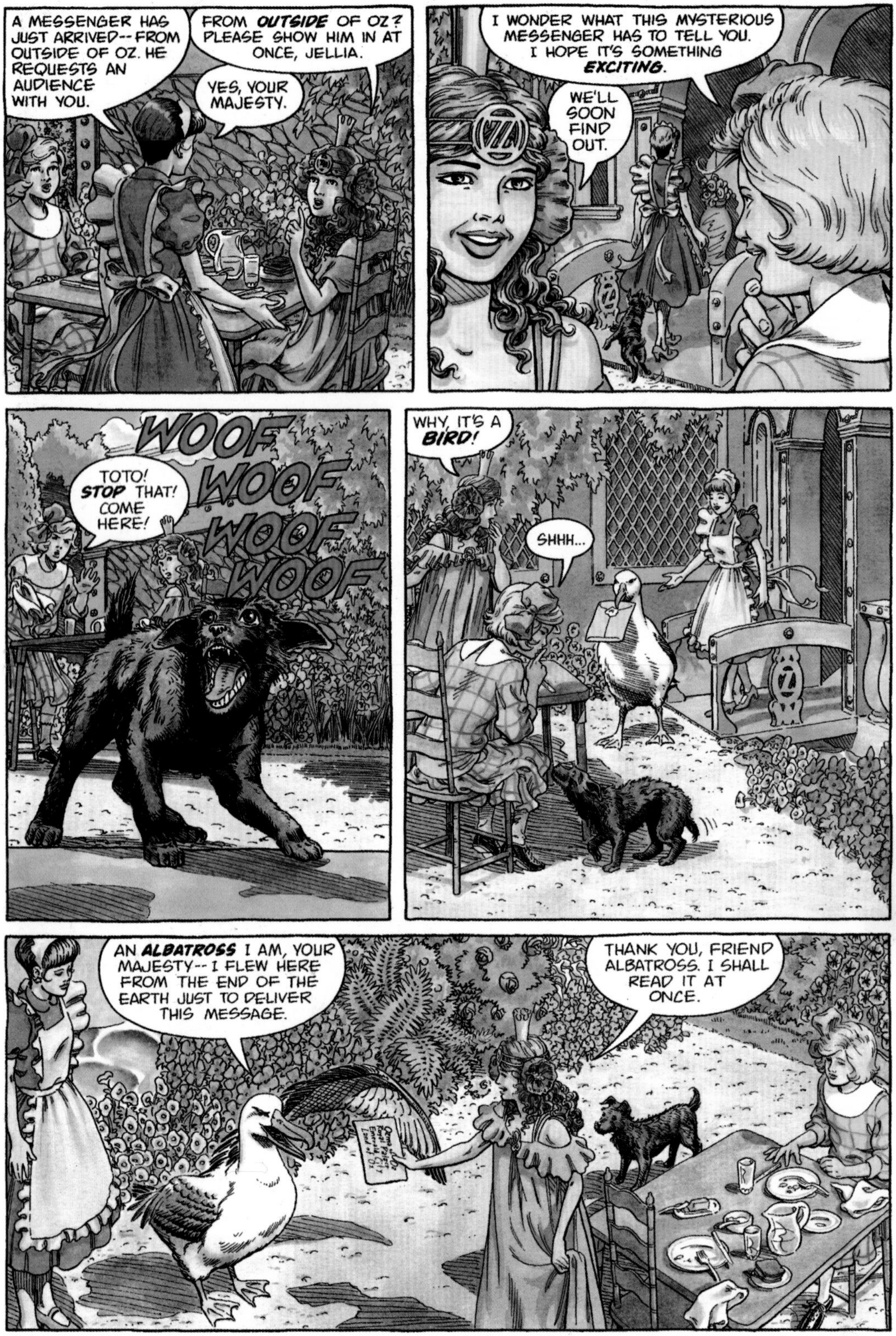
A MESSENGER HAS JUST ARRIVED-- FROM OUTSIDE OF OZ. HE REQUESTS AN AUDIENCE WITH YOU.
FROM OUTSIDE OF OZ? PLEASE SHOW HIM IN AT ONCE, JELLIA.
YES, YOUR MAJESTY.
I WONDER WHAT THIS MYSTERIOUS MESSENGER HAS TO TELL YOU. I HOPE IT'S SOMETHING EXCITING.
WE'LL SOON FIND OUT.
WOOF WOOF WOOF WOOF
TOTO! STOP THAT! COME HERE!
WHY, IT'S A BIRD!
SHHH...
AN ALBATROSS I AM, YOUR MAJESTY-- I FLEW HERE FROM THE END OF THE EARTH JUST TO DELIVER THIS MESSAGE.
THANK YOU, FRIEND ALBATROSS. I SHALL READ IT AT ONCE.

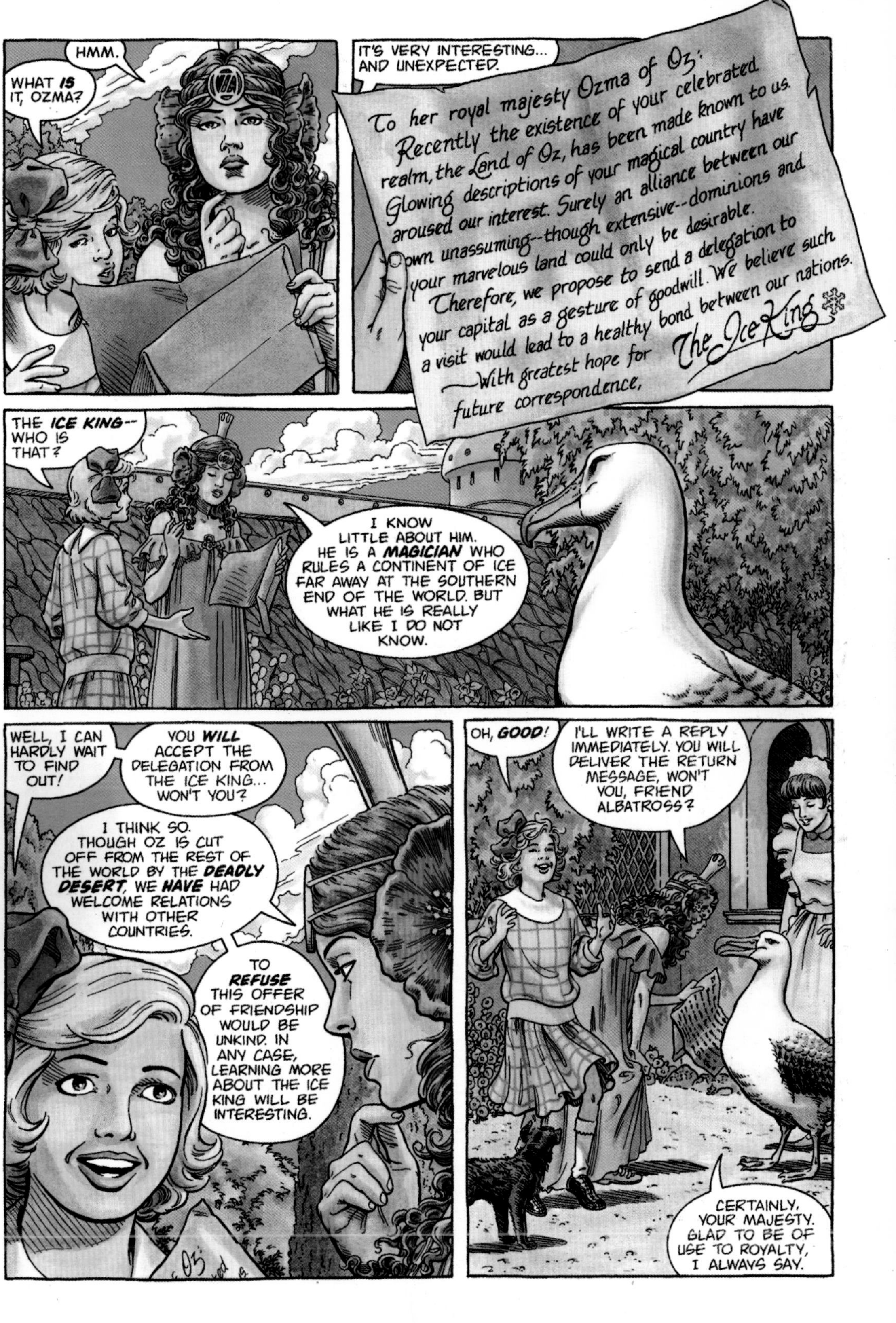
HMM.
WHAT IS IT, OZMA?
IT'S VERY INTERESTING... AND UNEXPECTED.
To her royal majesty Ozma of Oz:
Recently the existence of your celebrated realm, the Land of Oz, has been made known to us. Glowing descriptions of your magical country have aroused our interest. Surely an alliance between our own unassuming--though extensive--dominions and your marvelous land could only be desirable.
Therefore, we propose to send a delegation to your capital as a gesture of goodwill. We believe such a visit would lead to a healthy bond between our nations.
—With greatest hope for future correspondence,
The Ice King
THE ICE KING-- WHO IS THAT?
I KNOW LITTLE ABOUT HIM. HE IS A MAGICIAN WHO RULES A CONTINENT OF ICE FAR AWAY AT THE SOUTHERN END OF THE WORLD. BUT WHAT HE IS REALLY LIKE I DO NOT KNOW.
WELL, I CAN HARDLY WAIT TO FIND OUT!
YOU WILL ACCEPT THE DELEGATION FROM THE ICE KING... WON'T YOU?
I THINK SO. THOUGH OZ IS CUT OFF FROM THE REST OF THE WORLD BY THE DEADLY DESERT, WE HAVE HAD WELCOME RELATIONS WITH OTHER COUNTRIES.
TO REFUSE THIS OFFER OF FRIENDSHIP WOULD BE UNKIND. IN ANY CASE, LEARNING MORE ABOUT THE ICE KING WILL BE INTERESTING.
OH, GOOD!
I'LL WRITE A REPLY IMMEDIATELY. YOU WILL DELIVER THE RETURN MESSAGE, WON'T YOU, FRIEND ALBATROSS?
CERTAINLY, YOUR MAJESTY. GLAD TO BE OF USE TO ROYALTY, I ALWAYS SAY.

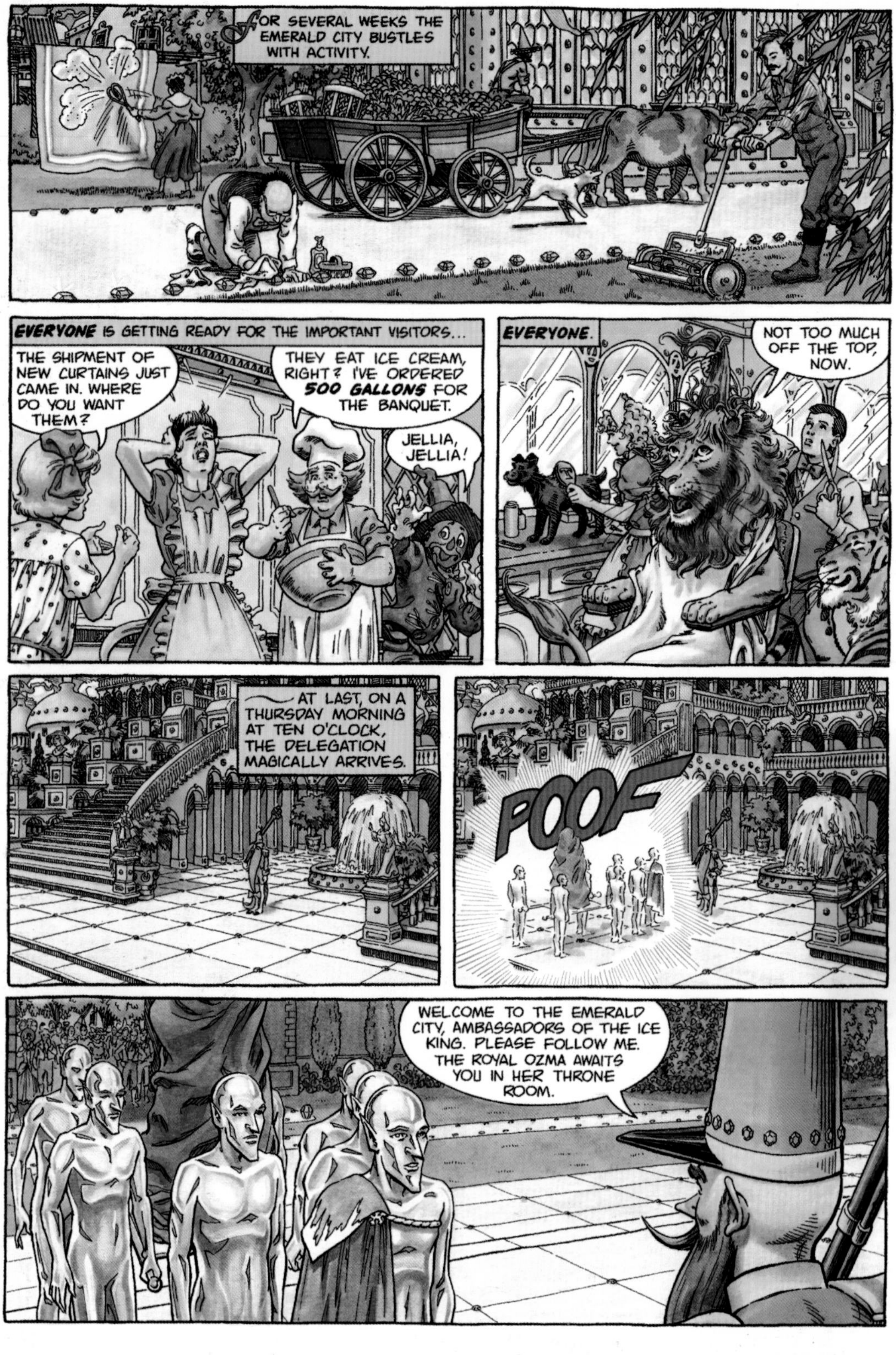

FOR SEVERAL WEEKS THE EMERALD CITY BUSTLES WITH ACTIVITY.
EVERYONE IS GETTING READY FOR THE IMPORTANT VISITORS...
THE SHIPMENT OF NEW CURTAINS JUST CAME IN. WHERE DO YOU WANT THEM?
THEY EAT ICE CREAM, RIGHT? I'VE ORDERED 500 GALLONS FOR THE BANQUET.
JELLIA, JELLIA!
EVERYONE.
NOT TOO MUCH OFF THE TOP, NOW.
—AT LAST, ON A THURSDAY MORNING AT TEN O'CLOCK, THE DELEGATION MAGICALLY ARRIVES.
POOF
WELCOME TO THE EMERALD CITY, AMBASSADORS OF THE ICE KING. PLEASE FOLLOW ME. THE ROYAL OZMA AWAITS YOU IN HER THRONE ROOM.

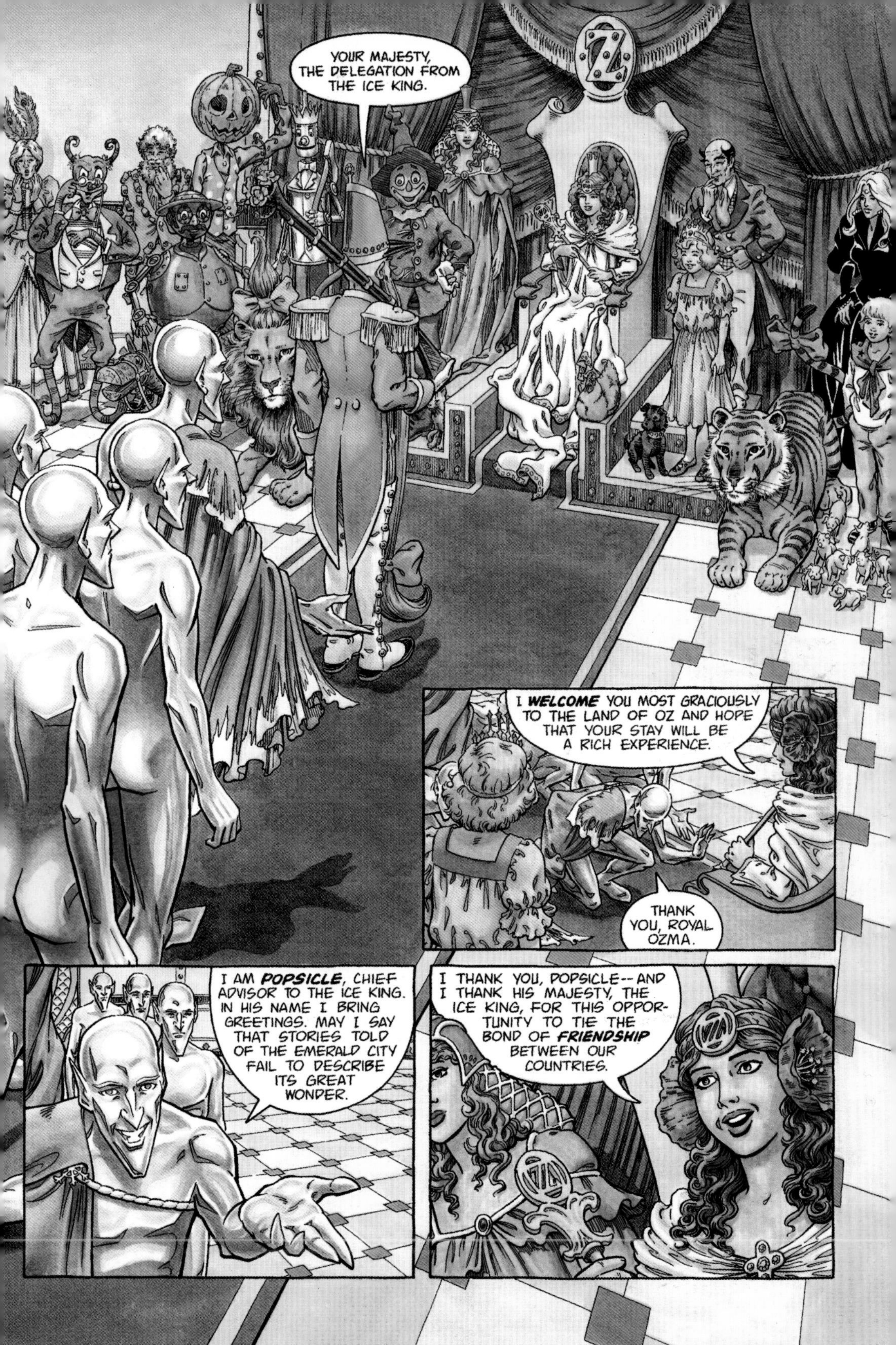
YOUR MAJESTY, THE DELEGATION FROM THE ICE KING.
I **WELCOME** YOU MOST GRACIOUSLY TO THE LAND OF OZ AND HOPE THAT YOUR STAY WILL BE A RICH EXPERIENCE.
THANK YOU, ROYAL OZMA.
I AM **POPSICLE**, CHIEF ADVISOR TO THE ICE KING. IN HIS NAME I BRING GREETINGS. MAY I SAY THAT STORIES TOLD OF THE EMERALD CITY FAIL TO DESCRIBE ITS GREAT WONDER.
I THANK YOU, POPSICLE-- AND I THANK HIS MAJESTY, THE ICE KING, FOR THIS OPPOR-TUNITY TO TIE THE BOND OF **FRIENDSHIP** BETWEEN OUR COUNTRIES.

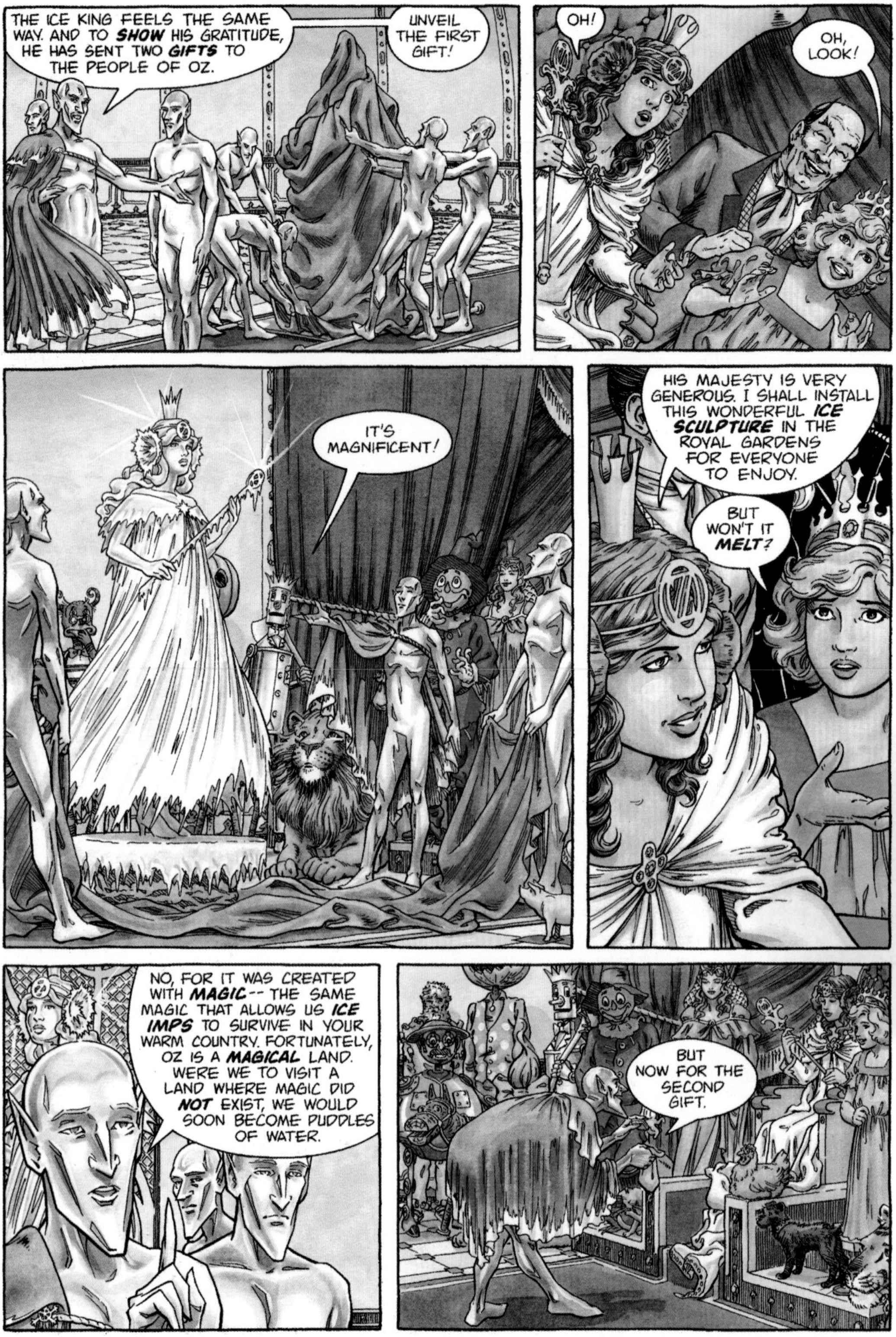
THE ICE KING FEELS THE SAME WAY. AND TO SHOW HIS GRATITUDE, HE HAS SENT TWO GIFTS TO THE PEOPLE OF OZ.
UNVEIL THE FIRST GIFT!
OH!
OH, LOOK!
IT'S MAGNIFICENT!
HIS MAJESTY IS VERY GENEROUS. I SHALL INSTALL THIS WONDERFUL ICE SCULPTURE IN THE ROYAL GARDENS FOR EVERYONE TO ENJOY.
BUT WON'T IT MELT?
NO, FOR IT WAS CREATED WITH MAGIC-- THE SAME MAGIC THAT ALLOWS US ICE IMPS TO SURVIVE IN YOUR WARM COUNTRY. FORTUNATELY, OZ IS A MAGICAL LAND. WERE WE TO VISIT A LAND WHERE MAGIC DID NOT EXIST, WE WOULD SOON BECOME PUDDLES OF WATER.
BUT NOW FOR THE SECOND GIFT.

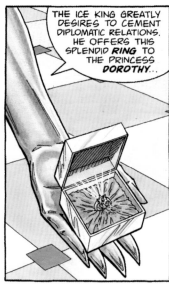

THE ICE KING GREATLY DESIRES TO CEMENT DIPLOMATIC RELATIONS. HE OFFERS THIS SPLENDID *RING* TO THE PRINCESS *DOROTHY*...

...AS A PROPOSAL OF *MARRIAGE!*

*WHAT?!*

I ASSURE YOU, IT IS QUITE *CUSTOMARY* FOR A PRINCESS OF ONE NATION TO WED THE RULER OF ANOTHER. IT ENSURES GOODWILL.

BUT I DON'T *WANT* TO MARRY THE ICE KING! I DON'T EVEN *KNOW* HIM! BESIDES, I'M TOO YOUNG TO MARRY.

SNIFF-- WELL, THE ICE KING WILL BE *VASTLY* DISAPPOINTED BY YOUR REFUSAL. PERHAPS--

*CLICK!*

PERHAPS *LATER* WHEN RELATIONS ARE MORE FIRMLY ESTABLISHED WE WILL DISCUSS THIS GENEROUS PROPOSAL AT GREATER LENGTH.

IN THE MEANTIME WE HAVE MANY SIGHTS AND ACTIVITIES FOR YOU TO ENJOY. YOU WILL BE SHOWN TO A PALACE SUITE WHERE YOU MAY RE- FRESH YOURSELVES FOR THE GRAND BANQUET THIS AFTERNOON.

COURT IS *ADJOURNED.*

# Chapter Two Treachery

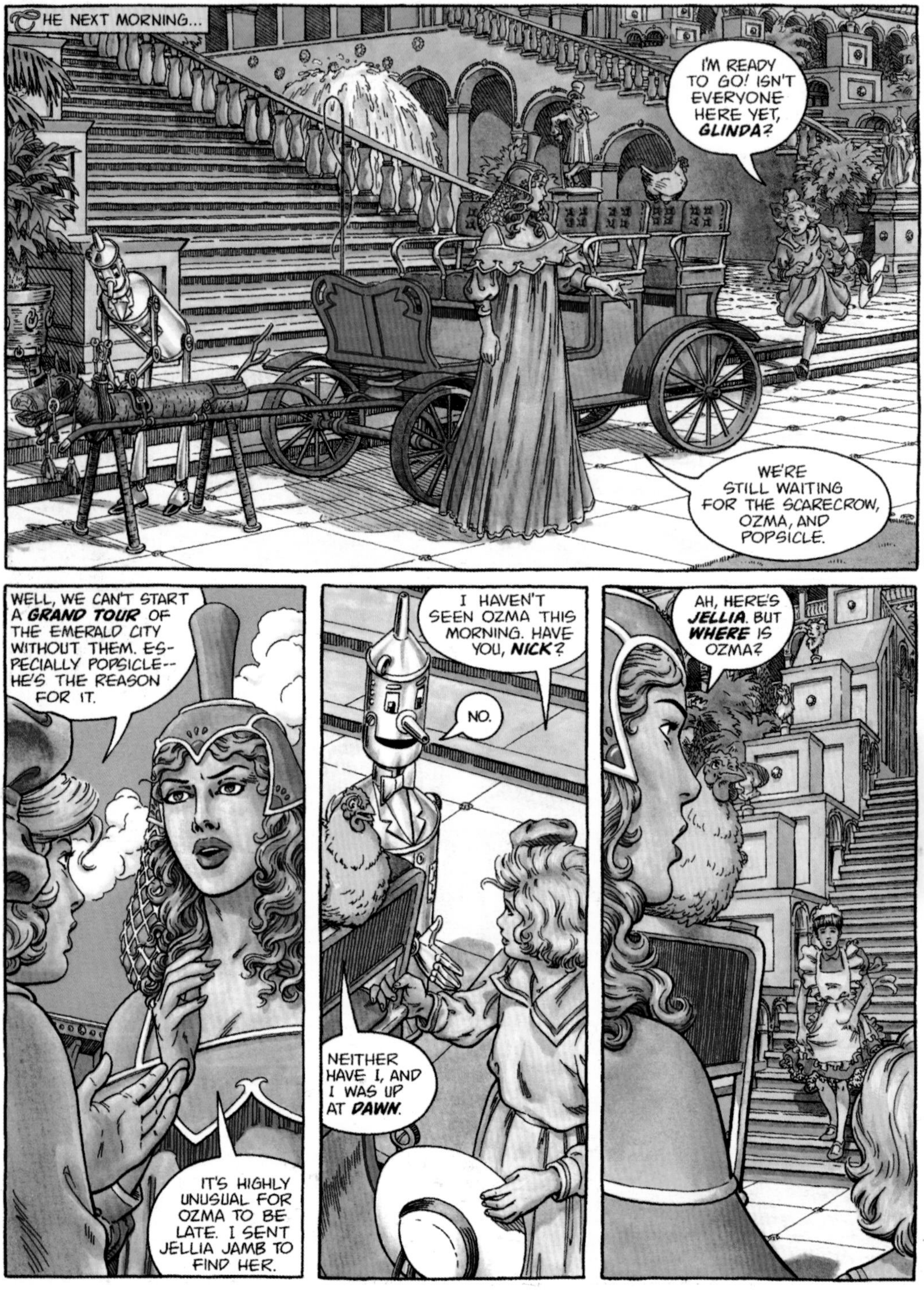
THE NEXT MORNING...
I'M READY TO GO! ISN'T EVERYONE HERE YET, GLINDA?
WE'RE STILL WAITING FOR THE SCARECROW, OZMA, AND POPSICLE.
WELL, WE CAN'T START A GRAND TOUR OF THE EMERALD CITY WITHOUT THEM. ESPECIALLY POPSICLE-- HE'S THE REASON FOR IT.
IT'S HIGHLY UNUSUAL FOR OZMA TO BE LATE. I SENT JELLIA JAMB TO FIND HER.
I HAVEN'T SEEN OZMA THIS MORNING. HAVE YOU, NICK?
NO.
NEITHER HAVE I, AND I WAS UP AT DAWN.
AH, HERE'S JELLIA. BUT WHERE IS OZMA?

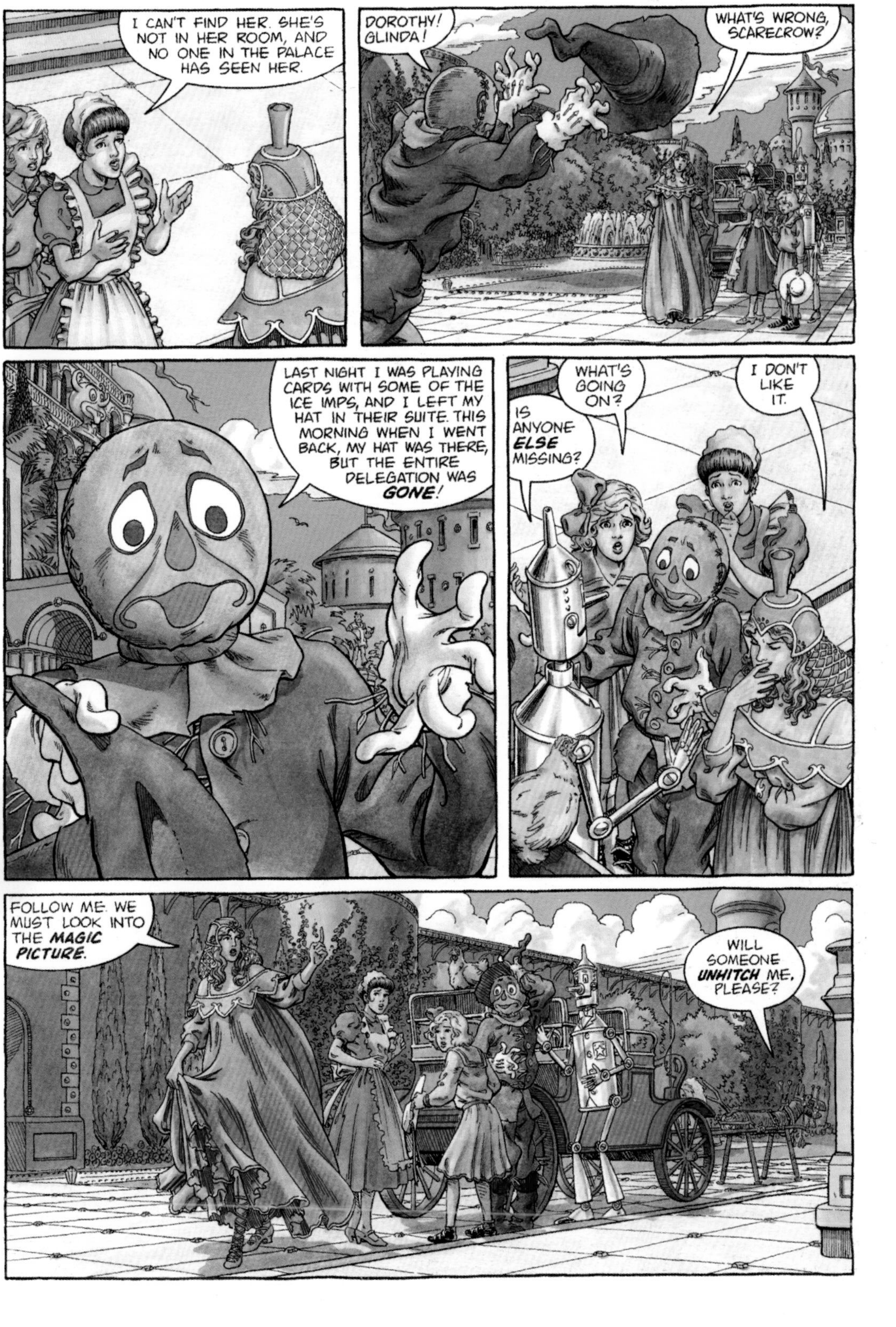
I CAN'T FIND HER. SHE'S NOT IN HER ROOM, AND NO ONE IN THE PALACE HAS SEEN HER.
DOROTHY! GLINDA!
WHAT'S WRONG, SCARECROW?
LAST NIGHT I WAS PLAYING CARDS WITH SOME OF THE ICE IMPS, AND I LEFT MY HAT IN THEIR SUITE. THIS MORNING WHEN I WENT BACK, MY HAT WAS THERE, BUT THE ENTIRE DELEGATION WAS **GONE**!
WHAT'S GOING ON?
IS ANYONE **ELSE** MISSING?
I DON'T LIKE IT.
FOLLOW ME. WE MUST LOOK INTO THE **MAGIC PICTURE**.
WILL SOMEONE **UNHITCH** ME, PLEASE?

MAGIC PICTURE, I COMMAND YOU--USE YOUR POWER TO SHOW THE LOCATION OF OZMA OF OZ.

OH, OZMA!

WHAT HAVE THEY DONE TO HER, GLINDA?

SHH, I DON'T THINK THEY'VE HURT HER.

THE FIENDS! AT TIMES LIKE THIS I ALMOST WISH I HAD NO HEART--

WHAT'S THAT?!

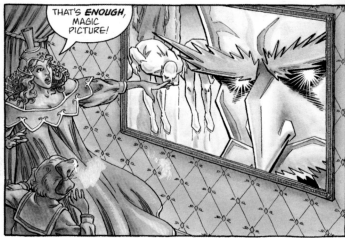

THAT'S ENOUGH, MAGIC PICTURE!

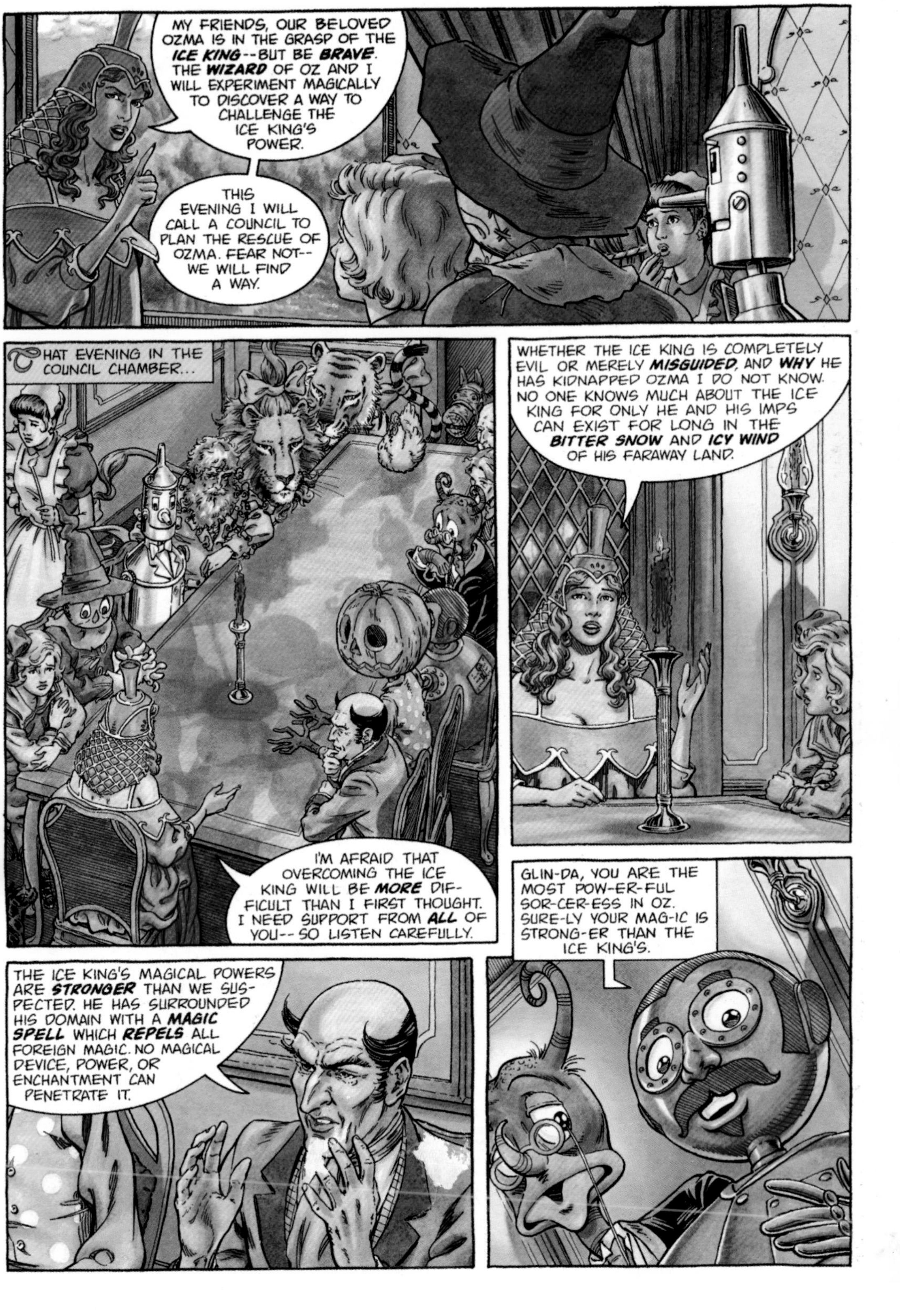

MY FRIENDS, OUR BELOVED OZMA IS IN THE GRASP OF THE **ICE KING**--BUT BE **BRAVE**. THE **WIZARD** OF OZ AND I WILL EXPERIMENT MAGICALLY TO DISCOVER A WAY TO CHALLENGE THE ICE KING'S POWER.
THIS EVENING I WILL CALL A COUNCIL TO PLAN THE RESCUE OF OZMA. FEAR NOT--WE WILL FIND A WAY.
THAT EVENING IN THE COUNCIL CHAMBER...
I'M AFRAID THAT OVERCOMING THE ICE KING WILL BE **MORE** DIFFICULT THAN I FIRST THOUGHT. I NEED SUPPORT FROM **ALL** OF YOU--SO LISTEN CAREFULLY.
WHETHER THE ICE KING IS COMPLETELY EVIL OR MERELY **MISGUIDED**, AND **WHY** HE HAS KIDNAPPED OZMA I DO NOT KNOW. NO ONE KNOWS MUCH ABOUT THE ICE KING FOR ONLY HE AND HIS IMPS CAN EXIST FOR LONG IN THE **BITTER SNOW** AND **ICY WIND** OF HIS FARAWAY LAND.
THE ICE KING'S MAGICAL POWERS ARE **STRONGER** THAN WE SUSPECTED. HE HAS SURROUNDED HIS DOMAIN WITH A **MAGIC SPELL** WHICH **REPELS** ALL FOREIGN MAGIC. NO MAGICAL DEVICE, POWER, OR ENCHANTMENT CAN PENETRATE IT.
GLIN-DA, YOU ARE THE MOST POW-ER-FUL SOR-CER-ESS IN OZ. SURE-LY YOUR MAG-IC IS STRONG-ER THAN THE ICE KING'S.

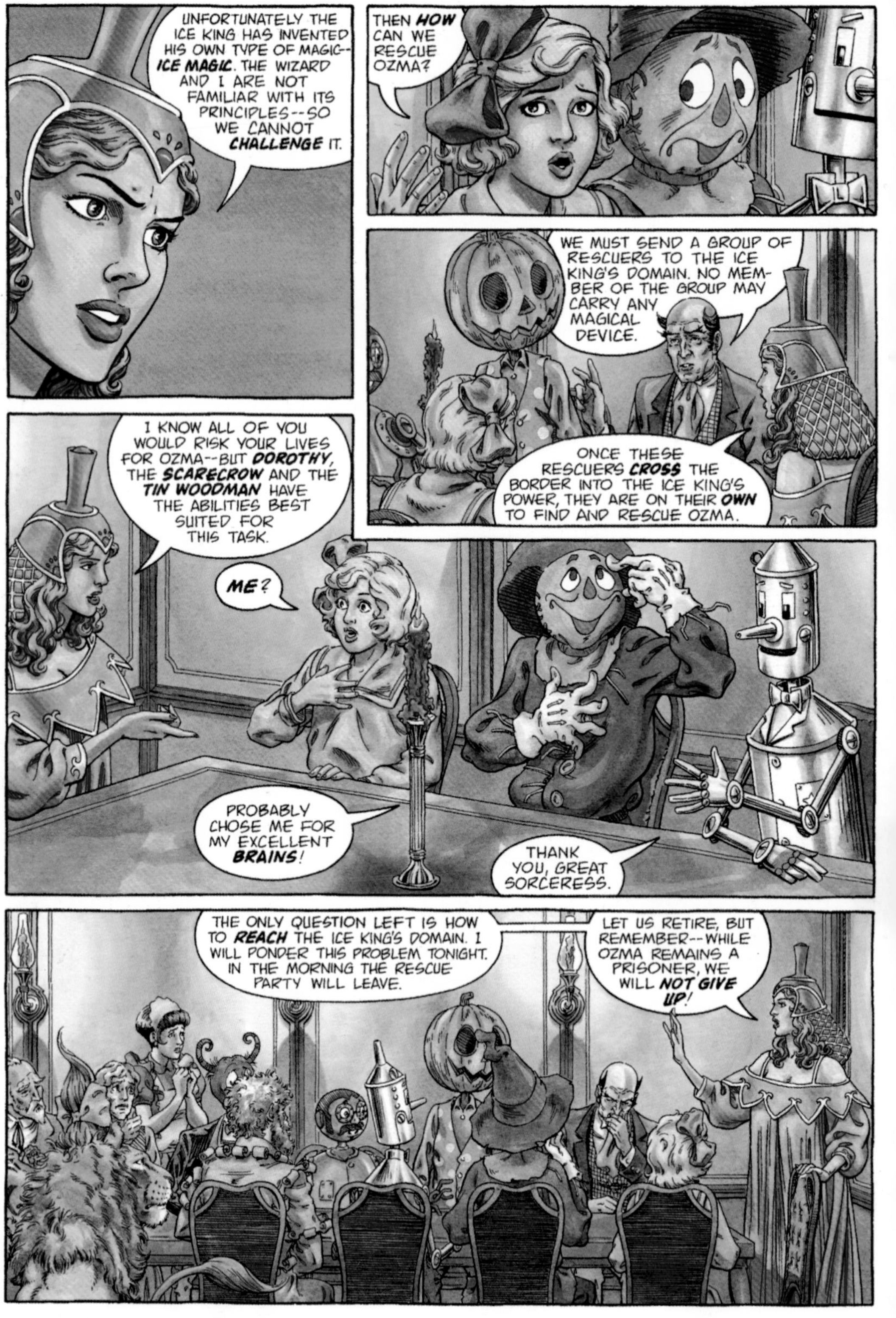
UNFORTUNATELY THE ICE KING HAS INVENTED HIS OWN TYPE OF MAGIC--ICE MAGIC. THE WIZARD AND I ARE NOT FAMILIAR WITH ITS PRINCIPLES--SO WE CANNOT CHALLENGE IT.
THEN HOW CAN WE RESCUE OZMA?
WE MUST SEND A GROUP OF RESCUERS TO THE ICE KING'S DOMAIN. NO MEMBER OF THE GROUP MAY CARRY ANY MAGICAL DEVICE.
ONCE THESE RESCUERS CROSS THE BORDER INTO THE ICE KING'S POWER, THEY ARE ON THEIR OWN TO FIND AND RESCUE OZMA.
I KNOW ALL OF YOU WOULD RISK YOUR LIVES FOR OZMA--BUT DOROTHY, THE SCARECROW AND THE TIN WOODMAN HAVE THE ABILITIES BEST SUITED FOR THIS TASK.
ME?
PROBABLY CHOSE ME FOR MY EXCELLENT BRAINS!
THANK YOU, GREAT SORCERESS.
THE ONLY QUESTION LEFT IS HOW TO REACH THE ICE KING'S DOMAIN. I WILL PONDER THIS PROBLEM TONIGHT. IN THE MORNING THE RESCUE PARTY WILL LEAVE.
LET US RETIRE, BUT REMEMBER--WHILE OZMA REMAINS A PRISONER, WE WILL NOT GIVE UP!

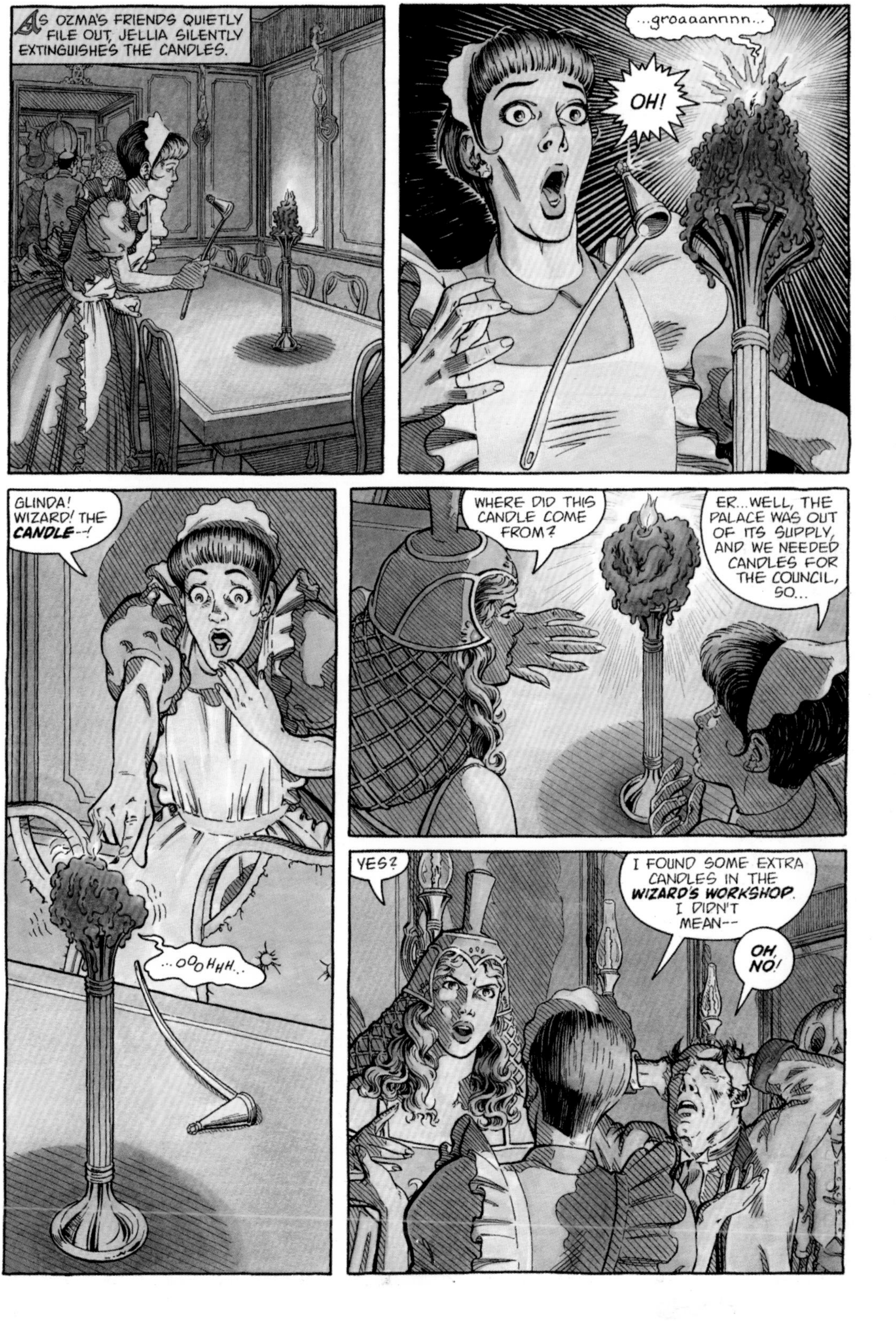
AS OZMA'S FRIENDS QUIETLY FILE OUT, JELLIA SILENTLY EXTINGUISHE'S THE CANDLES.
...groaaannnn...
OH!
GLINDA! WIZARD! THE CANDLE--!
...OOOHHH...
WHERE DID THIS CANDLE COME FROM?
ER...WELL, THE PALACE WAS OUT OF ITS SUPPLY, AND WE NEEDED CANDLES FOR THE COUNCIL, SO...
YES?
I FOUND SOME EXTRA CANDLES IN THE WIZARD'S WORKSHOP. I DIDN'T MEAN--
OH, NO!

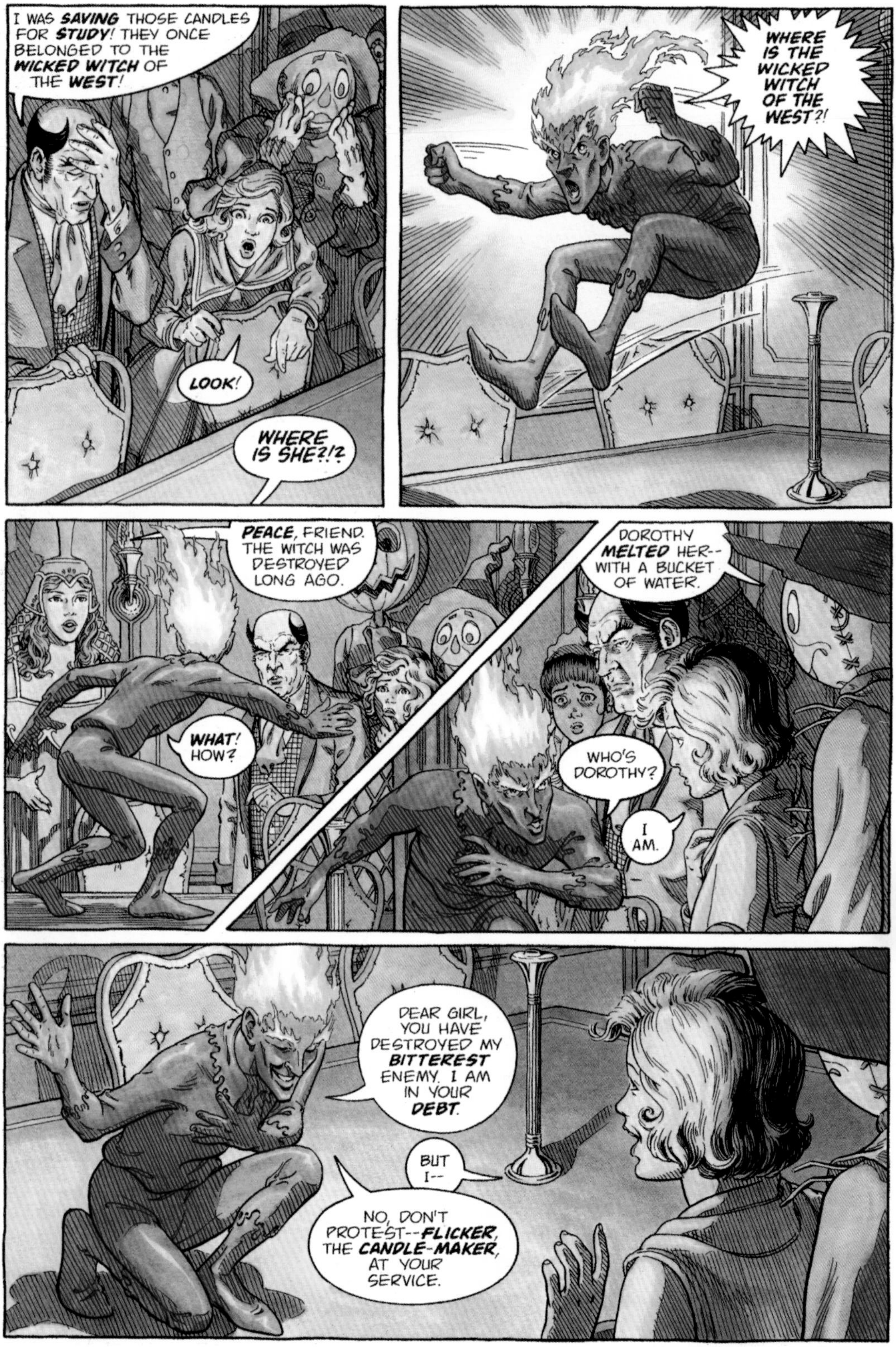

I WAS SAVING THOSE CANDLES FOR STUDY! THEY ONCE BELONGED TO THE WICKED WITCH OF THE WEST!
LOOK!
WHERE IS SHE?!?
WHERE IS THE WICKED WITCH OF THE WEST?!
PEACE, FRIEND. THE WITCH WAS DESTROYED LONG AGO.
WHAT! HOW?
DOROTHY MELTED HER-- WITH A BUCKET OF WATER.
WHO'S DOROTHY?
I AM.
DEAR GIRL, YOU HAVE DESTROYED MY BITTEREST ENEMY. I AM IN YOUR DEBT.
BUT I--
NO, DON'T PROTEST--FLICKER, THE CANDLE-MAKER, AT YOUR SERVICE.

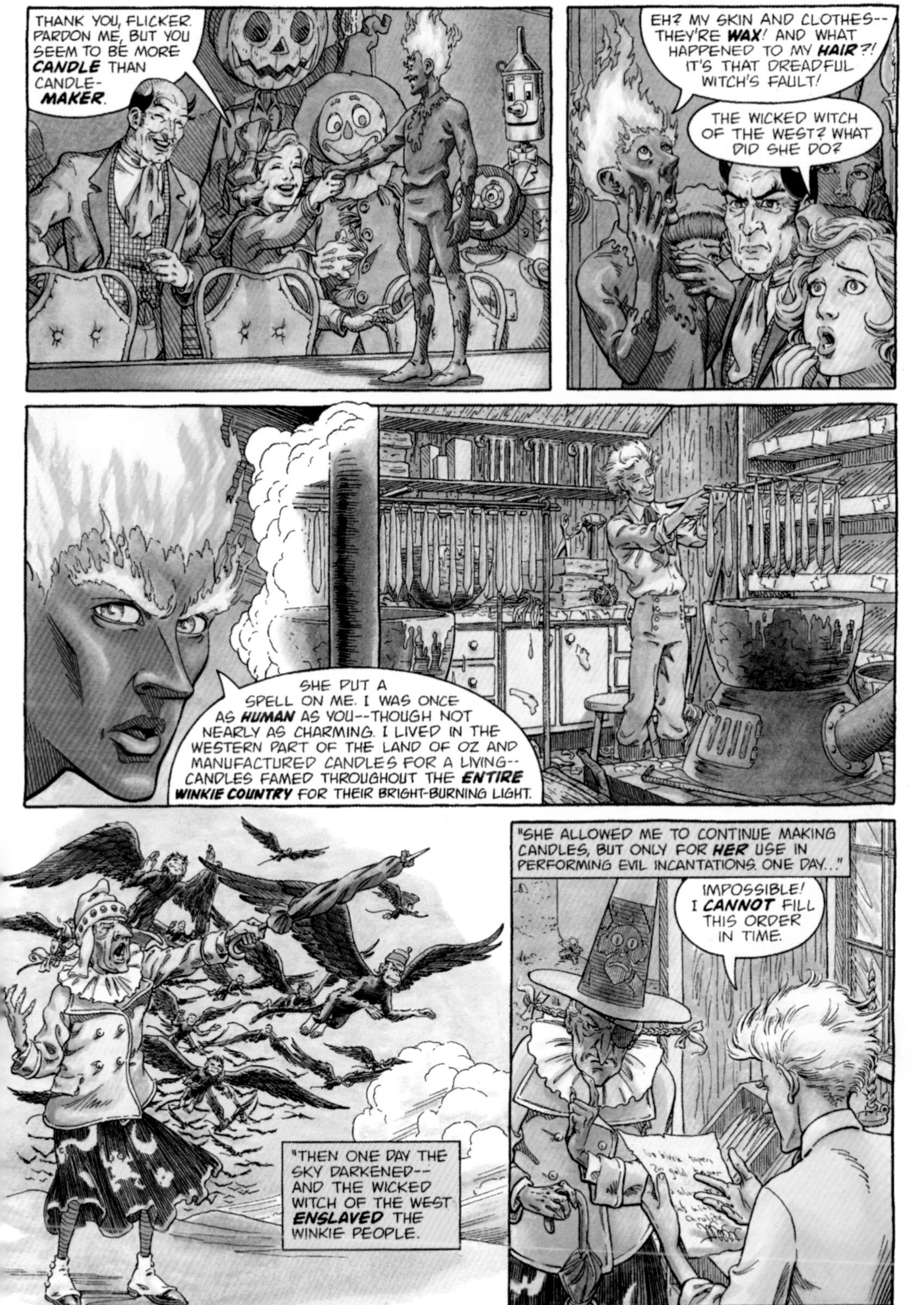
THANK YOU, FLICKER. PARDON ME, BUT YOU SEEM TO BE MORE CANDLE THAN CANDLE-MAKER.
EH? MY SKIN AND CLOTHES--THEY'RE WAX! AND WHAT HAPPENED TO MY HAIR?! IT'S THAT DREADFUL WITCH'S FAULT!
THE WICKED WITCH OF THE WEST? WHAT DID SHE DO?
SHE PUT A SPELL ON ME. I WAS ONCE AS HUMAN AS YOU--THOUGH NOT NEARLY AS CHARMING. I LIVED IN THE WESTERN PART OF THE LAND OF OZ AND MANUFACTURED CANDLES FOR A LIVING--CANDLES FAMED THROUGHOUT THE ENTIRE WINKIE COUNTRY FOR THEIR BRIGHT-BURNING LIGHT.
"THEN ONE DAY THE SKY DARKENED--AND THE WICKED WITCH OF THE WEST ENSLAVED THE WINKIE PEOPLE.
"SHE ALLOWED ME TO CONTINUE MAKING CANDLES, BUT ONLY FOR HER USE IN PERFORMING EVIL INCANTATIONS. ONE DAY..."
IMPOSSIBLE! I CANNOT FILL THIS ORDER IN TIME.

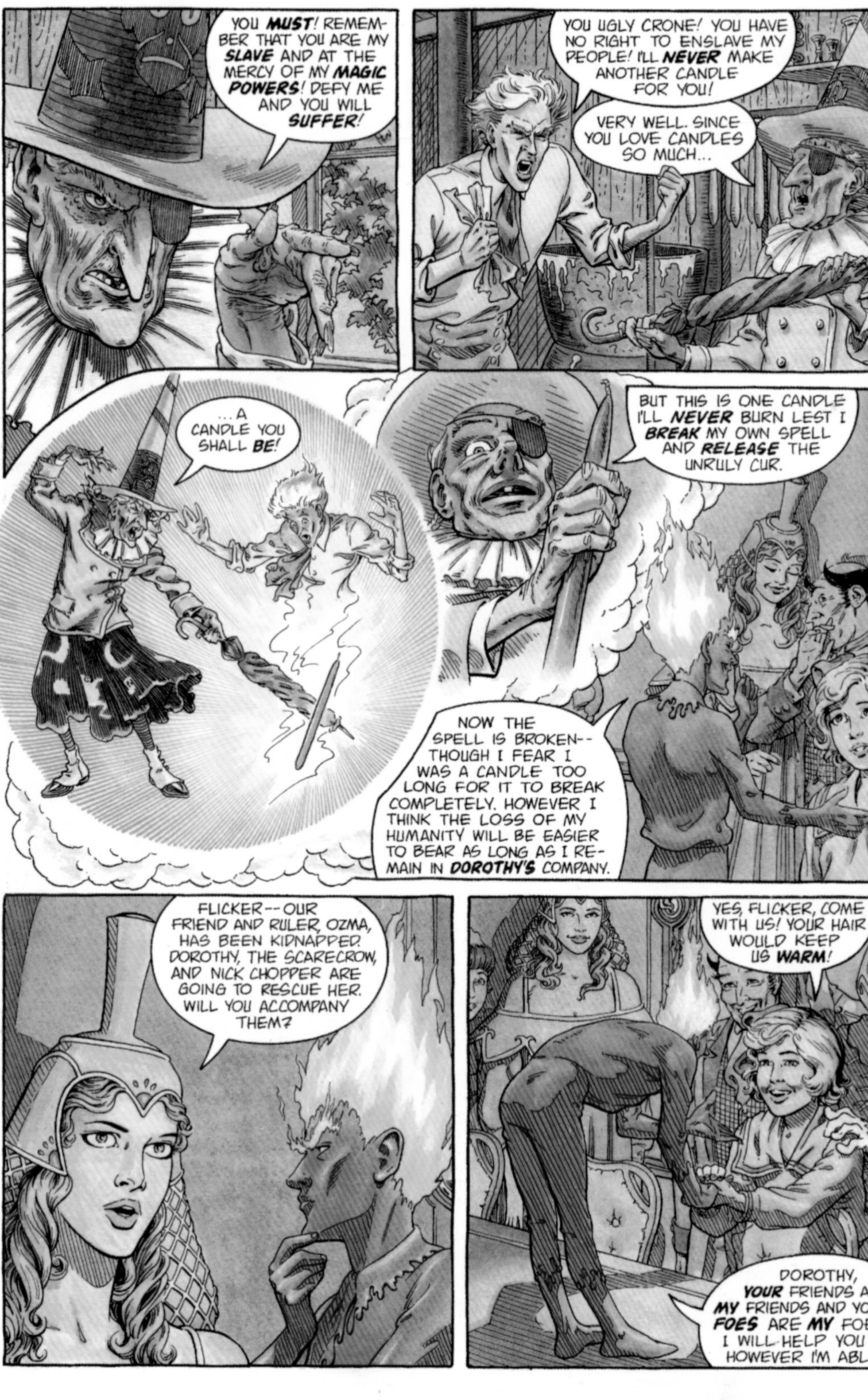
YOU MUST! REMEMBER THAT YOU ARE MY SLAVE AND AT THE MERCY OF MY MAGIC POWERS! DEFY ME AND YOU WILL SUFFER!
YOU UGLY CRONE! YOU HAVE NO RIGHT TO ENSLAVE MY PEOPLE! I'LL NEVER MAKE ANOTHER CANDLE FOR YOU!
VERY WELL. SINCE YOU LOVE CANDLES SO MUCH...
...A CANDLE YOU SHALL BE!
BUT THIS IS ONE CANDLE I'LL NEVER BURN LEST I BREAK MY OWN SPELL AND RELEASE THE UNRULY CUR.
NOW THE SPELL IS BROKEN--THOUGH I FEAR I WAS A CANDLE TOO LONG FOR IT TO BREAK COMPLETELY. HOWEVER I THINK THE LOSS OF MY HUMANITY WILL BE EASIER TO BEAR AS LONG AS I REMAIN IN DOROTHY'S COMPANY.
FLICKER--OUR FRIEND AND RULER, OZMA, HAS BEEN KIDNAPPED. DOROTHY, THE SCARECROW, AND NICK CHOPPER ARE GOING TO RESCUE HER. WILL YOU ACCOMPANY THEM?
YES, FLICKER, COME WITH US! YOUR HAIR WOULD KEEP US WARM!
DOROTHY, YOUR FRIENDS ARE MY FRIENDS AND YOUR FOES ARE MY FOES! I WILL HELP YOU HOWEVER I'M ABLE.

# Chapter Three The Land of Ice

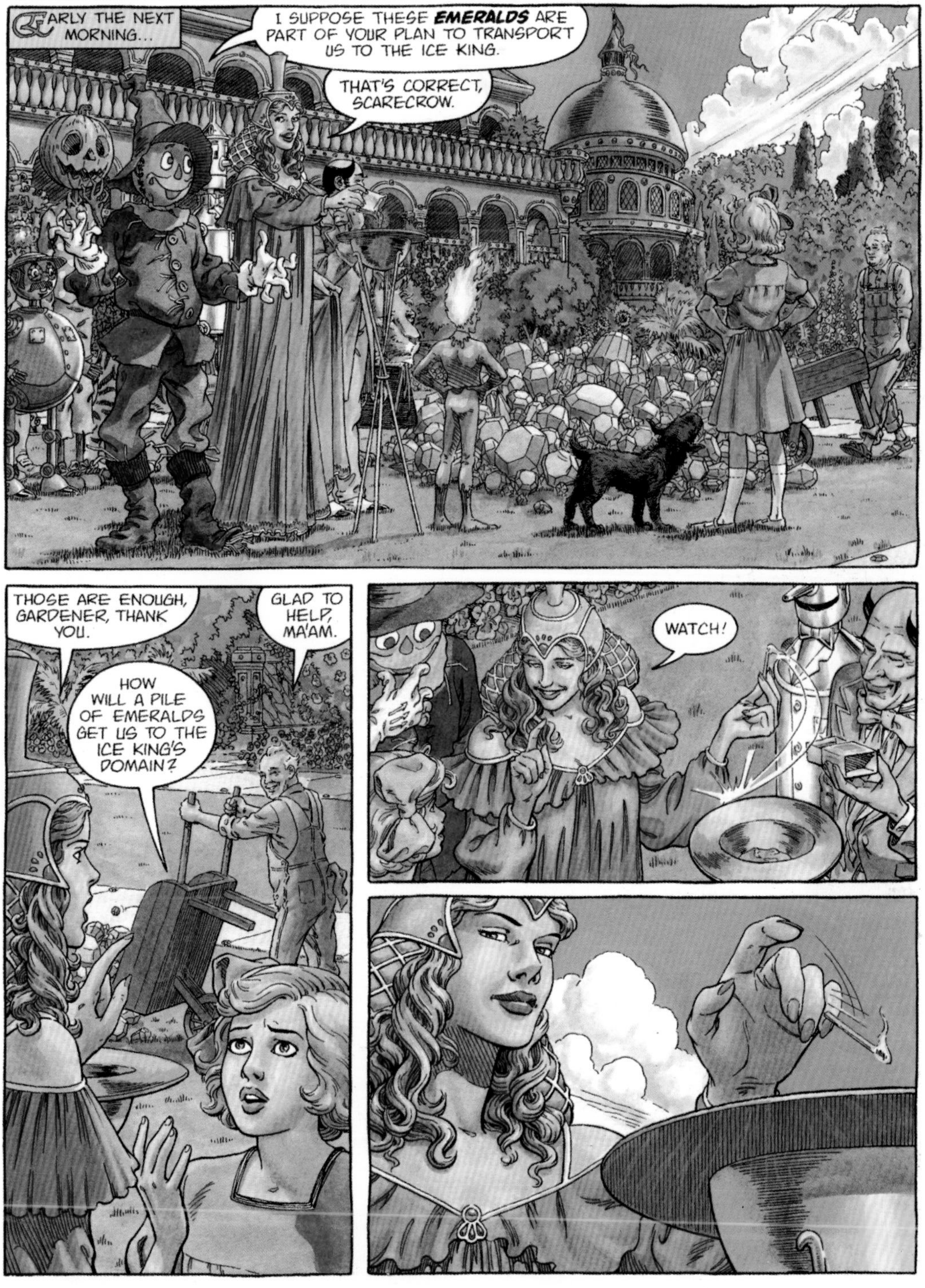
EARLY THE NEXT MORNING...
I SUPPOSE THESE **EMERALDS** ARE PART OF YOUR PLAN TO TRANSPORT US TO THE ICE KING.
THAT'S CORRECT, SCARECROW.
THOSE ARE ENOUGH, GARDENER, THANK YOU.
GLAD TO HELP, MA'AM.
HOW WILL A PILE OF EMERALDS GET US TO THE ICE KING'S DOMAIN?
WATCH!

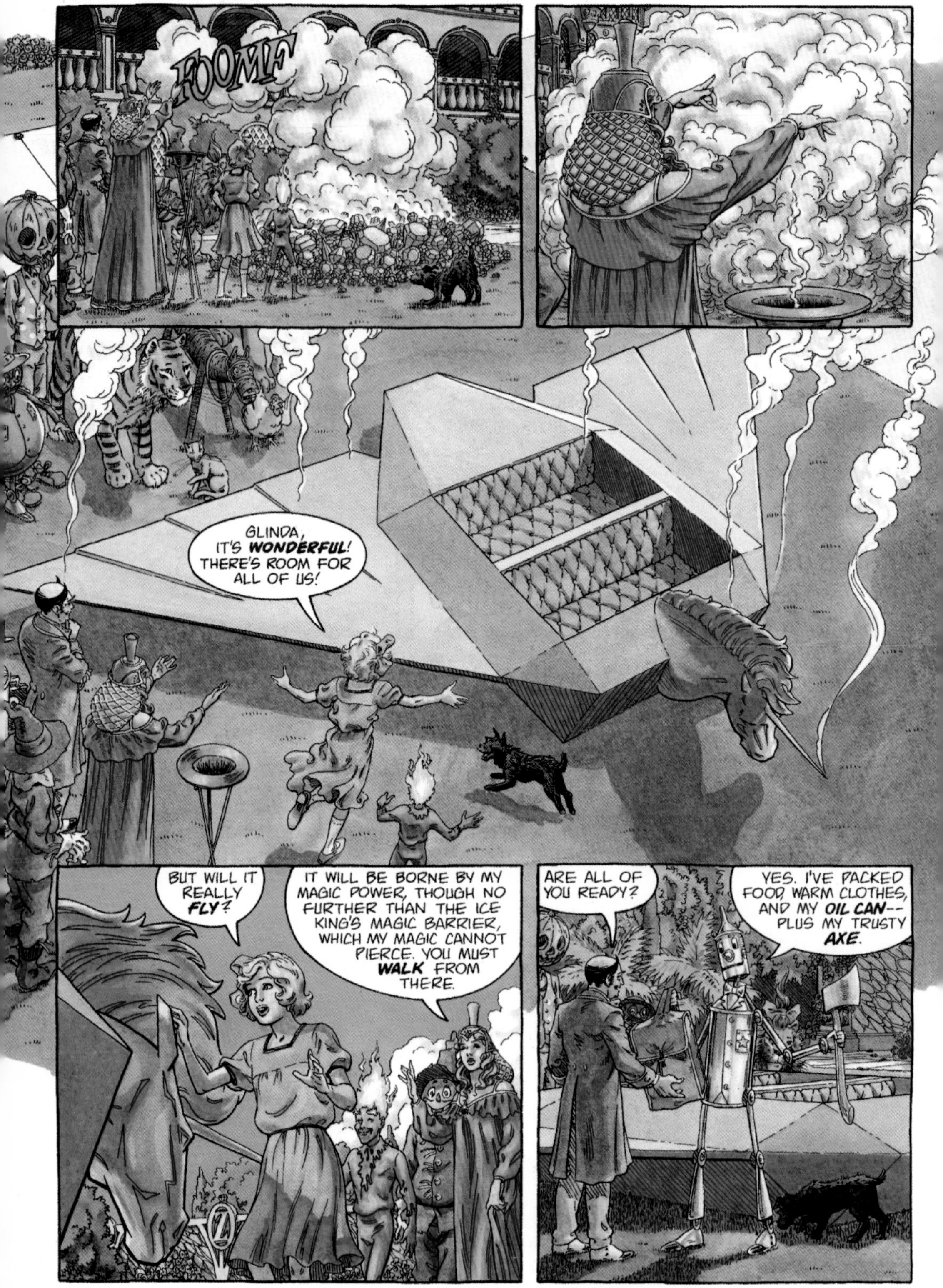
FOOMF
GLINDA, IT'S **WONDERFUL**! THERE'S ROOM FOR ALL OF US!
BUT WILL IT REALLY **FLY**?
IT WILL BE BORNE BY MY MAGIC POWER, THOUGH NO FURTHER THAN THE ICE KING'S MAGIC BARRIER, WHICH MY MAGIC CANNOT PIERCE. YOU MUST **WALK** FROM THERE.
ARE ALL OF YOU READY?
YES. I'VE PACKED FOOD, WARM CLOTHES, AND MY **OIL CAN**-- PLUS MY TRUSTY **AXE**.

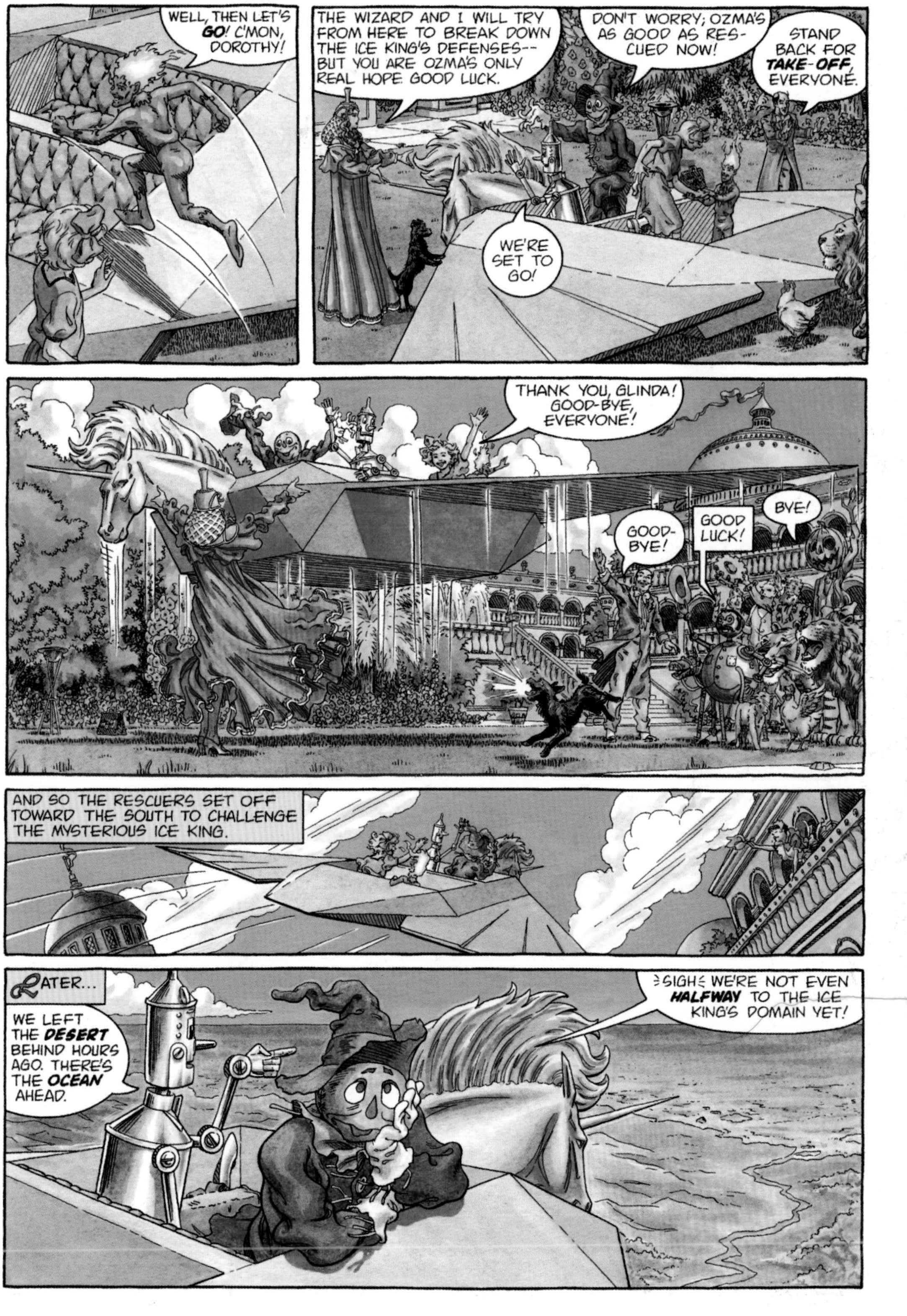
WELL, THEN LET'S **GO**! C'MON, DOROTHY!
THE WIZARD AND I WILL TRY FROM HERE TO BREAK DOWN THE ICE KING'S DEFENSES-- BUT YOU ARE OZMA'S ONLY REAL HOPE. GOOD LUCK.
DON'T WORRY; OZMA'S AS GOOD AS RESCUED NOW!
STAND BACK FOR **TAKE-OFF**, EVERYONE.
WE'RE SET TO GO!
THANK YOU, GLINDA! GOOD-BYE, EVERYONE!
GOOD-BYE!
GOOD LUCK!
BYE!
AND SO THE RESCUERS SET OFF TOWARD THE SOUTH TO CHALLENGE THE MYSTERIOUS ICE KING.
LATER...
WE LEFT THE **DESERT** BEHIND HOURS AGO. THERE'S THE **OCEAN** AHEAD.
SIGH WE'RE NOT EVEN **HALFWAY** TO THE ICE KING'S DOMAIN YET!

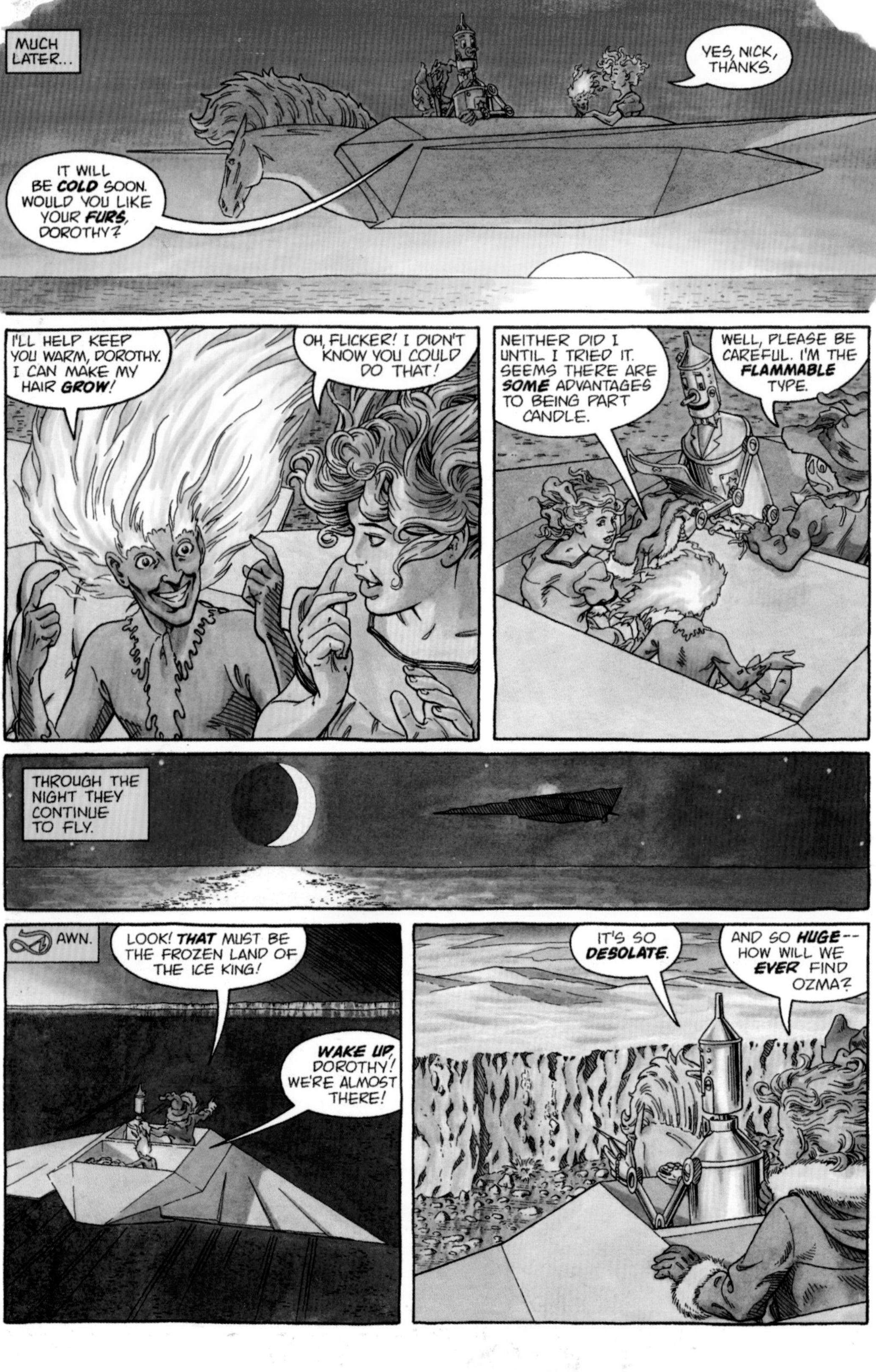
MUCH LATER...
YES, NICK, THANKS.
IT WILL BE COLD SOON. WOULD YOU LIKE YOUR FURS, DOROTHY?
I'LL HELP KEEP YOU WARM, DOROTHY. I CAN MAKE MY HAIR GROW!
OH, FLICKER! I DIDN'T KNOW YOU COULD DO THAT!
NEITHER DID I UNTIL I TRIED IT. SEEMS THERE ARE SOME ADVANTAGES TO BEING PART CANDLE.
WELL, PLEASE BE CAREFUL. I'M THE FLAMMABLE TYPE.
THROUGH THE NIGHT THEY CONTINUE TO FLY.
DAWN.
LOOK! THAT MUST BE THE FROZEN LAND OF THE ICE KING!
WAKE UP, DOROTHY! WE'RE ALMOST THERE!
IT'S SO DESOLATE.
AND SO HUGE-- HOW WILL WE EVER FIND OZMA?

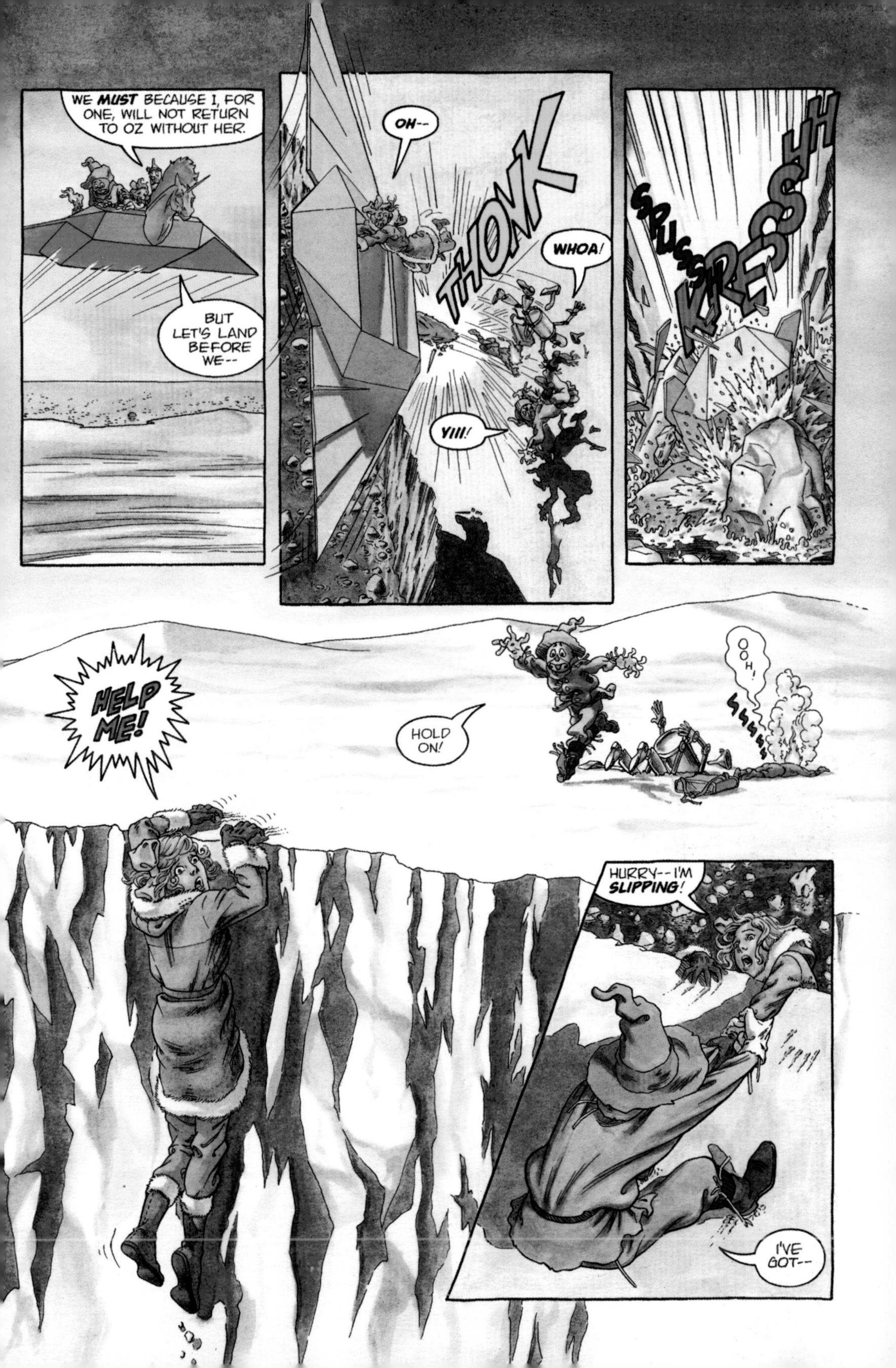

WE MUST BECAUSE I, FOR ONE, WILL NOT RETURN TO OZ WITHOUT HER.
BUT LET'S LAND BEFORE WE--
OH--
THONK
WHOA!
YIII!
SPLUSSH
KRESSHH
HELP ME!
HOLD ON!
OOH!
HURRY--I'M SLIPPING!
I'VE GOT--

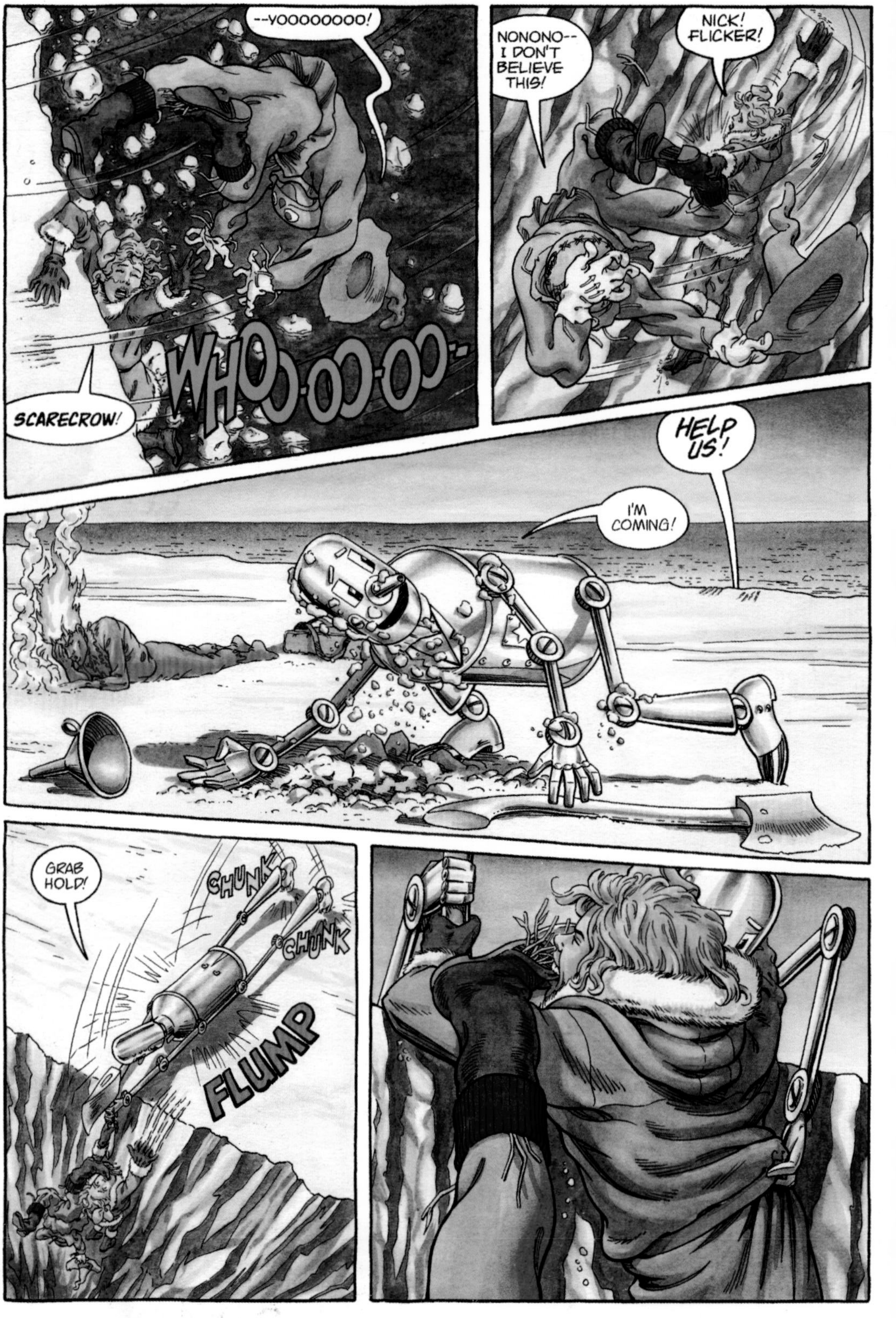
--YOOOOOOOO!
WHO-OO-OO-OO-
SCARECROW!
NONONO-- I DON'T BELIEVE THIS!
NICK! FLICKER!
HELP US!
I'M COMING!
GRAB HOLD!
CHUNK
CHUNK
FLUMP

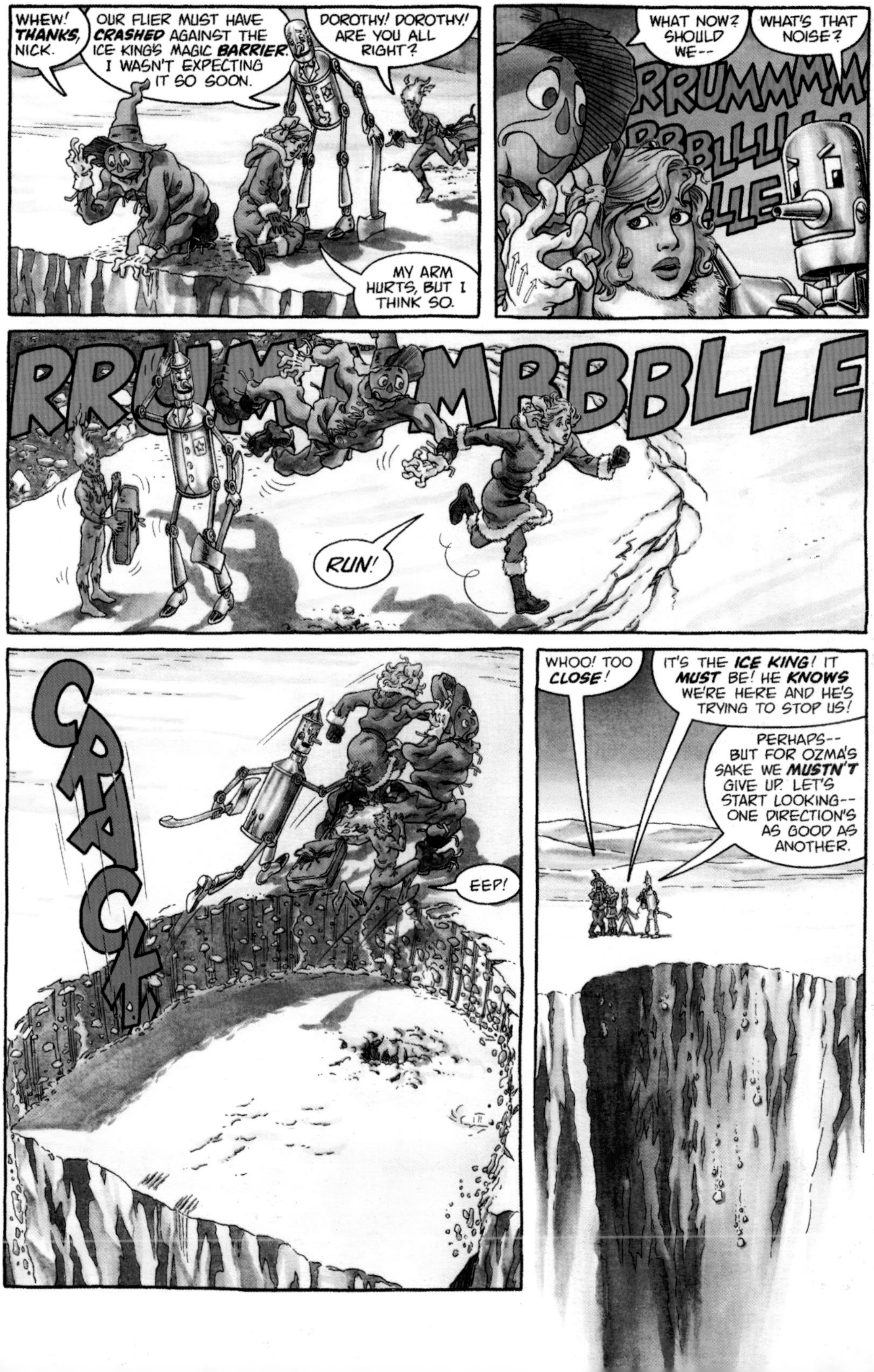
WHEW! THANKS, NICK.
OUR FLIER MUST HAVE CRASHED AGAINST THE ICE KING'S MAGIC BARRIER. I WASN'T EXPECTING IT SO SOON.
DOROTHY! DOROTHY! ARE YOU ALL RIGHT?
MY ARM HURTS, BUT I THINK SO.
WHAT NOW? SHOULD WE--
WHAT'S THAT NOISE?
RRUMMMM
BBLLLL
LLE
RRUMMMBBBLLE
RUN!
CRACK
EEP!
WHOO! TOO CLOSE!
IT'S THE ICE KING! IT MUST BE! HE KNOWS WE'RE HERE AND HE'S TRYING TO STOP US!
PERHAPS-- BUT FOR OZMA'S SAKE WE MUSTN'T GIVE UP. LET'S START LOOKING-- ONE DIRECTION'S AS GOOD AS ANOTHER.

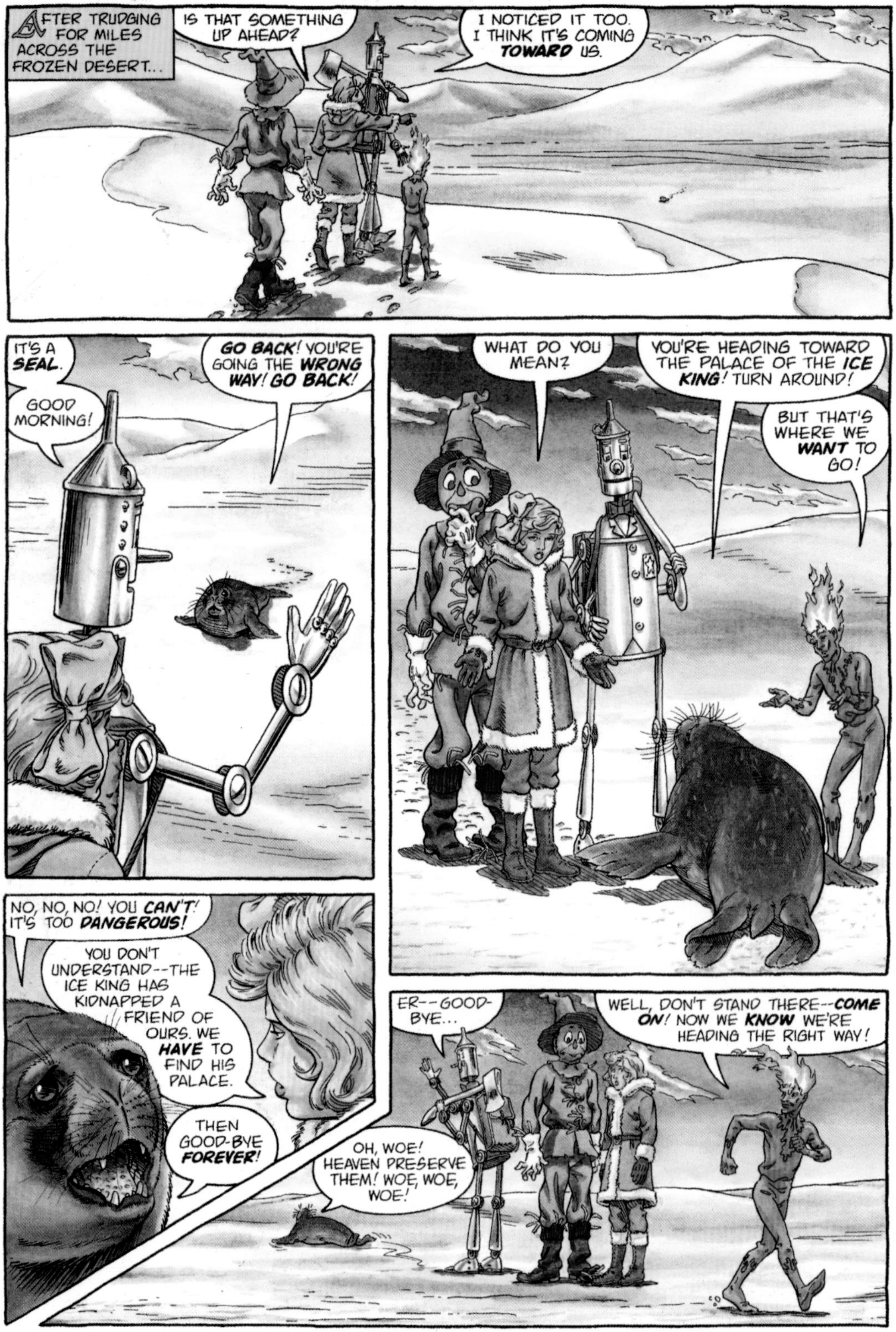

AFTER TRUDGING FOR MILES ACROSS THE FROZEN DESERT...
IS THAT SOMETHING UP AHEAD?
I NOTICED IT TOO. I THINK IT'S COMING TOWARD US.
IT'S A SEAL.
GOOD MORNING!
GO BACK! YOU'RE GOING THE WRONG WAY! GO BACK!
WHAT DO YOU MEAN?
YOU'RE HEADING TOWARD THE PALACE OF THE ICE KING! TURN AROUND!
BUT THAT'S WHERE WE WANT TO GO!
NO, NO, NO! YOU CAN'T! IT'S TOO DANGEROUS!
YOU DON'T UNDERSTAND--THE ICE KING HAS KIDNAPPED A FRIEND OF OURS. WE HAVE TO FIND HIS PALACE.
THEN GOOD-BYE FOREVER!
ER--GOOD-BYE...
OH, WOE! HEAVEN PRESERVE THEM! WOE, WOE, WOE!
WELL, DON'T STAND THERE--COME ON! NOW WE KNOW WE'RE HEADING THE RIGHT WAY!

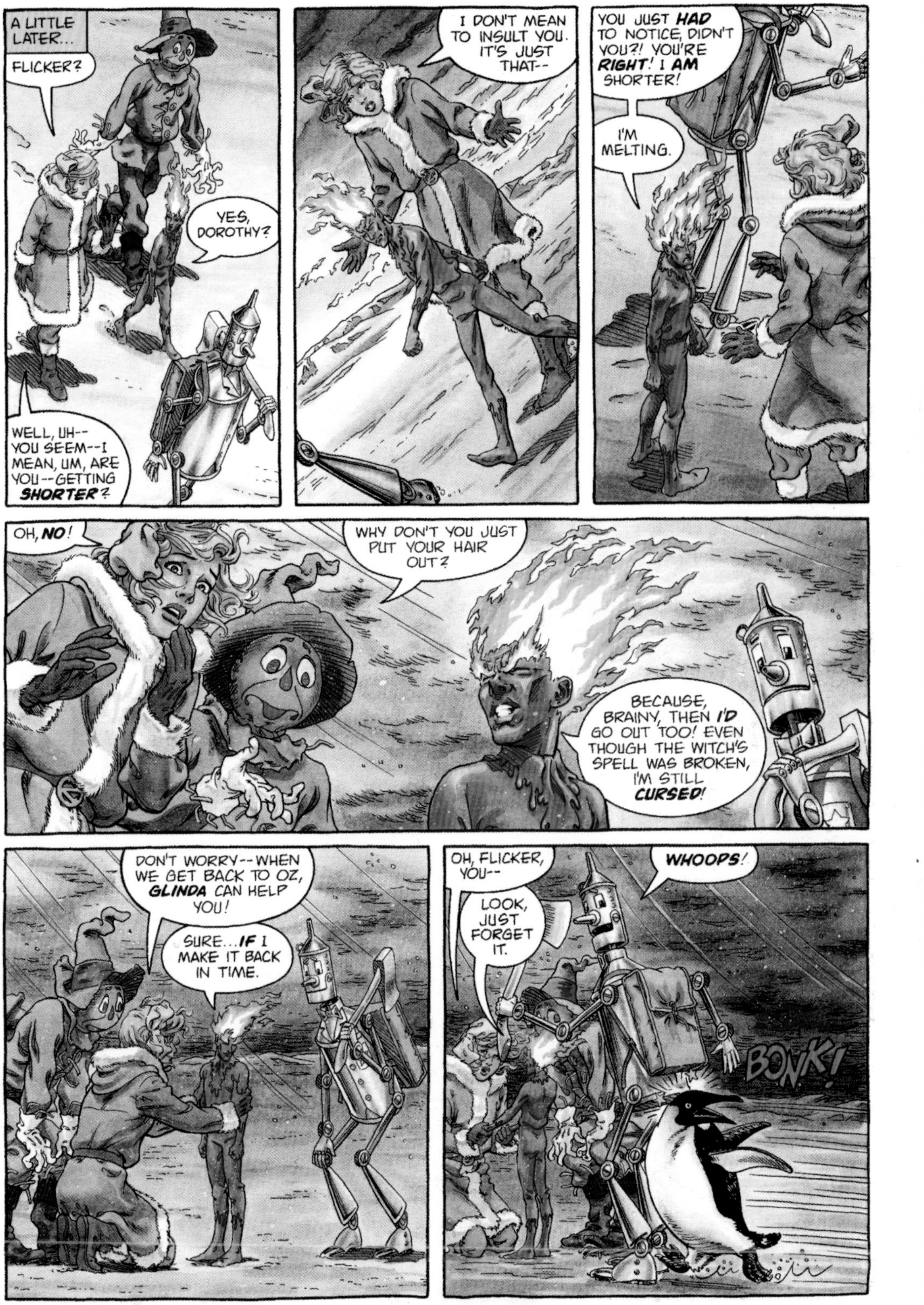
A LITTLE LATER...
FLICKER?
YES, DOROTHY?
WELL, UH-- YOU SEEM--I MEAN, UM, ARE YOU--GETTING **SHORTER**?
I DON'T MEAN TO INSULT YOU. IT'S JUST THAT--
YOU JUST **HAD** TO NOTICE, DIDN'T YOU?! YOU'RE **RIGHT**! I **AM** SHORTER!
I'M MELTING.
OH, **NO**!
WHY DON'T YOU JUST PUT YOUR HAIR OUT?
BECAUSE, BRAINY, THEN **I'D** GO OUT TOO! EVEN THOUGH THE WITCH'S SPELL WAS BROKEN, I'M STILL **CURSED**!
DON'T WORRY--WHEN WE GET BACK TO OZ, **GLINDA** CAN HELP YOU!
SURE... **IF** I MAKE IT BACK IN TIME.
OH, FLICKER, YOU--
LOOK, JUST FORGET IT.
**WHOOPS**!
BONK!

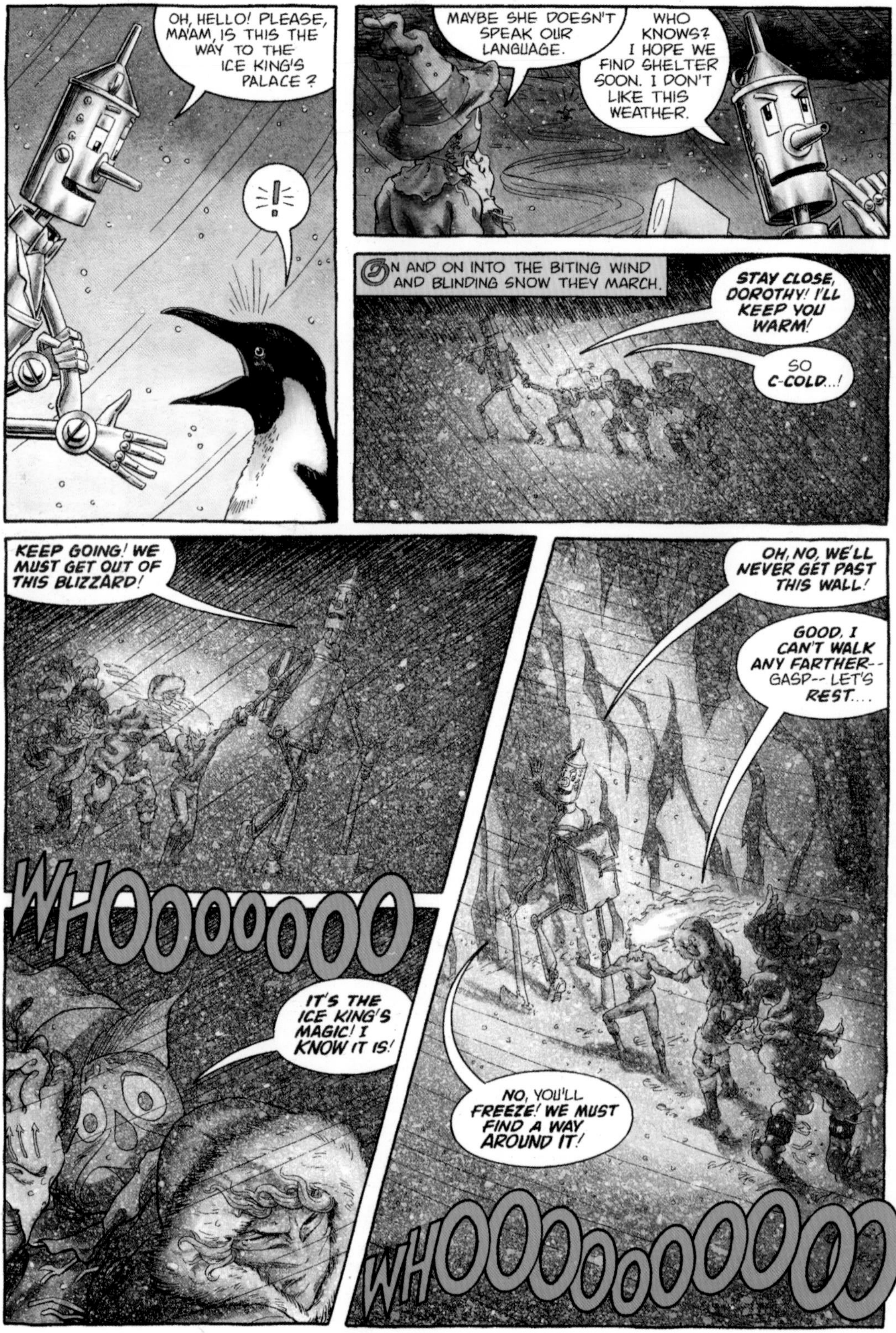

OH, HELLO! PLEASE, MA'AM, IS THIS THE WAY TO THE ICE KING'S PALACE?
!
MAYBE SHE DOESN'T SPEAK OUR LANGUAGE.
WHO KNOWS? I HOPE WE FIND SHELTER SOON. I DON'T LIKE THIS WEATHER.
ON AND ON INTO THE BITING WIND AND BLINDING SNOW THEY MARCH.
STAY CLOSE, DOROTHY! I'LL KEEP YOU WARM!
SO C-COLD...!
KEEP GOING! WE MUST GET OUT OF THIS BLIZZARD!
WHOOOOOOO
IT'S THE ICE KING'S MAGIC! I KNOW IT IS!
OH, NO, WE'LL NEVER GET PAST THIS WALL!
GOOD, I CAN'T WALK ANY FARTHER-- GASP-- LET'S REST....
NO, YOU'LL FREEZE! WE MUST FIND A WAY AROUND IT!
WHOOOOOOOOOOOO

# Chapter Four In the Ice Palace

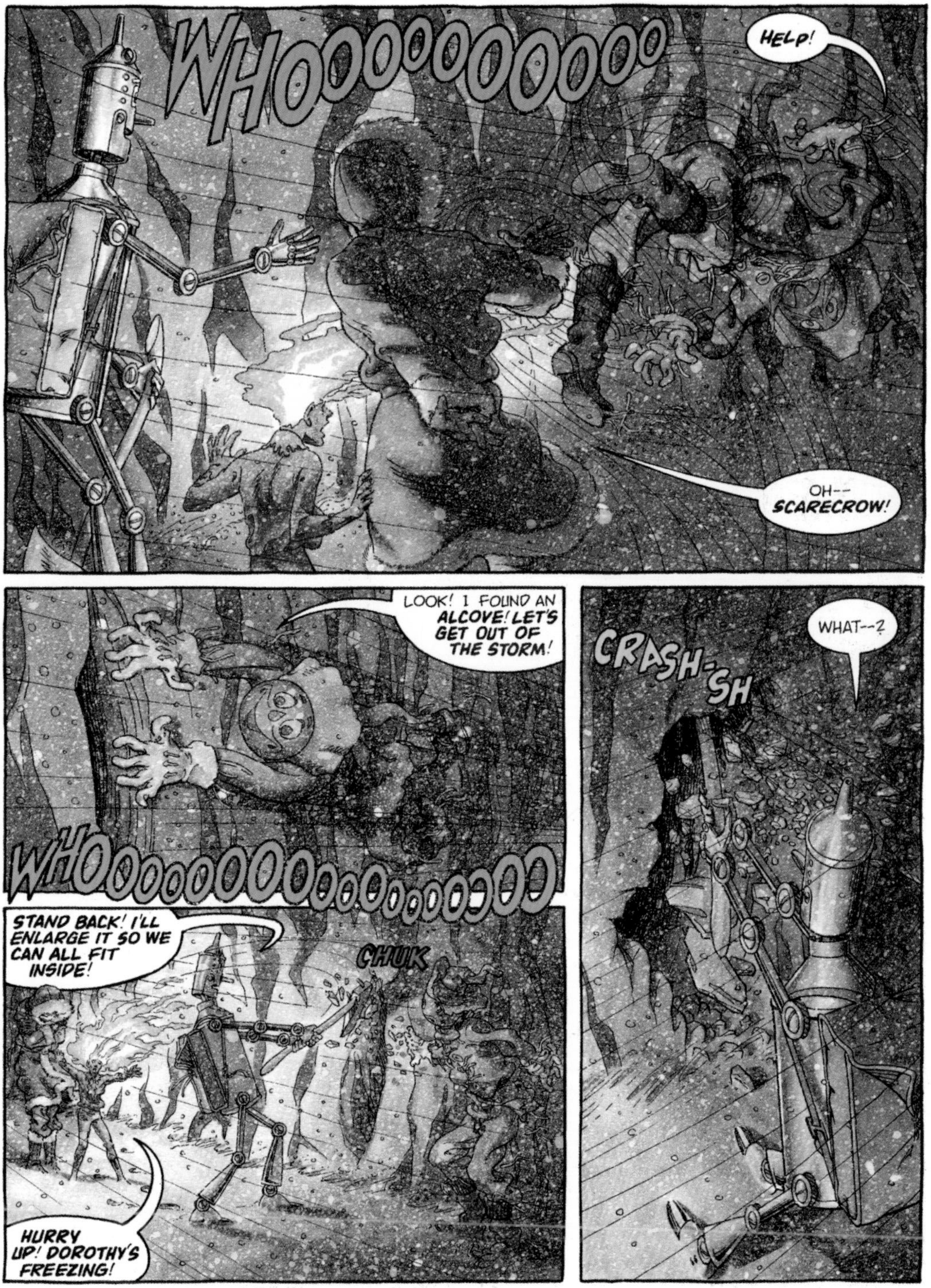
WHOOOOOOOOOO
HELP!
OH-- SCARECROW!
LOOK! I FOUND AN ALCOVE! LET'S GET OUT OF THE STORM!
WHOOOOOOOOOOOOOOOOO
STAND BACK! I'LL ENLARGE IT SO WE CAN ALL FIT INSIDE!
CHUK
HURRY UP! DOROTHY'S FREEZING!
WHAT--?
CRASH-SH

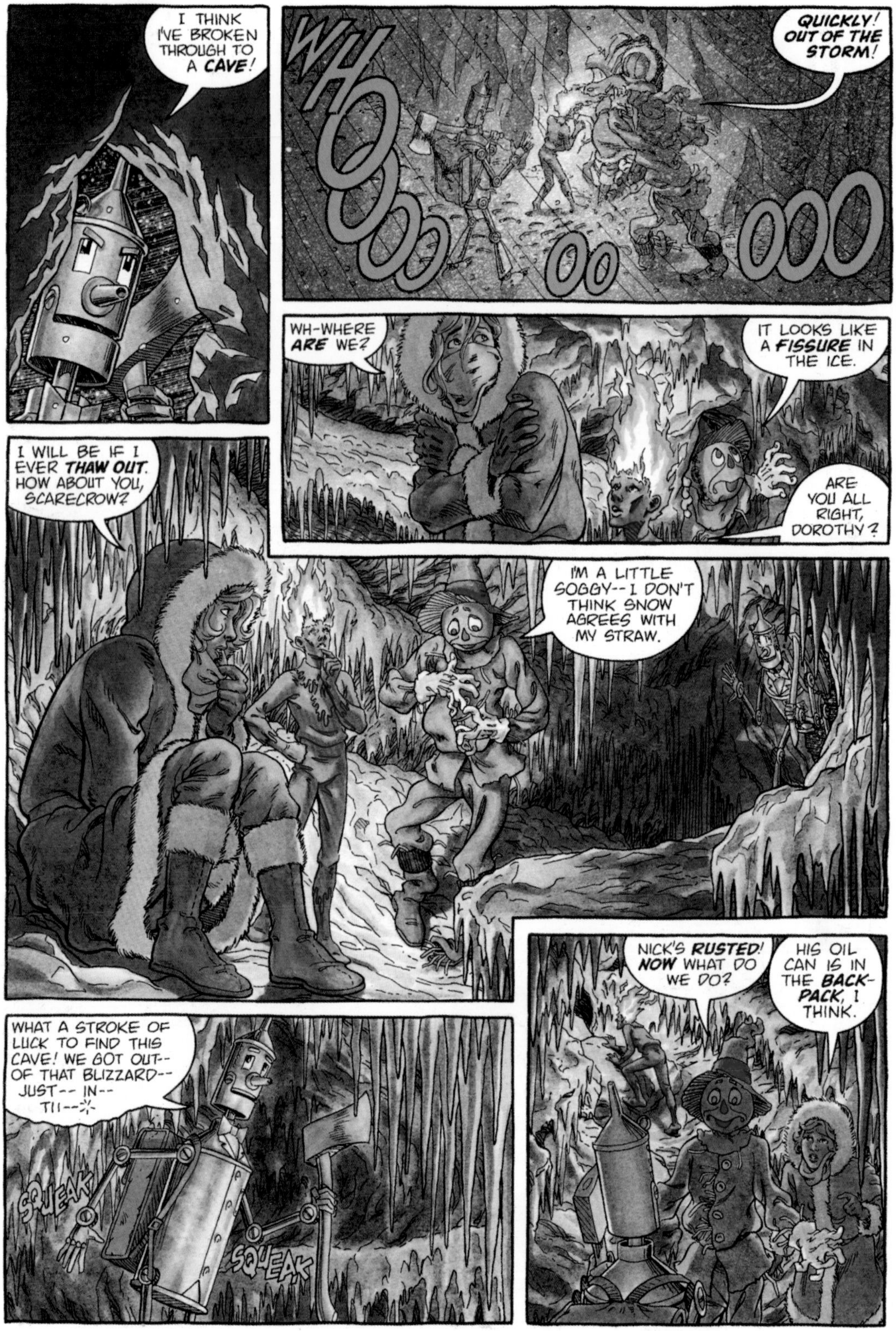
I THINK I'VE BROKEN THROUGH TO A **CAVE**!
WHOOOO
**QUICKLY! OUT OF THE STORM!**
OO
OOO
WH-WHERE **ARE** WE?
IT LOOKS LIKE A **FISSURE** IN THE ICE.
ARE YOU ALL RIGHT, DOROTHY?
I WILL BE IF I EVER **THAW OUT**. HOW ABOUT YOU, SCARECROW?
I'M A LITTLE SOGGY-- I DON'T THINK SNOW AGREES WITH MY STRAW.
WHAT A STROKE OF LUCK TO FIND THIS CAVE! WE GOT OUT-- OF THAT BLIZZARD-- JUST-- IN-- TI--
SQUEAK
SQUEAK
NICK'S **RUSTED**! **NOW** WHAT DO WE DO?
HIS OIL CAN IS IN THE **BACK-PACK**, I THINK.

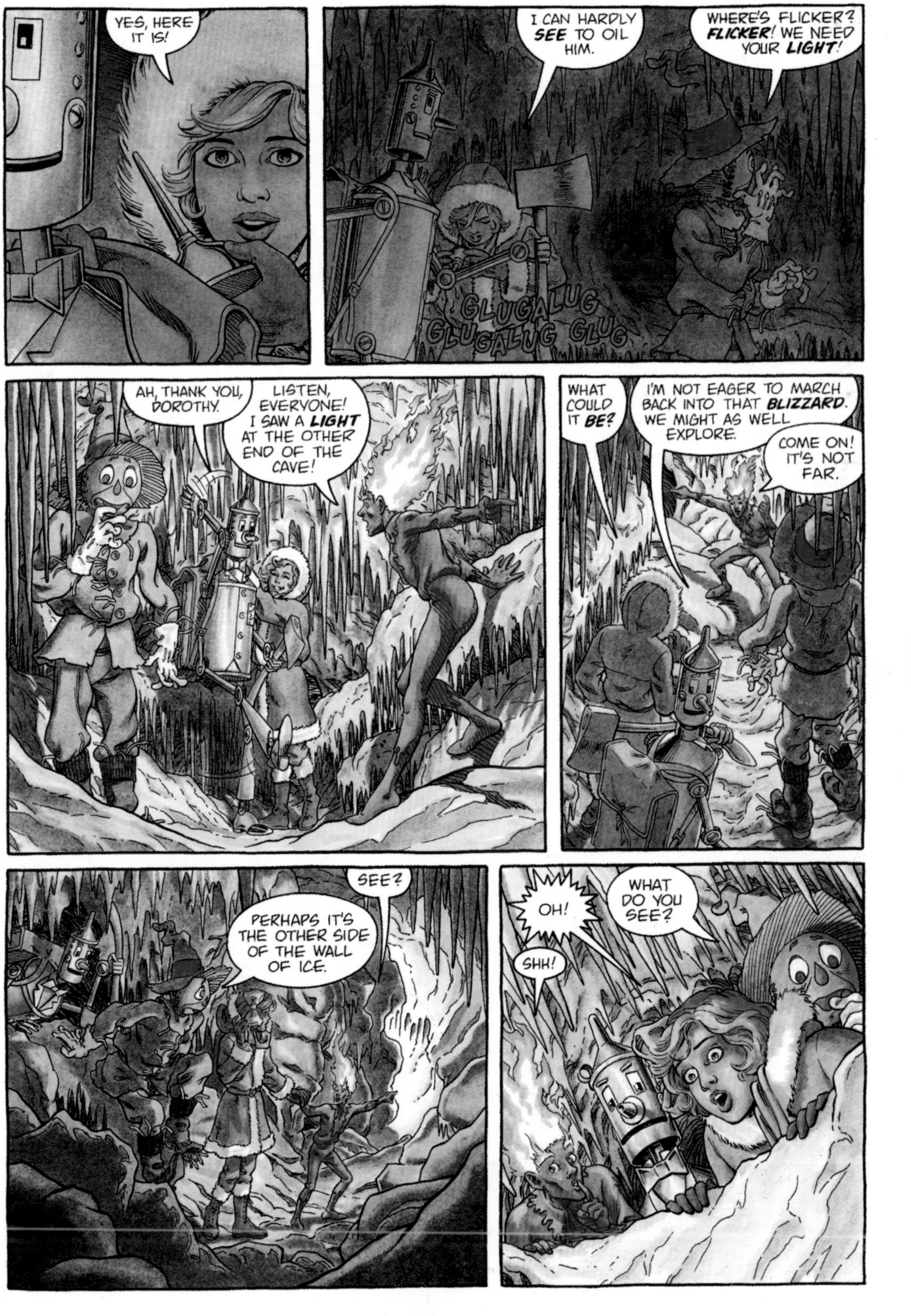
YES, HERE IT IS!
I CAN HARDLY SEE TO OIL HIM.
WHERE'S FLICKER? FLICKER! WE NEED YOUR LIGHT!
GLUGALUG GLUGALUG GLUG
AH, THANK YOU, DOROTHY.
LISTEN, EVERYONE! I SAW A LIGHT AT THE OTHER END OF THE CAVE!
WHAT COULD IT BE?
I'M NOT EAGER TO MARCH BACK INTO THAT BLIZZARD. WE MIGHT AS WELL EXPLORE.
COME ON! IT'S NOT FAR.
SEE?
PERHAPS IT'S THE OTHER SIDE OF THE WALL OF ICE.
OH!
WHAT DO YOU SEE?
SHH!

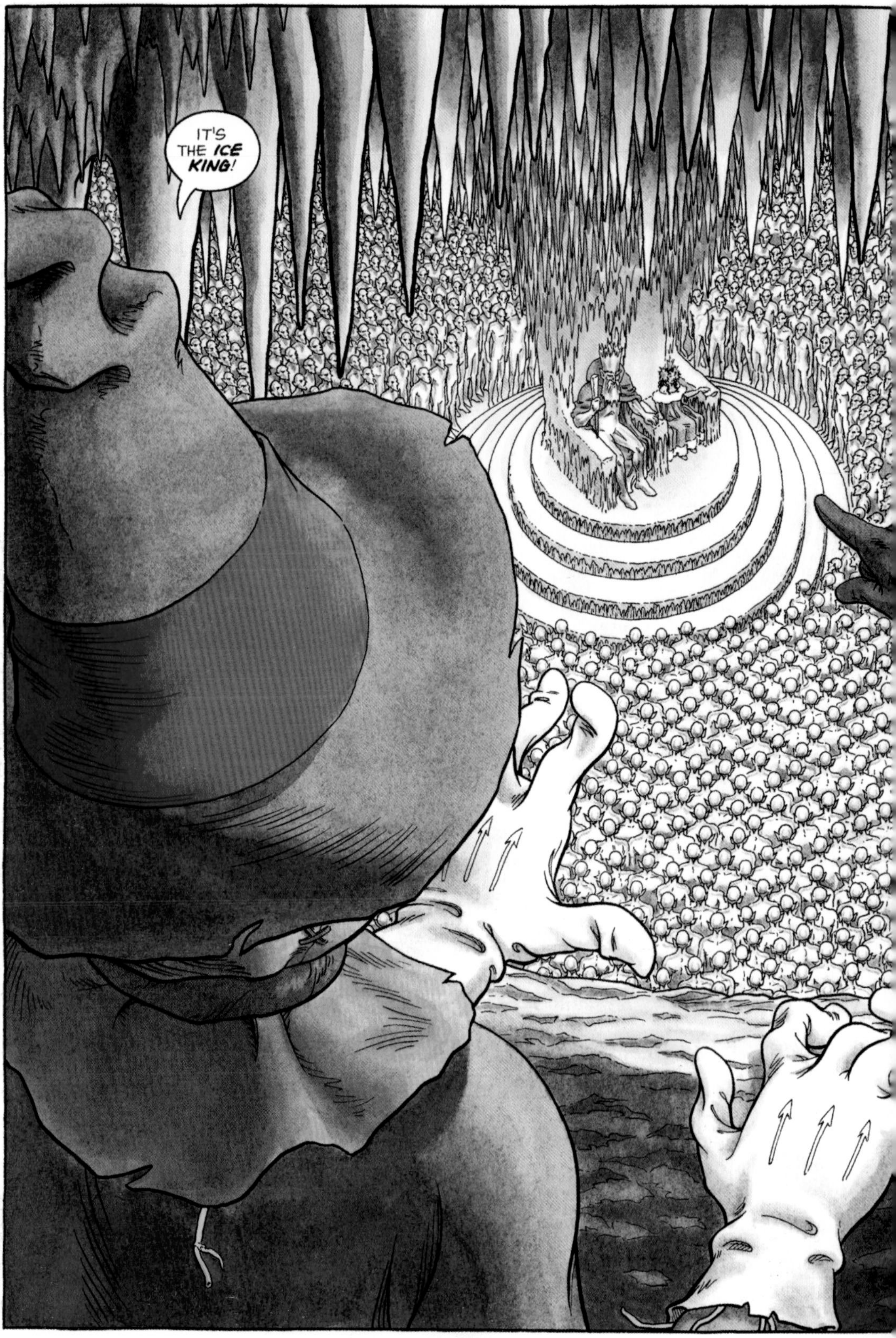
IT'S THE ICE KING!

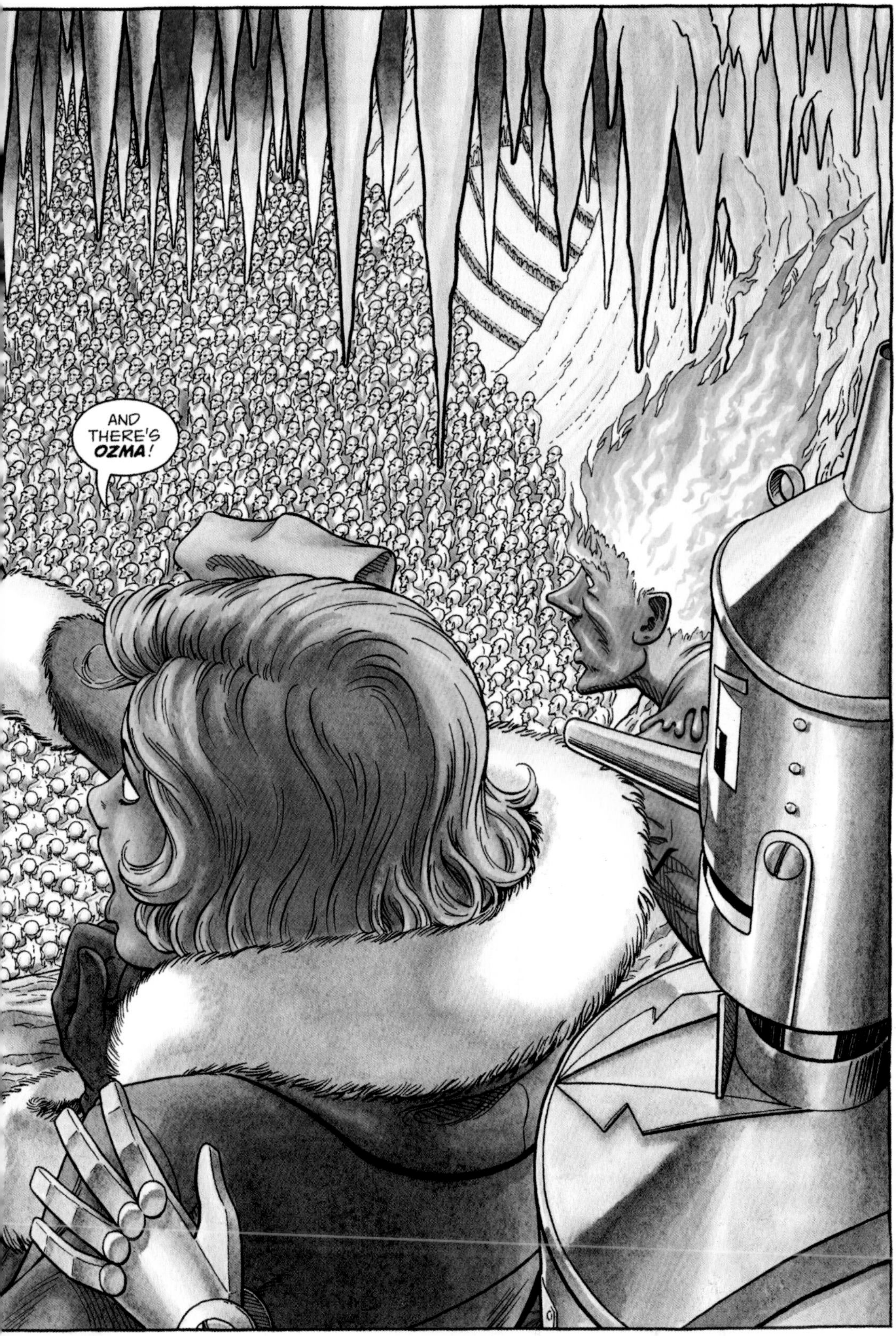
AND THERE'S *OZMA*!

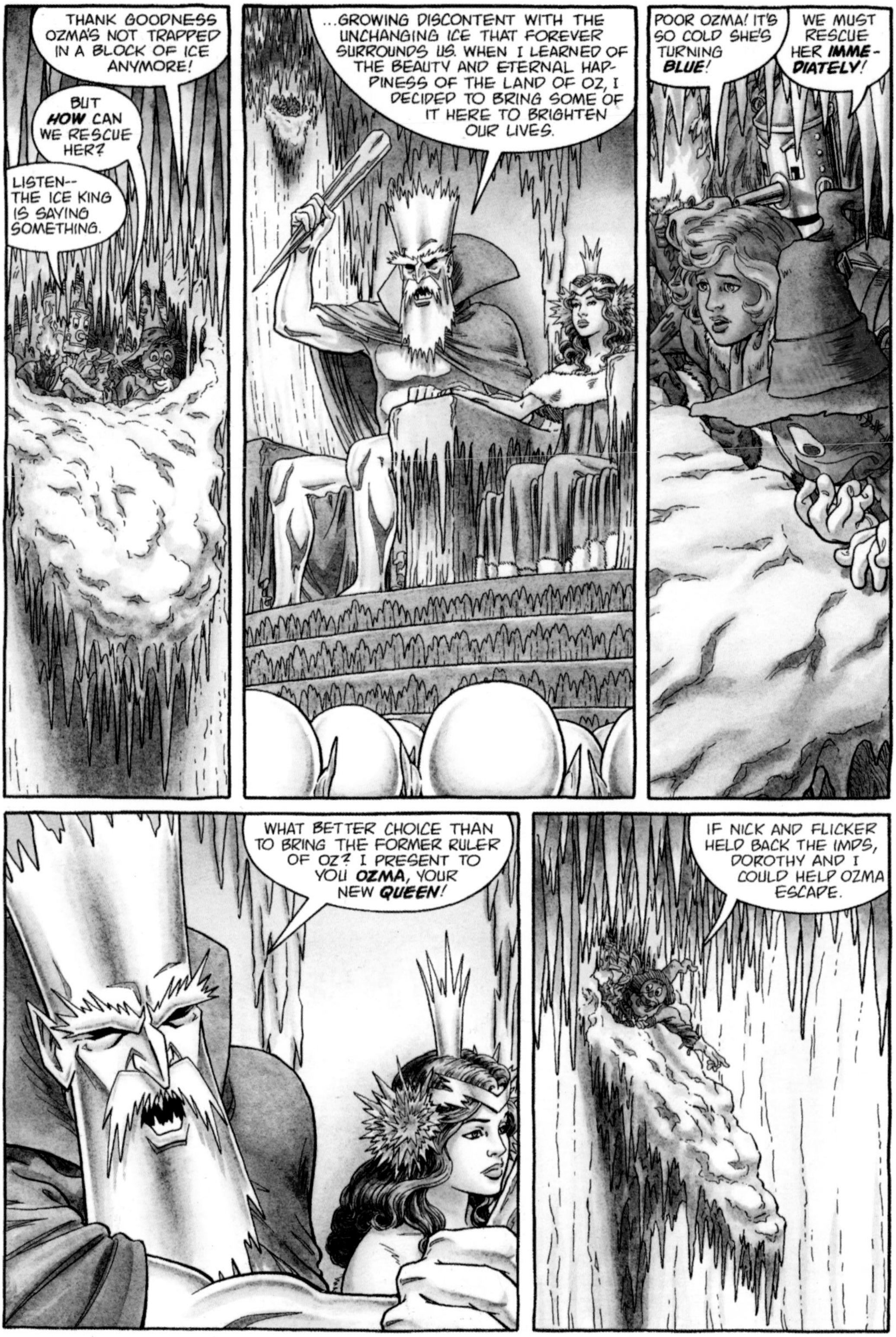
THANK GOODNESS OZMA'S NOT TRAPPED IN A BLOCK OF ICE ANYMORE!
BUT HOW CAN WE RESCUE HER?
LISTEN-- THE ICE KING IS SAYING SOMETHING.
...GROWING DISCONTENT WITH THE UNCHANGING ICE THAT FOREVER SURROUNDS US. WHEN I LEARNED OF THE BEAUTY AND ETERNAL HAPPINESS OF THE LAND OF OZ, I DECIDED TO BRING SOME OF IT HERE TO BRIGHTEN OUR LIVES.
POOR OZMA! IT'S SO COLD SHE'S TURNING BLUE!
WE MUST RESCUE HER IMMEDIATELY!
WHAT BETTER CHOICE THAN TO BRING THE FORMER RULER OF OZ? I PRESENT TO YOU OZMA, YOUR NEW QUEEN!
IF NICK AND FLICKER HELD BACK THE IMPS, DOROTHY AND I COULD HELP OZMA ESCAPE.

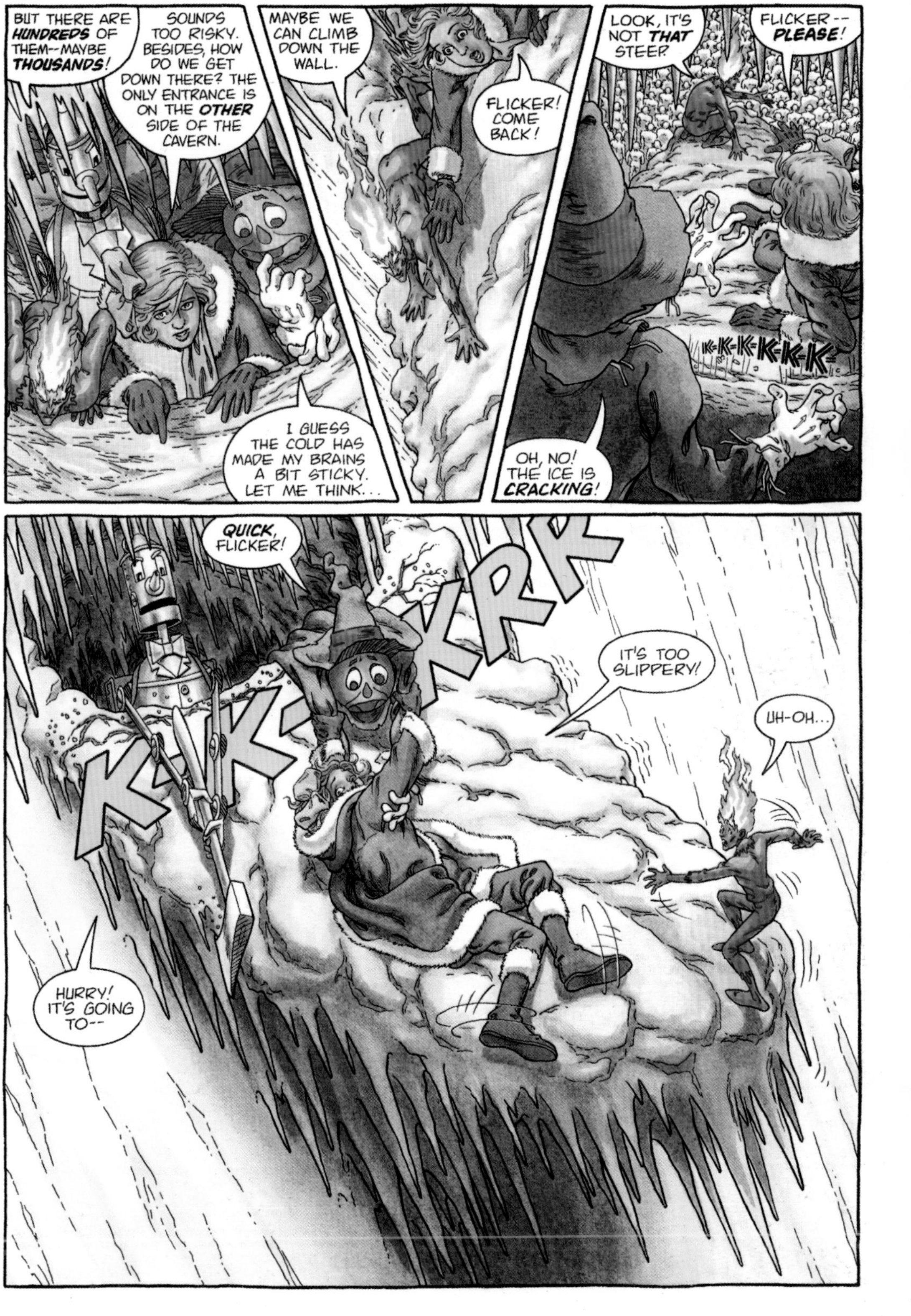
BUT THERE ARE HUNDREDS OF THEM--MAYBE THOUSANDS!
SOUNDS TOO RISKY. BESIDES, HOW DO WE GET DOWN THERE? THE ONLY ENTRANCE IS ON THE OTHER SIDE OF THE CAVERN.
I GUESS THE COLD HAS MADE MY BRAINS A BIT STICKY. LET ME THINK...
MAYBE WE CAN CLIMB DOWN THE WALL.
FLICKER! COME BACK!
LOOK, IT'S NOT THAT STEEP.
FLICKER-- PLEASE!
K-K-K-K-K-K-K-
OH, NO! THE ICE IS CRACKING!
QUICK, FLICKER!
K-K-KRRR
IT'S TOO SLIPPERY!
UH-OH...
HURRY! IT'S GOING TO--

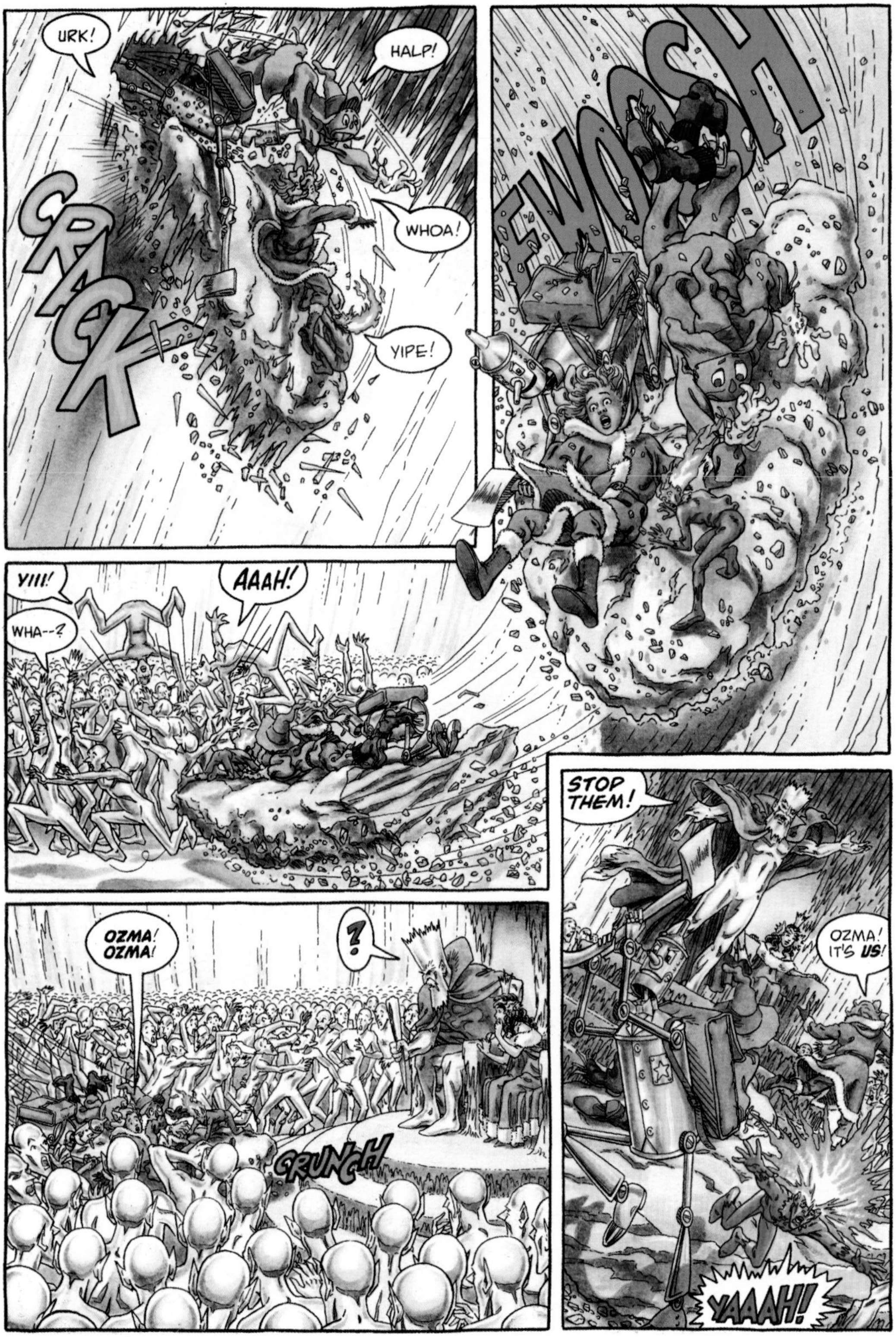
URK!
HALP!
WHOA!
YIPE!
CRACK
FWOOSH
YIII!
WHA--?
AAAH!
STOP THEM!
OZMA! IT'S US!
YAAAH!
OZMA! OZMA!
?
CRUNCH!

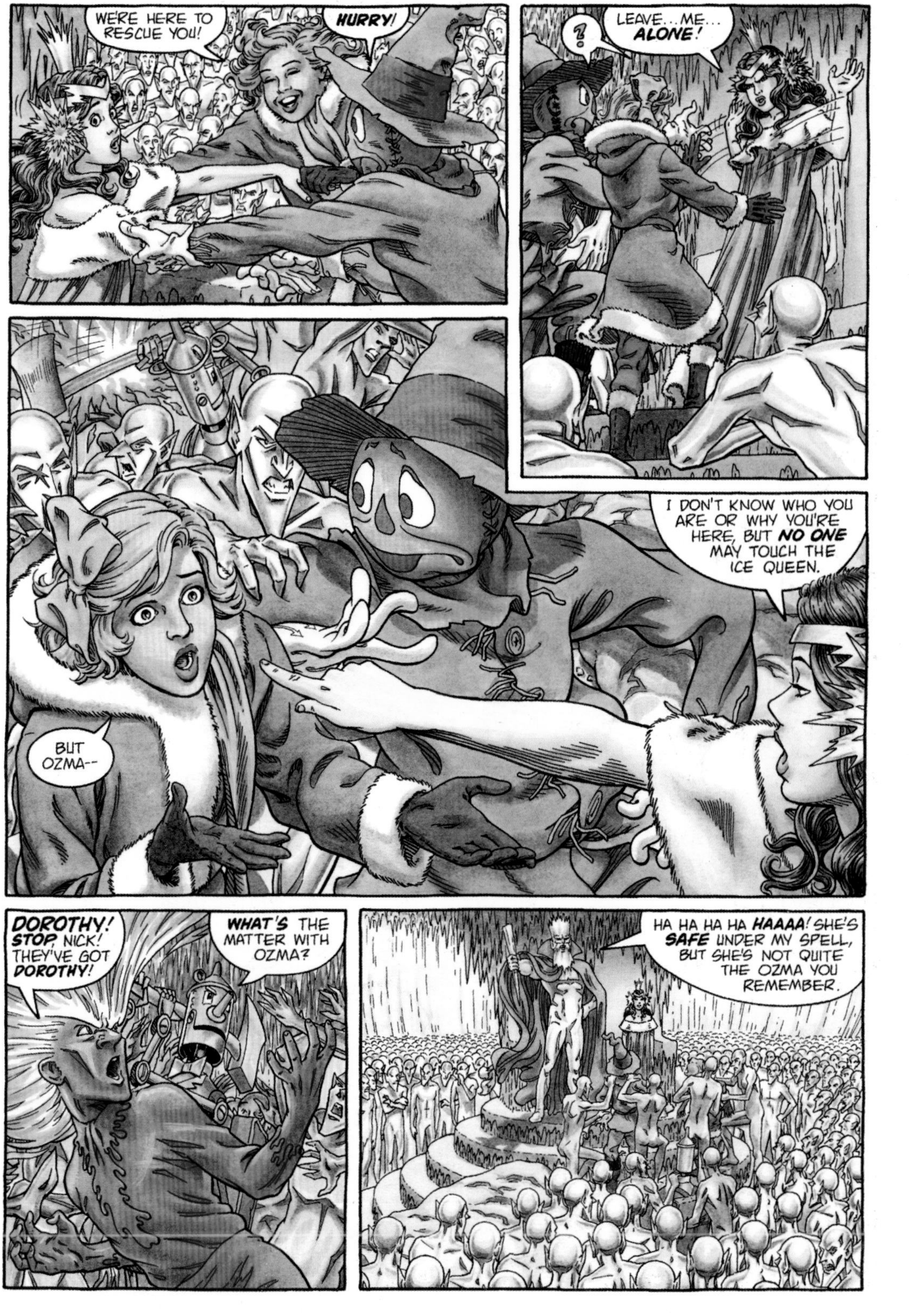
WE'RE HERE TO RESCUE YOU!
HURRY!
?
LEAVE... ME... ALONE!
I DON'T KNOW WHO YOU ARE OR WHY YOU'RE HERE, BUT NO ONE MAY TOUCH THE ICE QUEEN.
BUT OZMA--
DOROTHY! STOP, NICK! THEY'VE GOT DOROTHY!
WHAT'S THE MATTER WITH OZMA?
HA HA HA HA HAAAA! SHE'S SAFE UNDER MY SPELL, BUT SHE'S NOT QUITE THE OZMA YOU REMEMBER.

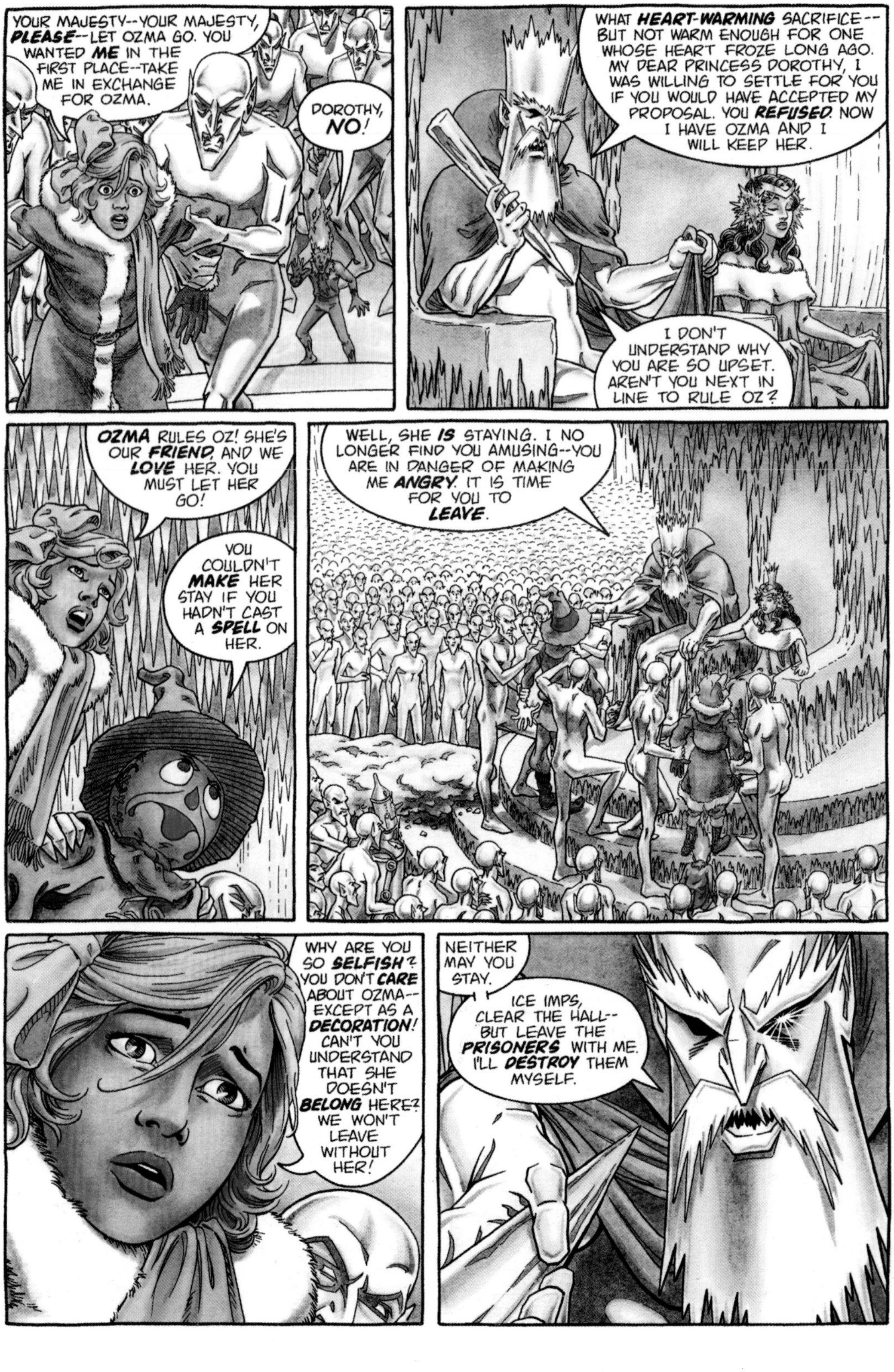
YOUR MAJESTY--YOUR MAJESTY, PLEASE--LET OZMA GO. YOU WANTED ME IN THE FIRST PLACE--TAKE ME IN EXCHANGE FOR OZMA.
DOROTHY, NO!
WHAT HEART-WARMING SACRIFICE--BUT NOT WARM ENOUGH FOR ONE WHOSE HEART FROZE LONG AGO. MY DEAR PRINCESS DOROTHY, I WAS WILLING TO SETTLE FOR YOU IF YOU WOULD HAVE ACCEPTED MY PROPOSAL. YOU REFUSED. NOW I HAVE OZMA AND I WILL KEEP HER.
I DON'T UNDERSTAND WHY YOU ARE SO UPSET. AREN'T YOU NEXT IN LINE TO RULE OZ?
OZMA RULES OZ! SHE'S OUR FRIEND, AND WE LOVE HER. YOU MUST LET HER GO!
YOU COULDN'T MAKE HER STAY IF YOU HADN'T CAST A SPELL ON HER.
WELL, SHE IS STAYING. I NO LONGER FIND YOU AMUSING--YOU ARE IN DANGER OF MAKING ME ANGRY. IT IS TIME FOR YOU TO LEAVE.
WHY ARE YOU SO SELFISH? YOU DON'T CARE ABOUT OZMA--EXCEPT AS A DECORATION! CAN'T YOU UNDERSTAND THAT SHE DOESN'T BELONG HERE? WE WON'T LEAVE WITHOUT HER!
NEITHER MAY YOU STAY.
ICE IMPS, CLEAR THE HALL--BUT LEAVE THE PRISONERS WITH ME. I'LL DESTROY THEM MYSELF.

# Chapter Five The Ice King's Power

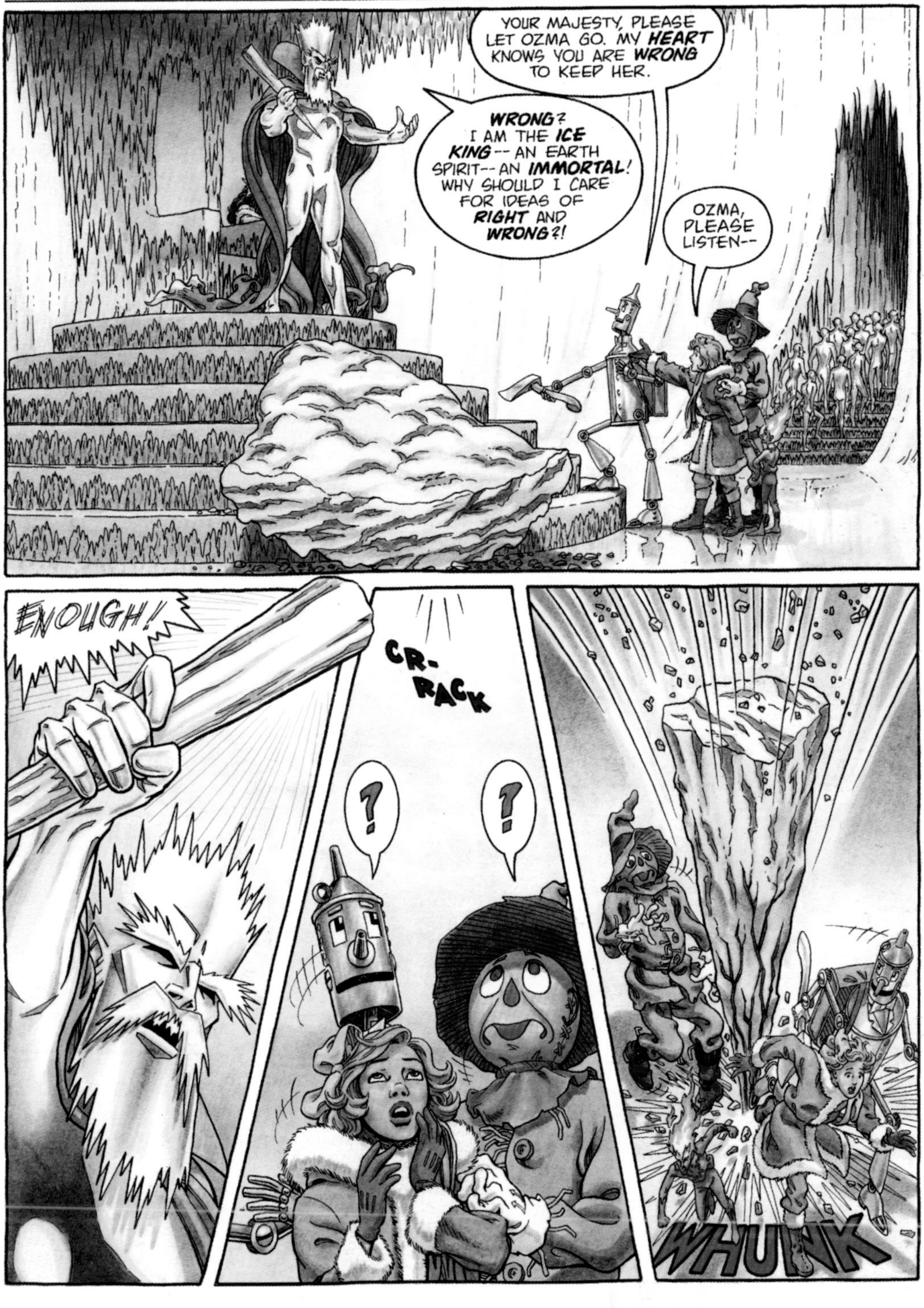
YOUR MAJESTY, PLEASE LET OZMA GO. MY **HEART** KNOWS YOU ARE **WRONG** TO KEEP HER.
**WRONG?** I AM THE **ICE KING**--AN EARTH SPIRIT--AN **IMMORTAL!** WHY SHOULD I CARE FOR IDEAS OF **RIGHT** AND **WRONG?!**
OZMA, PLEASE LISTEN--
ENOUGH!
CR-RACK
?
?
WHUNK

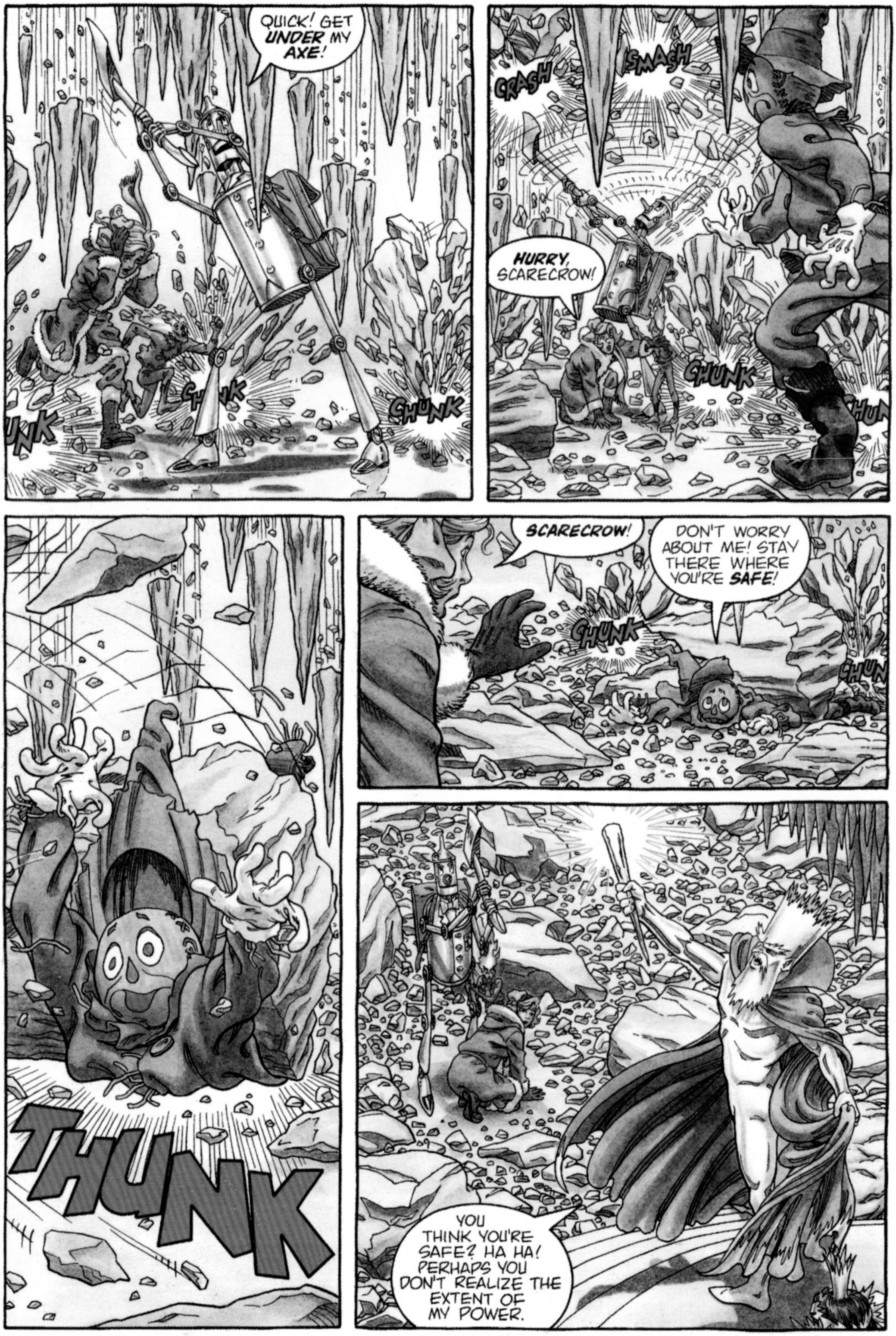
QUICK! GET **UNDER** MY **AXE**!
CHUNK
CHUNK
CRASH
SMASH
**HURRY**, SCARECROW!
CHUNK
THUNK
**SCARECROW**!
DON'T WORRY ABOUT ME! STAY THERE WHERE YOU'RE **SAFE**!
CHUNK
YOU THINK YOU'RE SAFE? HA HA! PERHAPS YOU DON'T REALIZE THE EXTENT OF MY POWER.

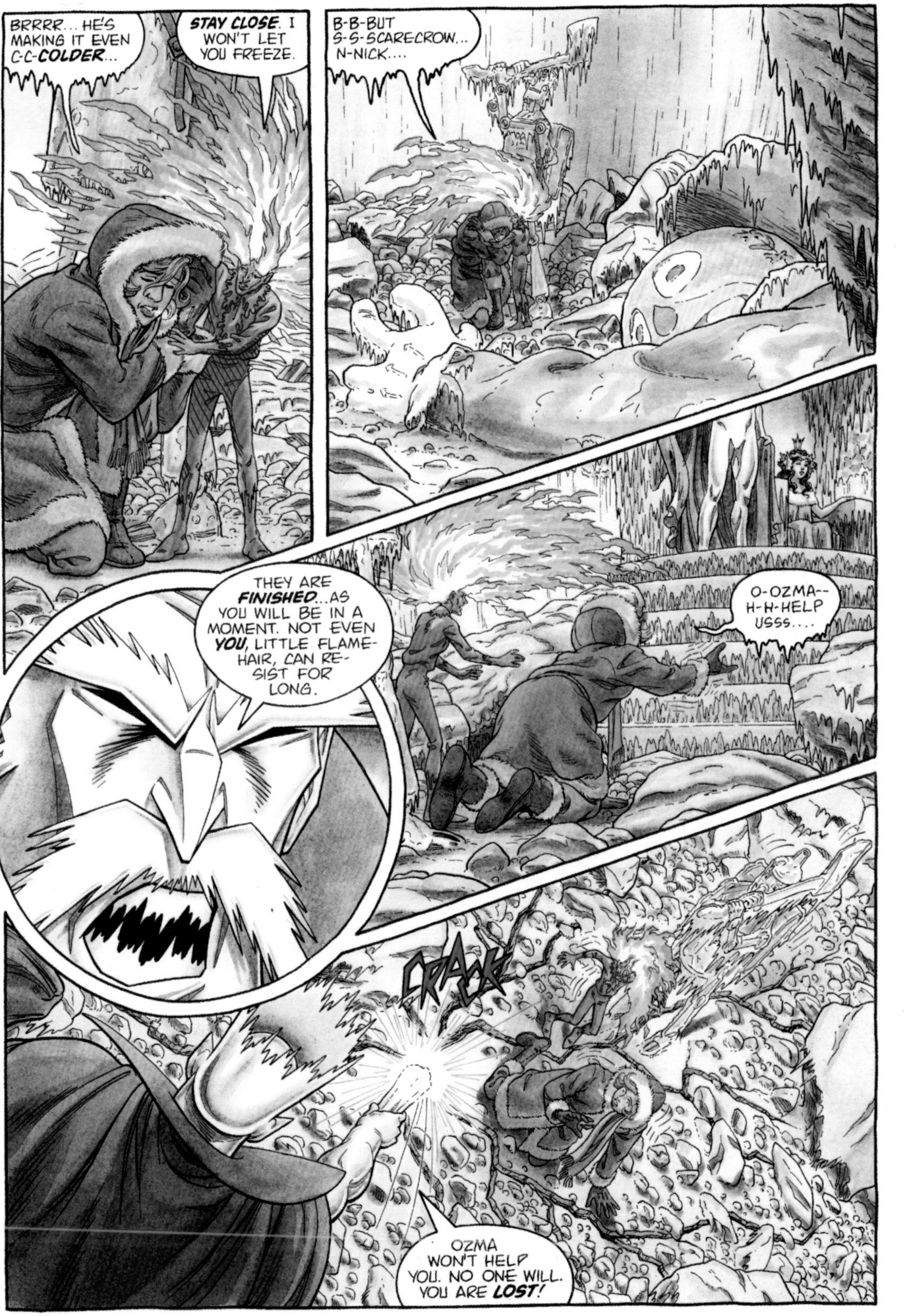
BRRRR... HE'S MAKING IT EVEN C-C-**COLDER**...
**STAY CLOSE**. I WON'T LET YOU FREEZE.
B-B-BUT S-S-SCARECROW... N-NICK....
THEY ARE **FINISHED**...AS YOU WILL BE IN A MOMENT. NOT EVEN **YOU**, LITTLE FLAME-HAIR, CAN RE-SIST FOR LONG.
O-OZMA-- H-H-HELP USSS....
CRACK
OZMA WON'T HELP YOU. NO ONE WILL. YOU ARE **LOST**!

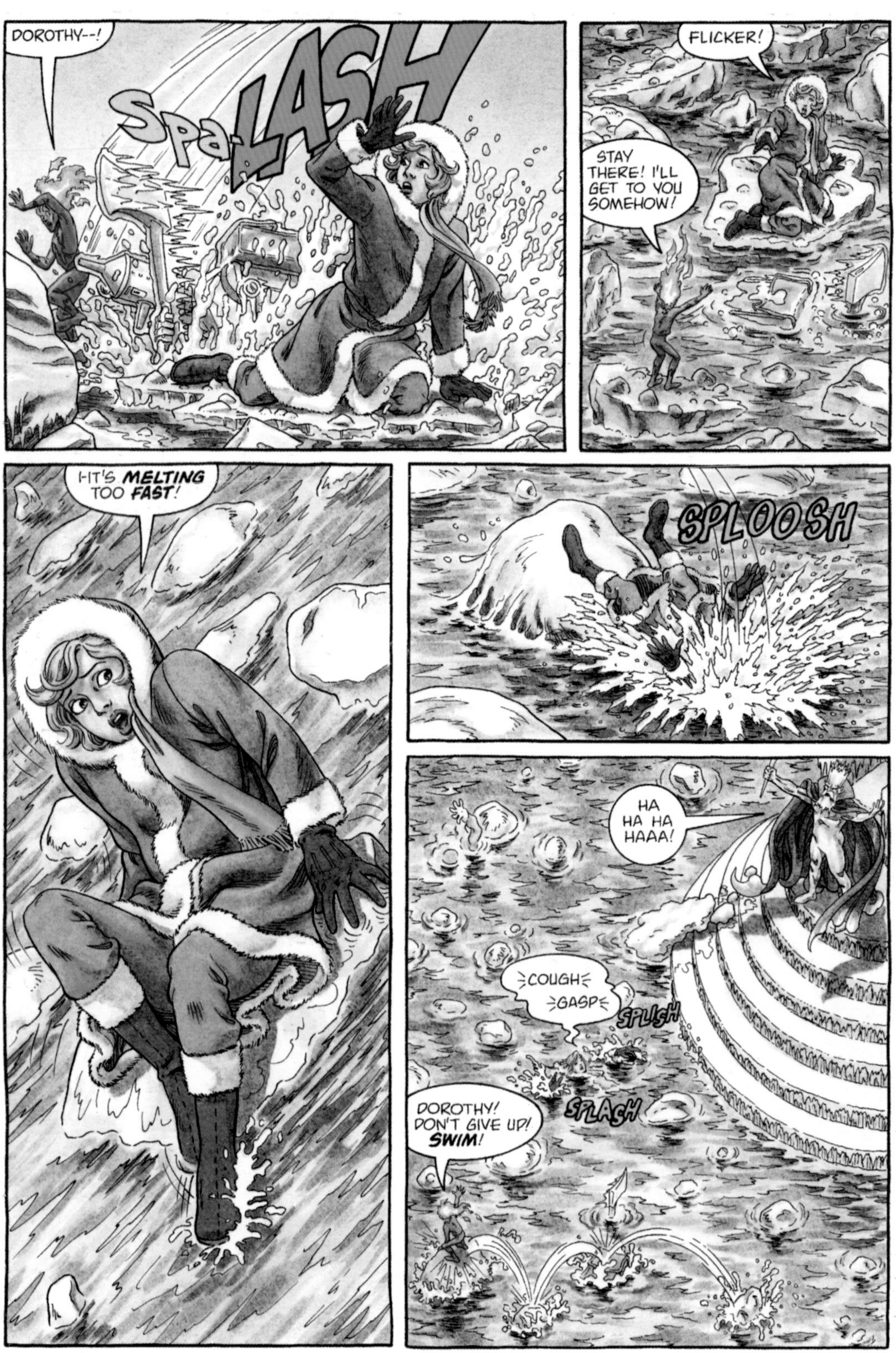
DOROTHY--!
SPA-LASH
FLICKER!
STAY THERE! I'LL GET TO YOU SOMEHOW!
I-IT'S MELTING TOO FAST!
SPLOOSH
HA HA HA HAAA!
COUGH
GASP
SPLISH
SPLASH
DOROTHY! DON'T GIVE UP! SWIM!

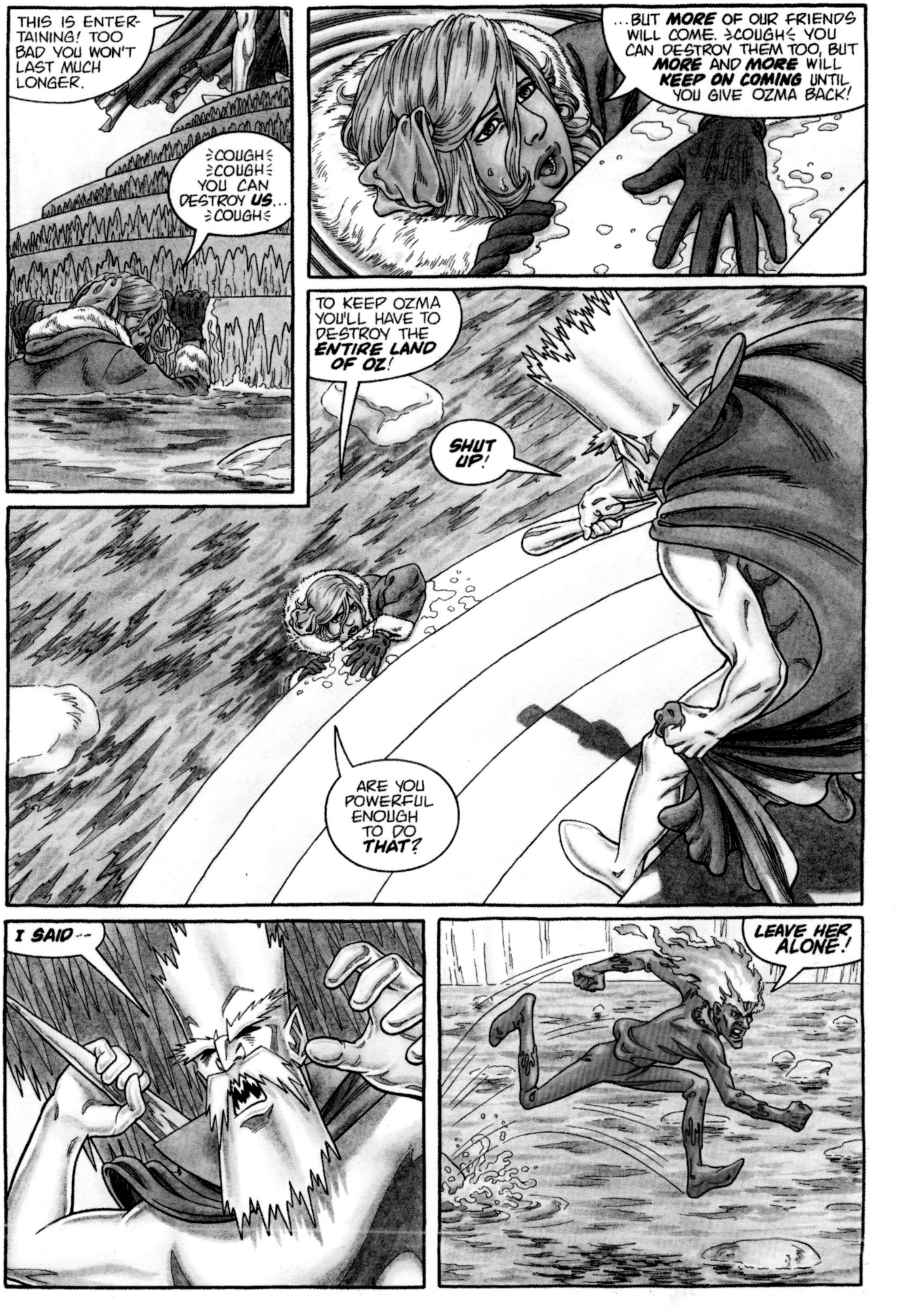
THIS IS ENTERTAINING! TOO BAD YOU WON'T LAST MUCH LONGER.
≷COUGH≶ ≷COUGH≶ YOU CAN DESTROY **US**... ≷COUGH≶
...BUT **MORE** OF OUR FRIENDS WILL COME. ≷COUGH≶ YOU CAN DESTROY THEM TOO, BUT **MORE** AND **MORE** WILL **KEEP ON COMING** UNTIL YOU GIVE OZMA BACK!
TO KEEP OZMA YOU'LL HAVE TO DESTROY THE **ENTIRE LAND OF OZ**!
**SHUT UP**!
ARE YOU POWERFUL ENOUGH TO DO **THAT**?
**I SAID**--
**LEAVE HER ALONE**!

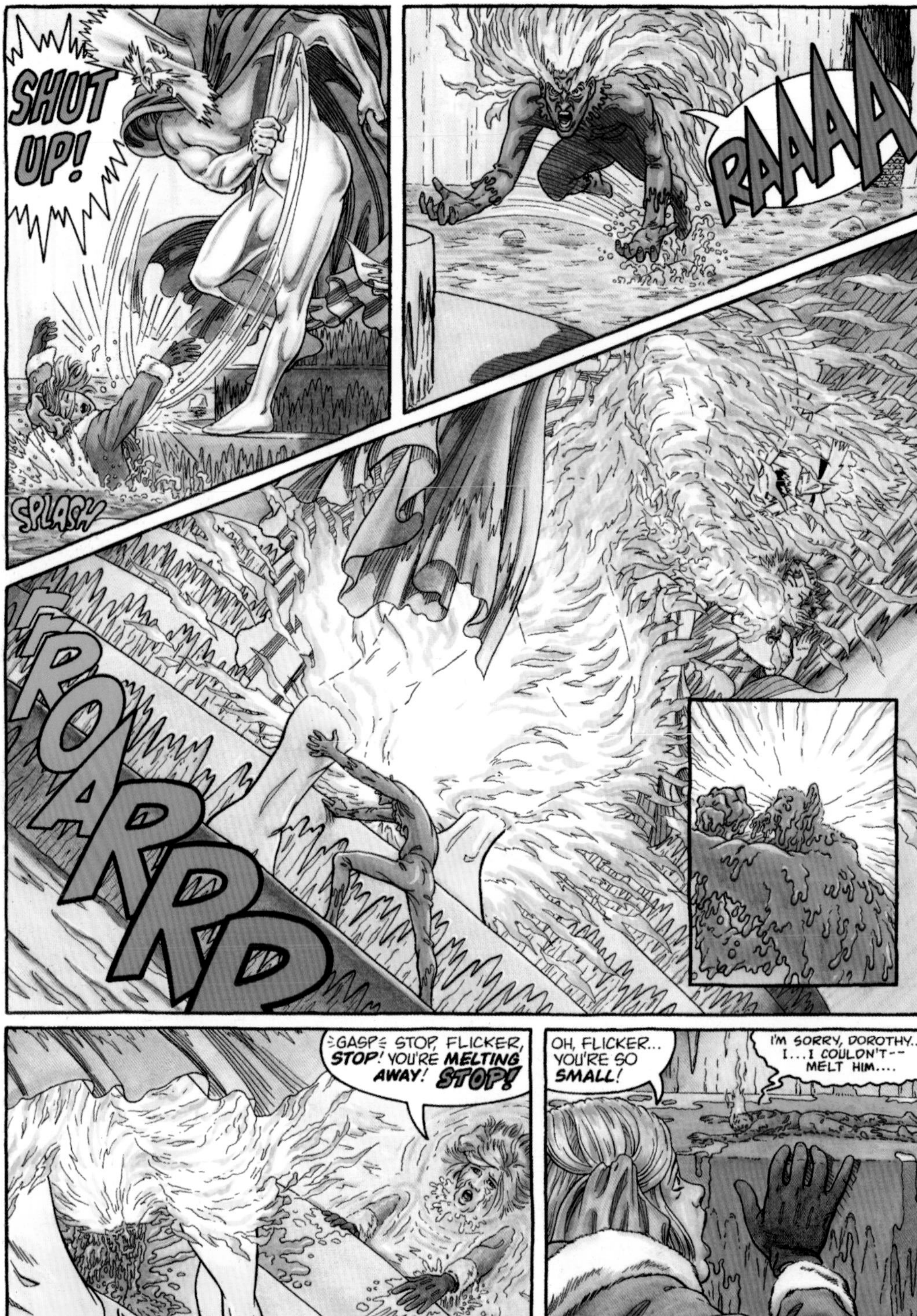
SHUT UP!
SPLASH
RAAAA
rrROARRRR
=GASP= STOP, FLICKER, STOP! YOU'RE MELTING AWAY! STOP!
AAAHHRRRR...
OH, FLICKER... YOU'RE SO SMALL!
I'M SORRY, DOROTHY... I... I COULDN'T-- MELT HIM....

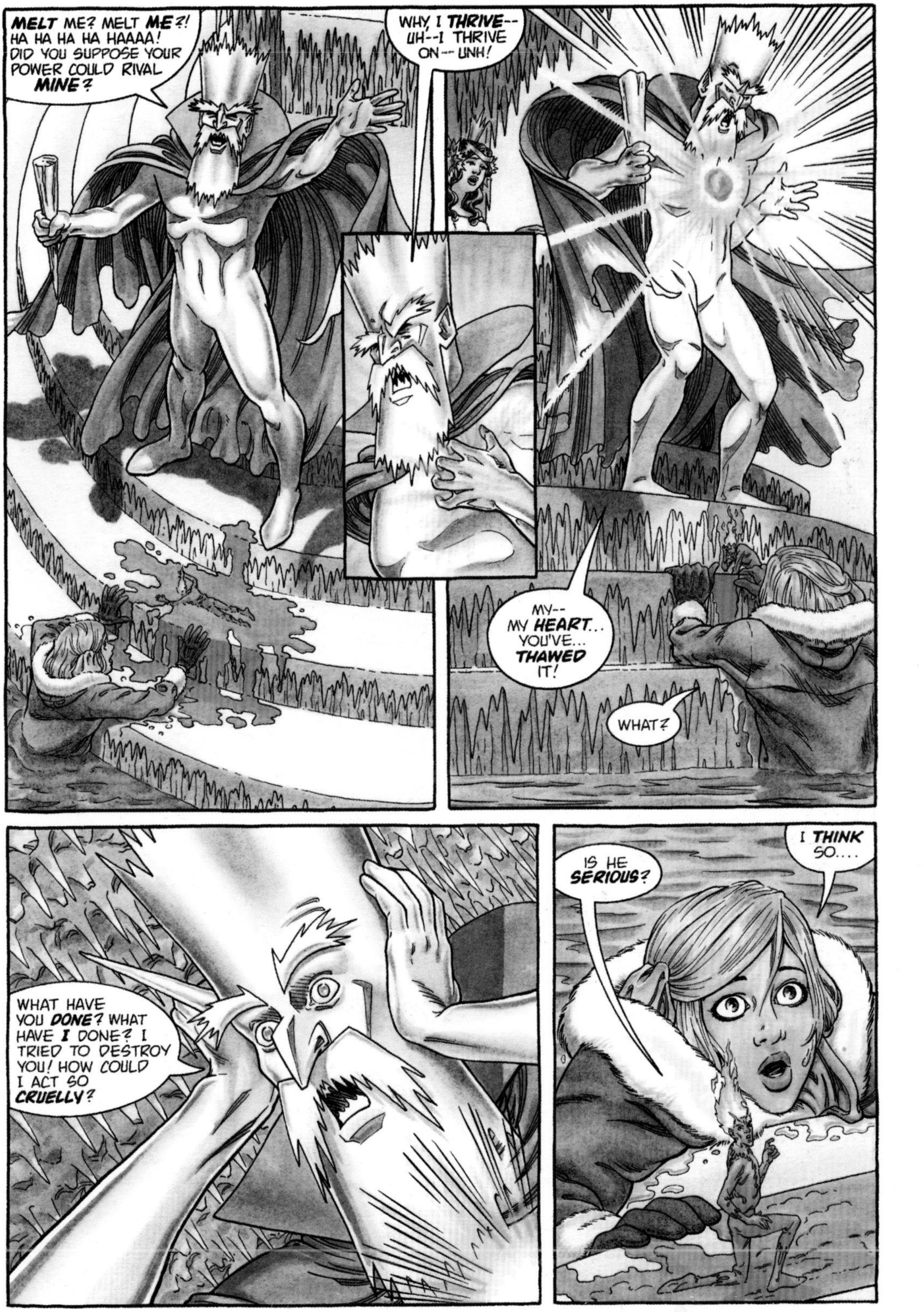
MELT ME? MELT ME?! HA HA HA HA HAAAA! DID YOU SUPPOSE YOUR POWER COULD RIVAL MINE?
WHY, I THRIVE-- UH--I THRIVE ON-- UNH!
MY-- MY HEART... YOU'VE... THAWED IT!
WHAT?
WHAT HAVE YOU DONE? WHAT HAVE I DONE? I TRIED TO DESTROY YOU! HOW COULD I ACT SO CRUELLY?
IS HE SERIOUS?
I THINK SO....

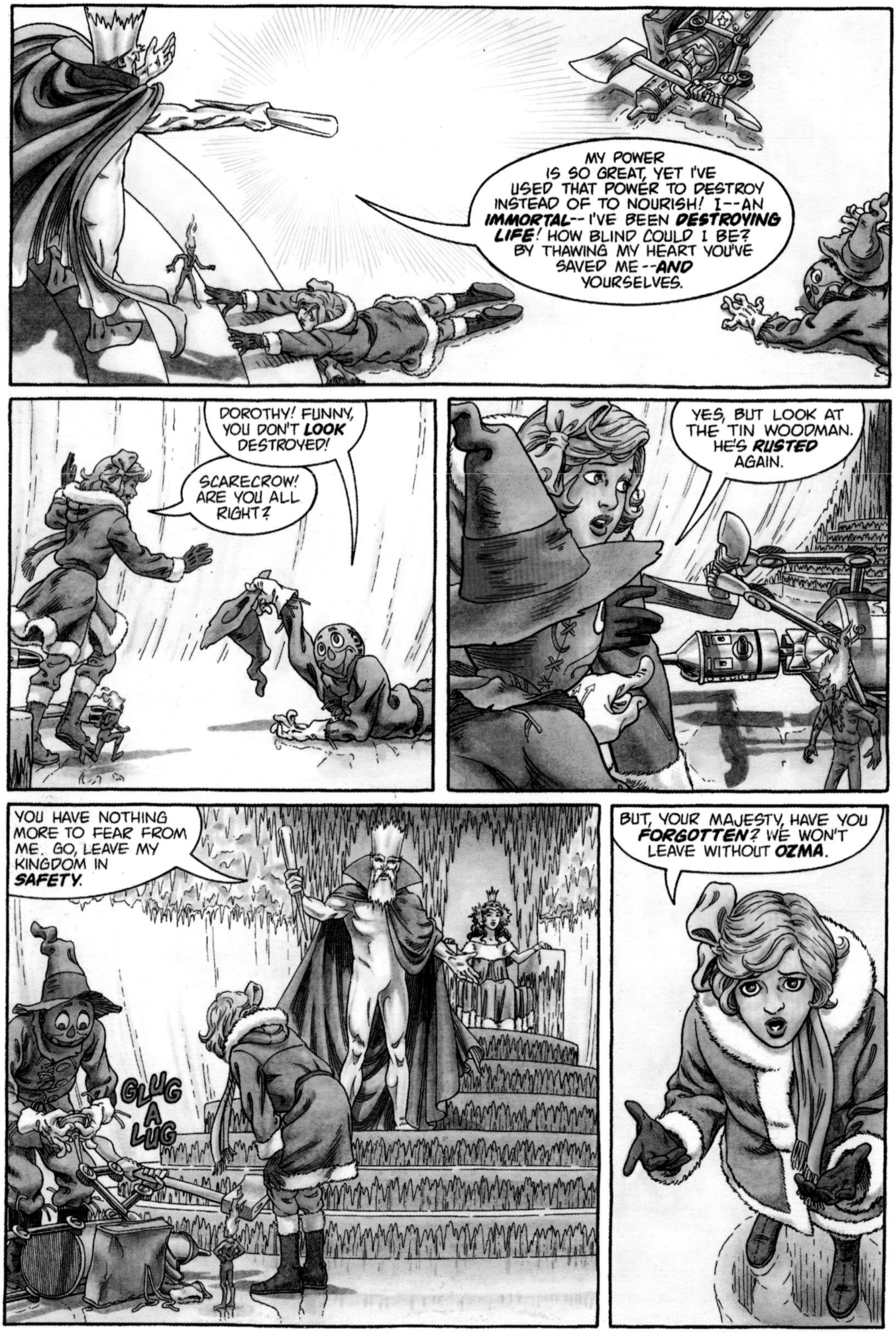
MY POWER IS SO GREAT, YET I'VE USED THAT POWER TO DESTROY INSTEAD OF TO NOURISH! I--AN **IMMORTAL**-- I'VE BEEN **DESTROYING LIFE**! HOW BLIND COULD I BE? BY THAWING MY HEART YOU'VE SAVED ME--**AND** YOURSELVES.
DOROTHY! FUNNY, YOU DON'T **LOOK** DESTROYED!
SCARECROW! ARE YOU ALL RIGHT?
YES, BUT LOOK AT THE TIN WOODMAN. HE'S **RUSTED** AGAIN.
YOU HAVE NOTHING MORE TO FEAR FROM ME. GO, LEAVE MY KINGDOM IN **SAFETY**.
GLUG A LUG
BUT, YOUR MAJESTY, HAVE YOU **FORGOTTEN**? WE WON'T LEAVE WITHOUT **OZMA**.

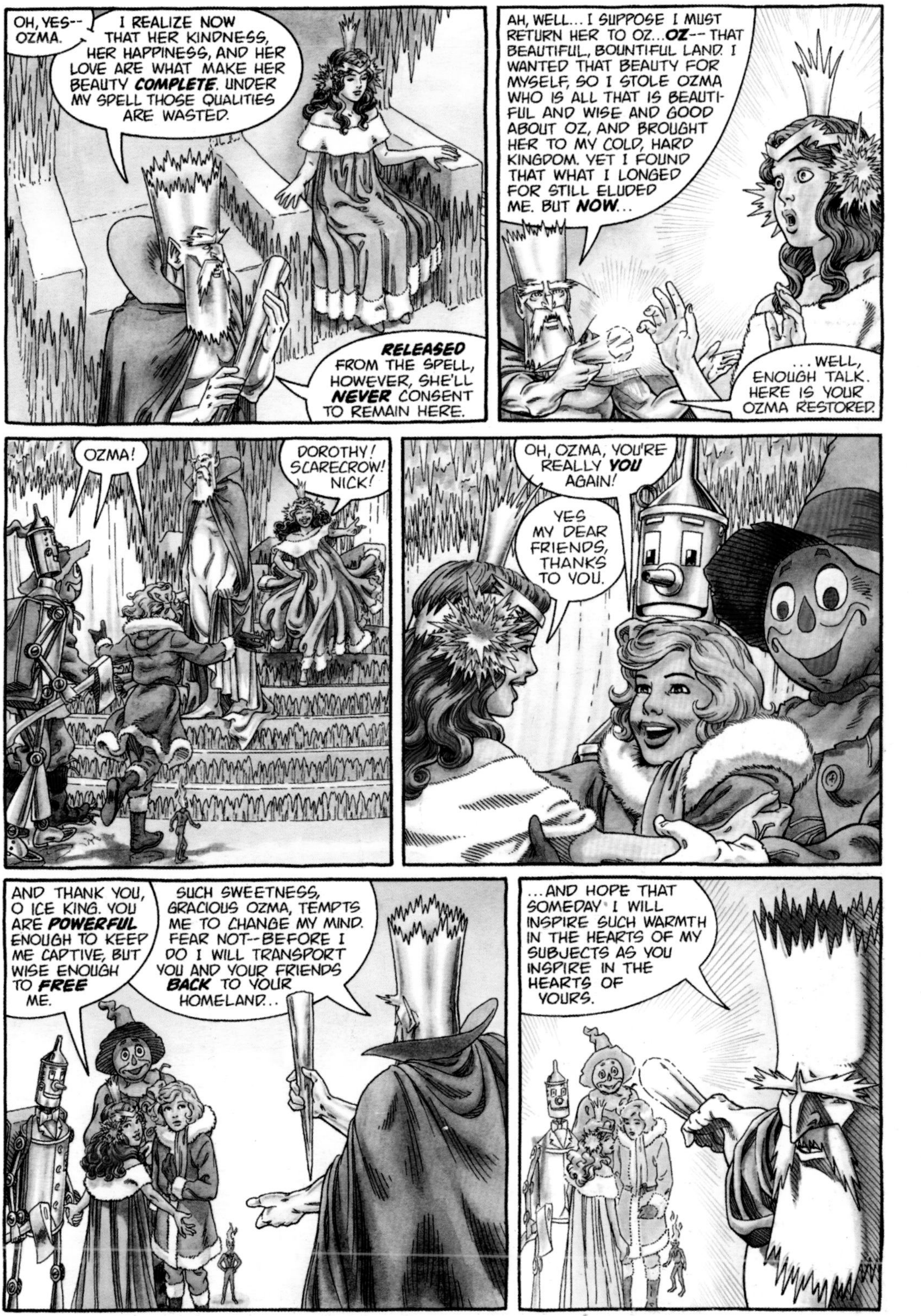
OH, YES-- OZMA.
I REALIZE NOW THAT HER KINDNESS, HER HAPPINESS, AND HER LOVE ARE WHAT MAKE HER BEAUTY COMPLETE. UNDER MY SPELL THOSE QUALITIES ARE WASTED.
RELEASED FROM THE SPELL, HOWEVER, SHE'LL NEVER CONSENT TO REMAIN HERE.
AH, WELL... I SUPPOSE I MUST RETURN HER TO OZ...OZ-- THAT BEAUTIFUL, BOUNTIFUL LAND. I WANTED THAT BEAUTY FOR MYSELF, SO I STOLE OZMA WHO IS ALL THAT IS BEAUTIFUL AND WISE AND GOOD ABOUT OZ, AND BROUGHT HER TO MY COLD, HARD KINGDOM. YET I FOUND THAT WHAT I LONGED FOR STILL ELUDED ME. BUT NOW...
...WELL, ENOUGH TALK. HERE IS YOUR OZMA RESTORED.
OZMA!
DOROTHY! SCARECROW! NICK!
OH, OZMA, YOU'RE REALLY YOU AGAIN!
YES MY DEAR FRIENDS, THANKS TO YOU.
AND THANK YOU, O ICE KING. YOU ARE POWERFUL ENOUGH TO KEEP ME CAPTIVE, BUT WISE ENOUGH TO FREE ME.
SUCH SWEETNESS, GRACIOUS OZMA, TEMPTS ME TO CHANGE MY MIND. FEAR NOT--BEFORE I DO I WILL TRANSPORT YOU AND YOUR FRIENDS BACK TO YOUR HOMELAND...
...AND HOPE THAT SOMEDAY I WILL INSPIRE SUCH WARMTH IN THE HEARTS OF MY SUBJECTS AS YOU INSPIRE IN THE HEARTS OF YOURS.

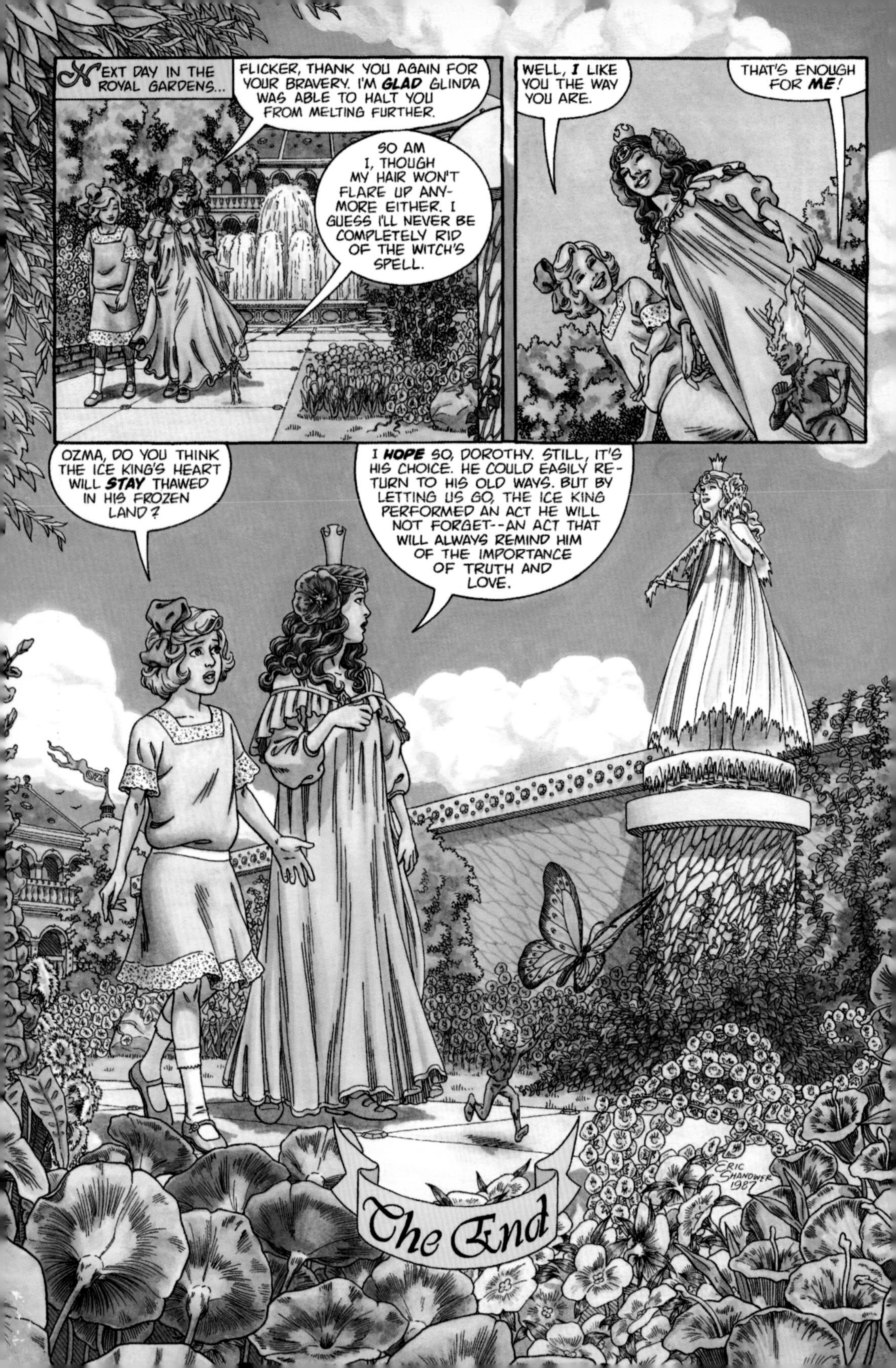

NEXT DAY IN THE ROYAL GARDENS...
FLICKER, THANK YOU AGAIN FOR YOUR BRAVERY. I'M GLAD GLINDA WAS ABLE TO HALT YOU FROM MELTING FURTHER.
SO AM I, THOUGH MY HAIR WON'T FLARE UP ANY-MORE EITHER. I GUESS I'LL NEVER BE COMPLETELY RID OF THE WITCH'S SPELL.
WELL, I LIKE YOU THE WAY YOU ARE.
THAT'S ENOUGH FOR ME!
OZMA, DO YOU THINK THE ICE KING'S HEART WILL STAY THAWED IN HIS FROZEN LAND?
I HOPE SO, DOROTHY. STILL, IT'S HIS CHOICE. HE COULD EASILY RE-TURN TO HIS OLD WAYS. BUT BY LETTING US GO, THE ICE KING PERFORMED AN ACT HE WILL NOT FORGET--AN ACT THAT WILL ALWAYS REMIND HIM OF THE IMPORTANCE OF TRUTH AND LOVE.
ERIC SHANOWER 1987
The End

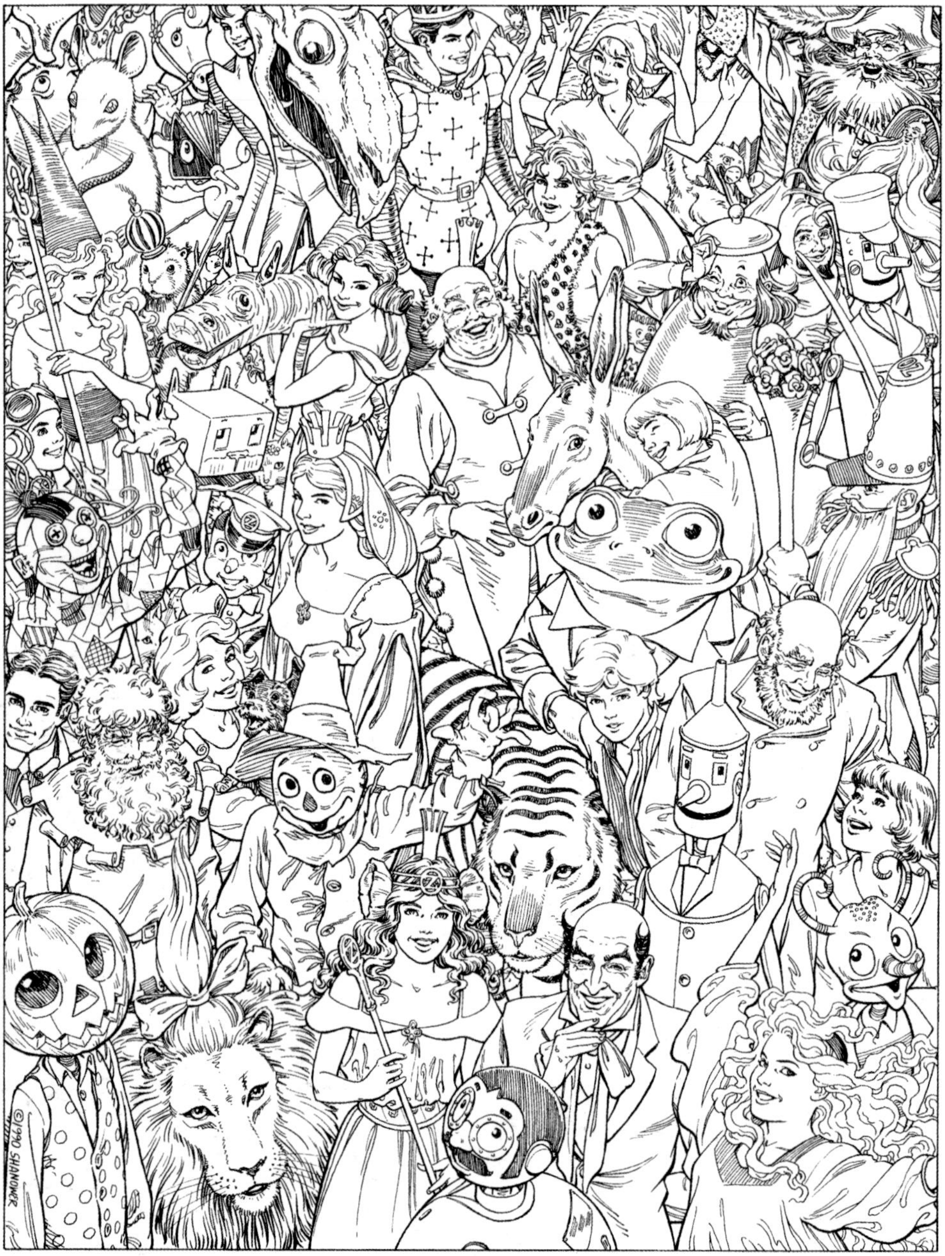
©1990 SHANOWER

# Art Gallery

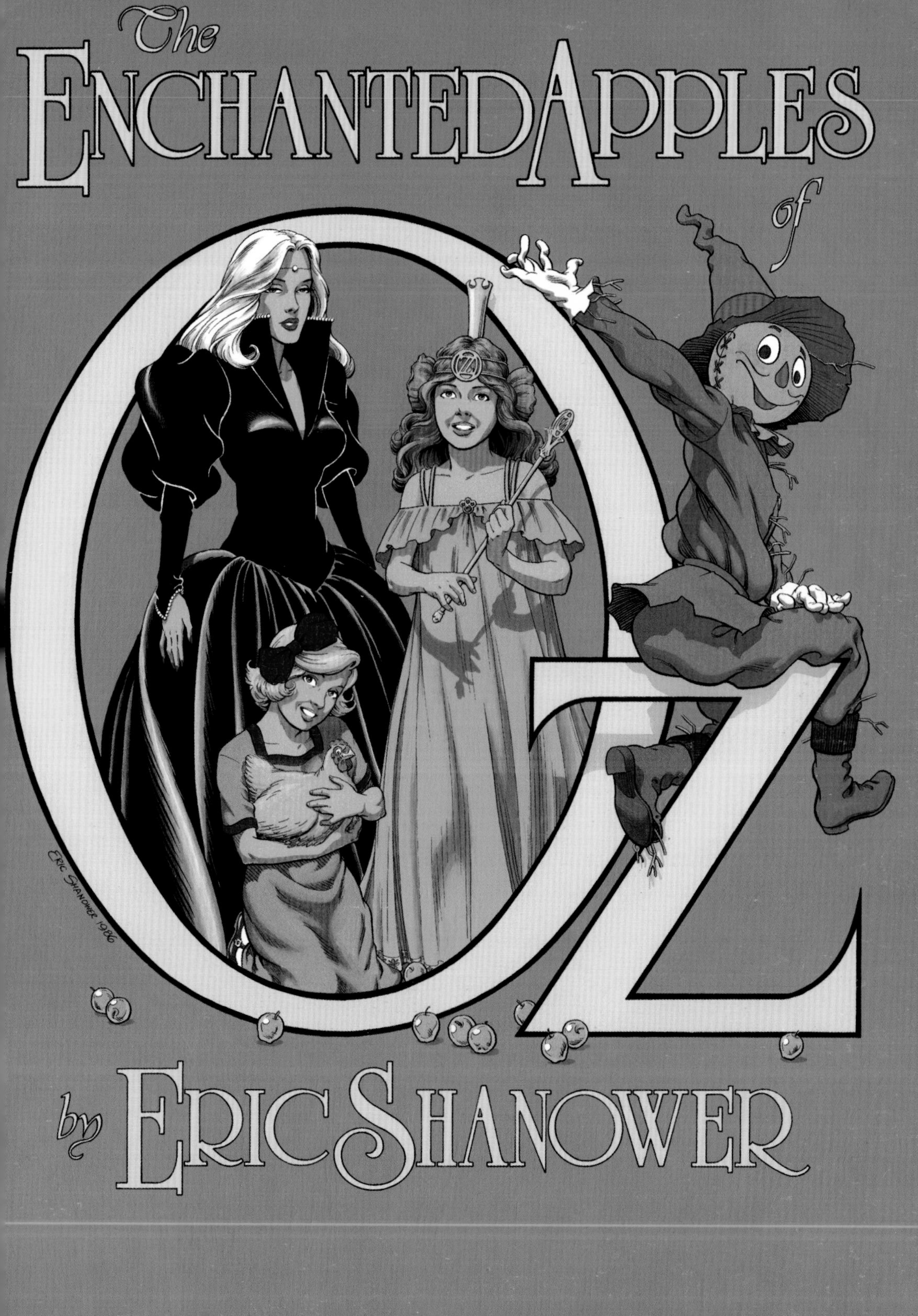
The Enchanted Apples of Oz
by Eric Shanower
Eric Shanower 1986

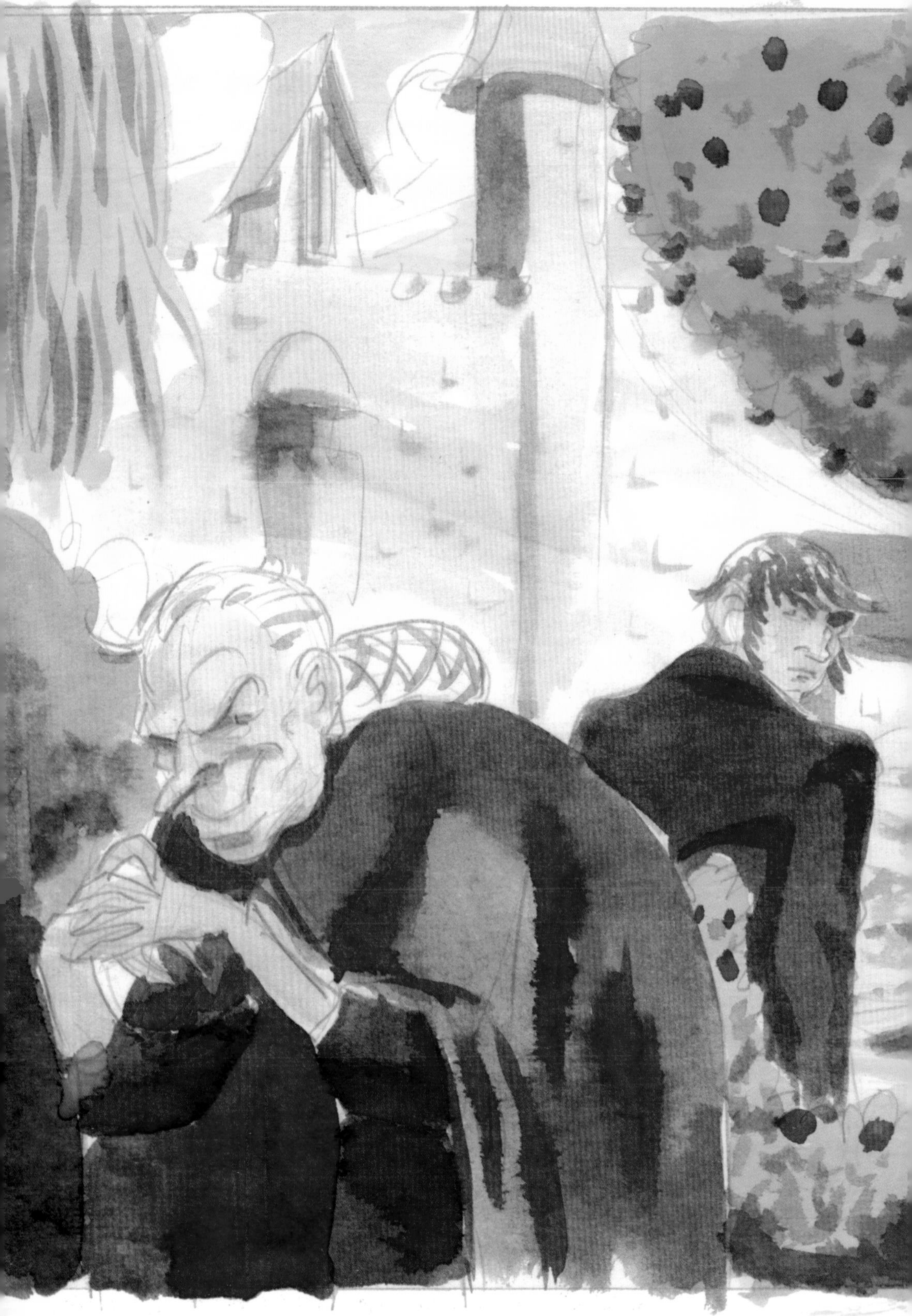

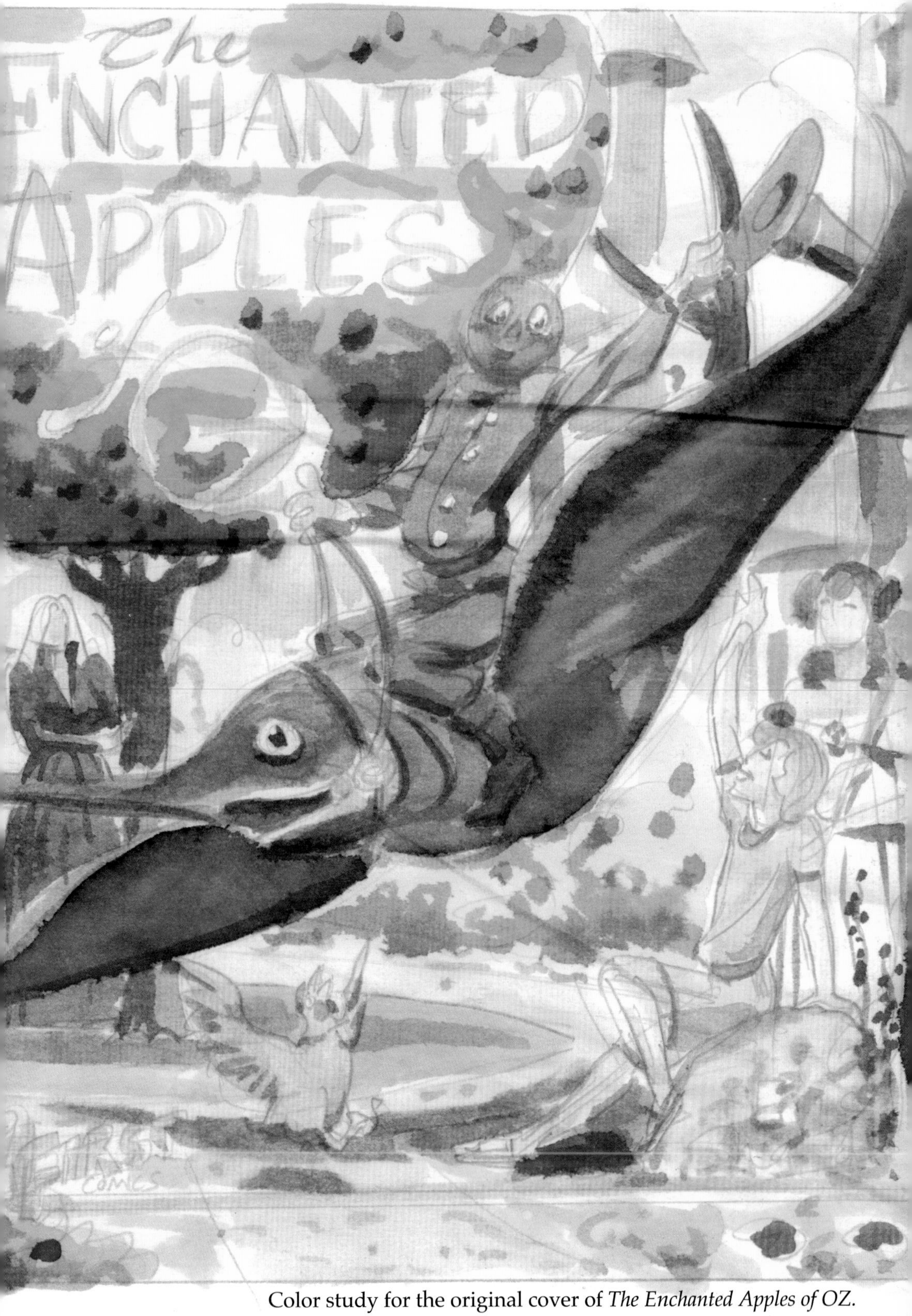
The
ENCHANTED
APPLES
of OZ

Color study for the original cover of *The Enchanted Apples of OZ*.

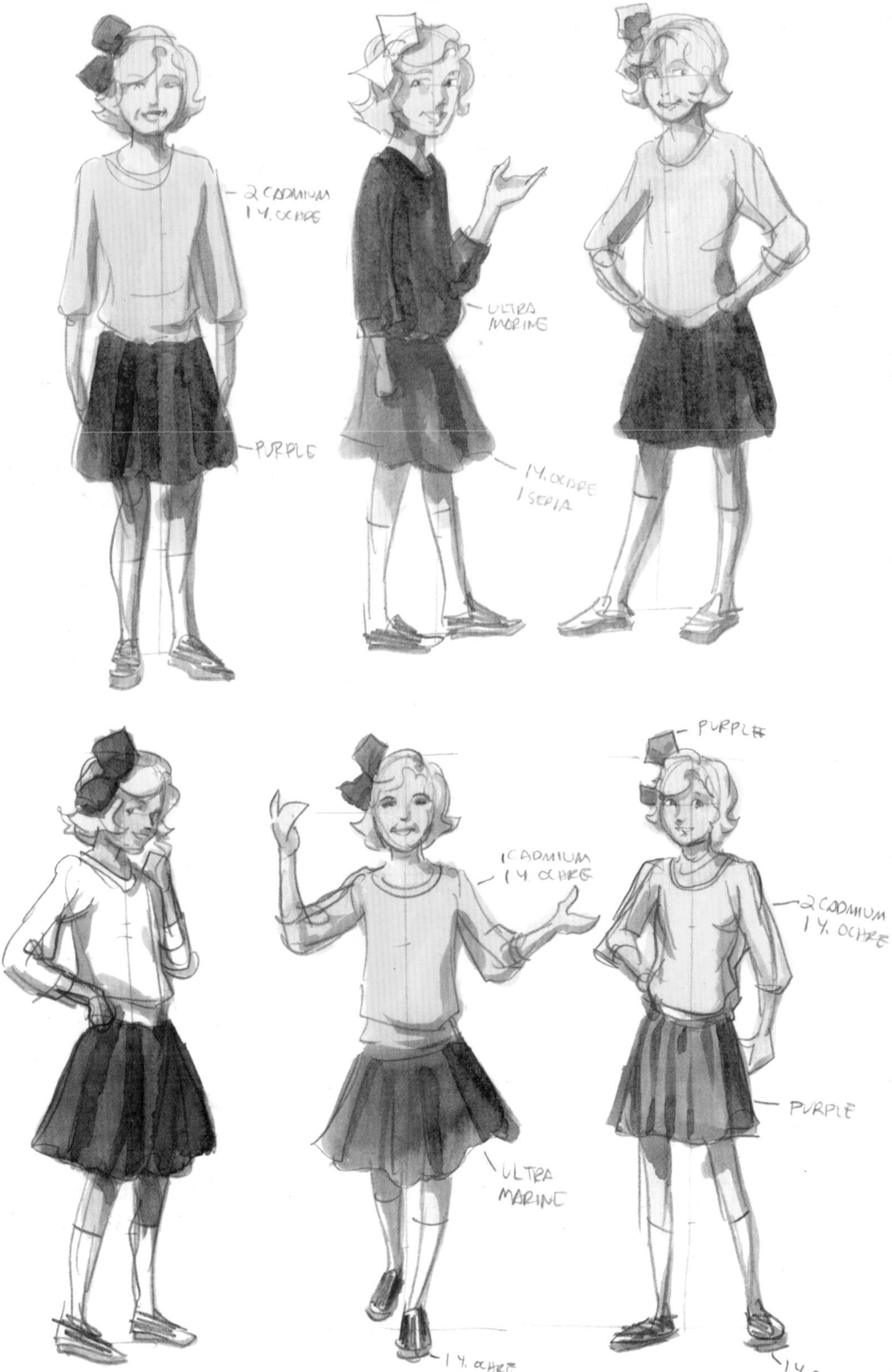
2 CADMIUM
1 Y. OCHRE
PURPLE
ULTRA MARINE
1 Y. OCHRE
1 SEPIA
PURPLE
1 CADMIUM
1 Y. OCHRE
ULTRA MARINE
1 Y. OCHRE
1 SEPIA
2 CADMIUM
1 Y. OCHRE
PURPLE
1 Y. OCHRE
1 SEPIA

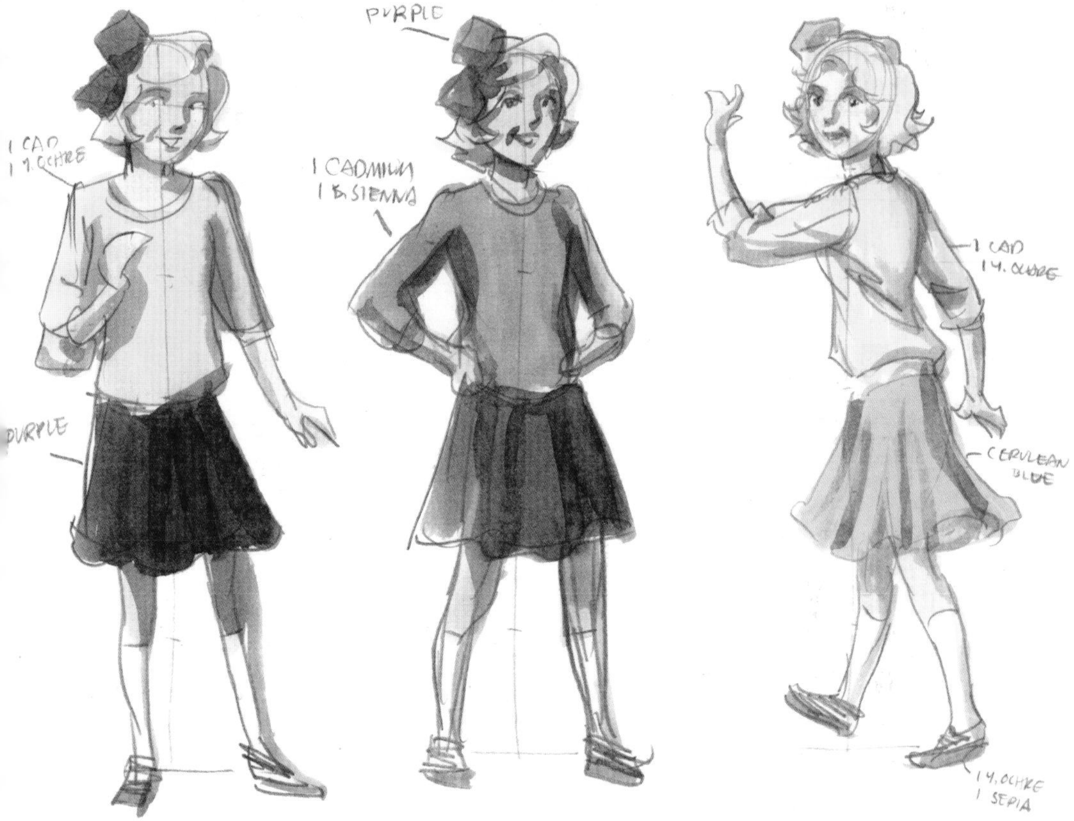
PURPLE
1 CAD
1 Y. OCHRE
PURPLE
1 CADMIUM
1 B. SIENNA
1 CAD
1 Y. OCHRE
CERULEAN BLUE
1 Y. OCHRE
1 SEPIA

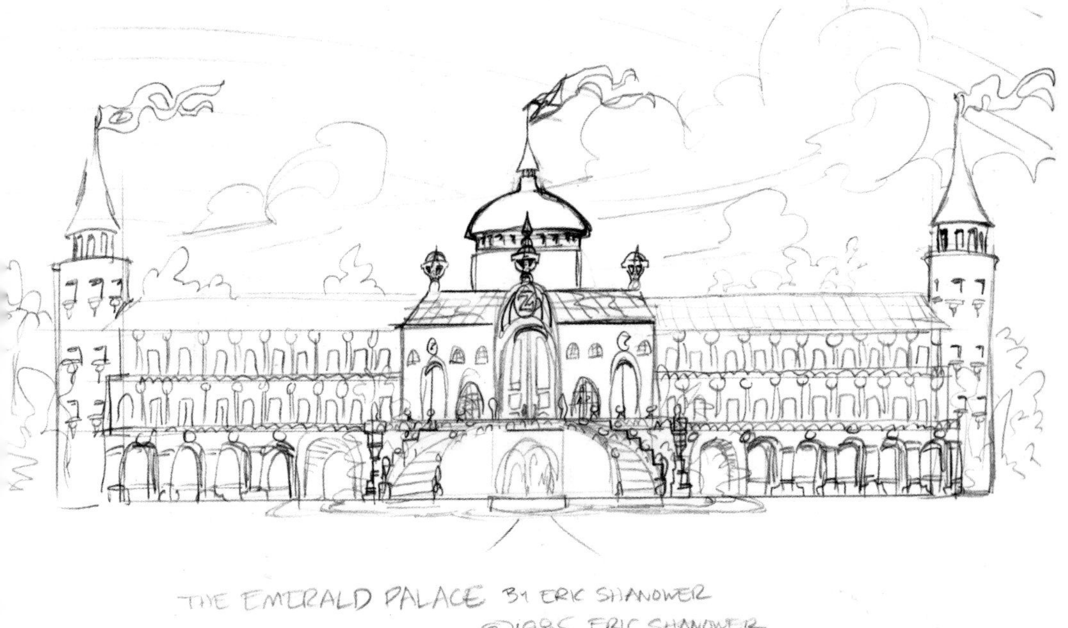
THE EMERALD PALACE BY ERIC SHANOWER
©1985 ERIC SHANOWER
AUG. 7, 1985

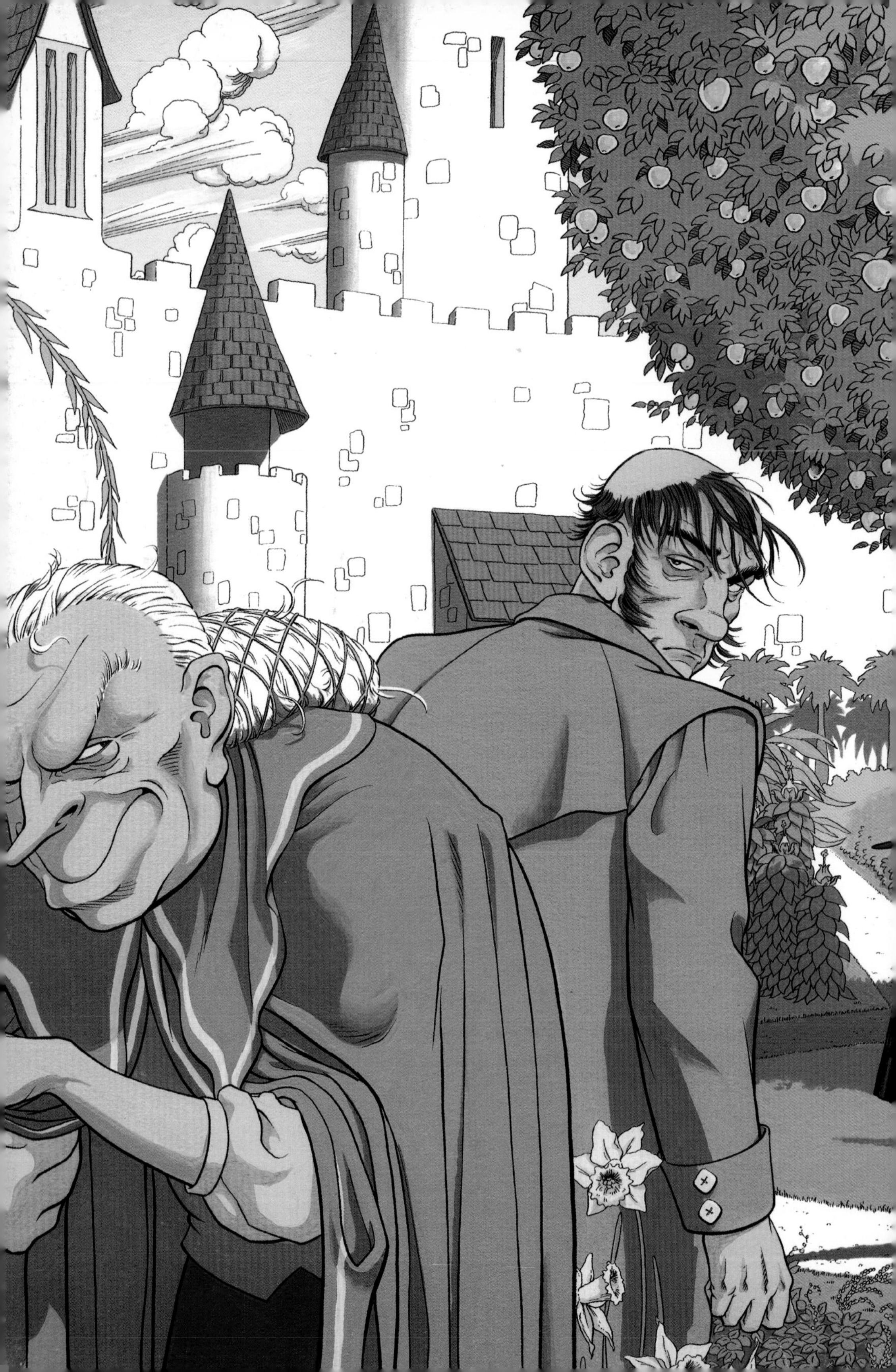

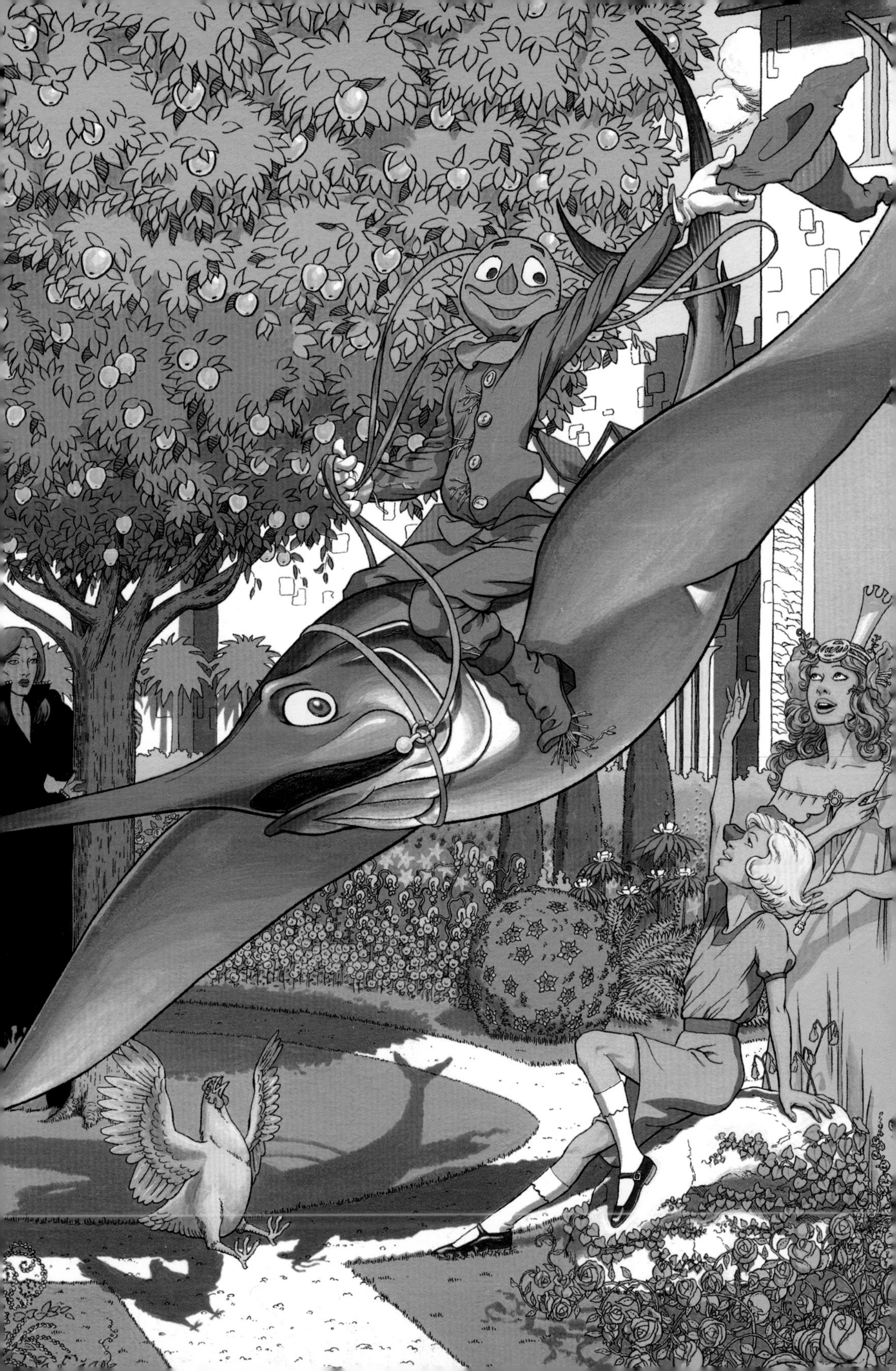

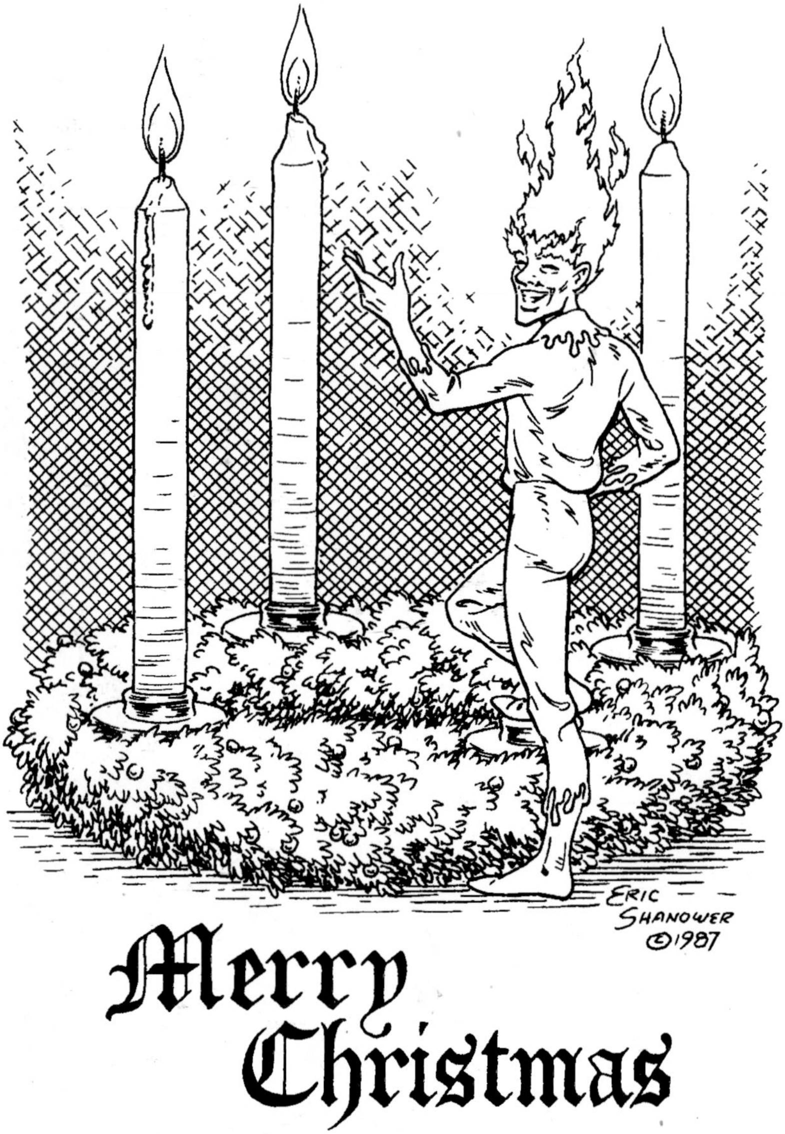
ERIC
SHANOWER
©1987

# Merry Christmas

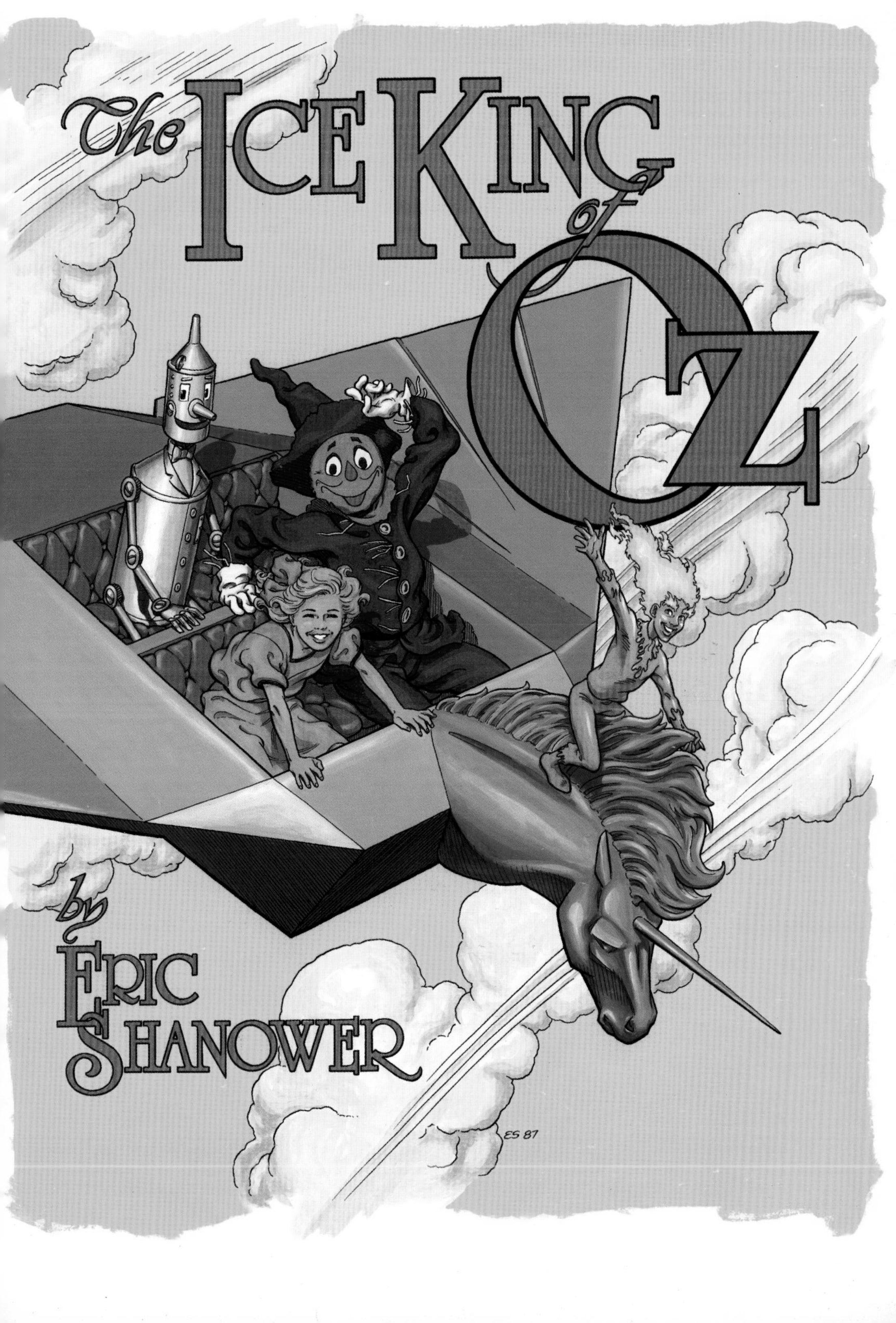
The Ice King of Oz
by
Eric Shanower
ES 87

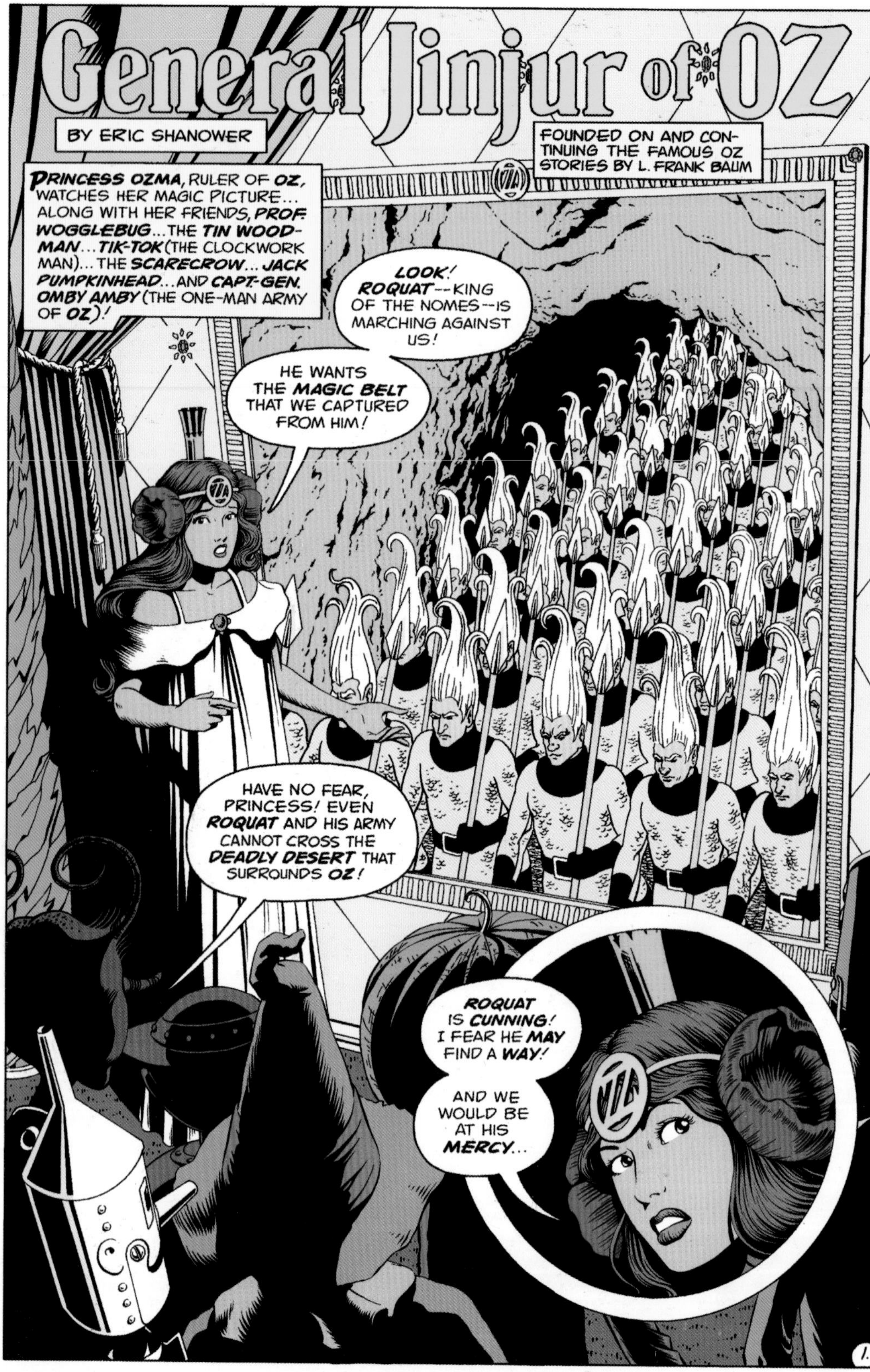

General Jinjur of OZ
BY ERIC SHANOWER
FOUNDED ON AND CONTINUING THE FAMOUS OZ STORIES BY L. FRANK BAUM
PRINCESS OZMA, RULER OF OZ, WATCHES HER MAGIC PICTURE... ALONG WITH HER FRIENDS, PROF. WOGGLEBUG... THE TIN WOODMAN... TIK-TOK (THE CLOCKWORK MAN)... THE SCARECROW... JACK PUMPKINHEAD... AND CAPT.-GEN. OMBY AMBY (THE ONE-MAN ARMY OF OZ)!
LOOK! ROQUAT--KING OF THE NOMES--IS MARCHING AGAINST US!
HE WANTS THE MAGIC BELT THAT WE CAPTURED FROM HIM!
HAVE NO FEAR, PRINCESS! EVEN ROQUAT AND HIS ARMY CANNOT CROSS THE DEADLY DESERT THAT SURROUNDS OZ!
ROQUAT IS CUNNING! I FEAR HE MAY FIND A WAY!
AND WE WOULD BE AT HIS MERCY...
1.

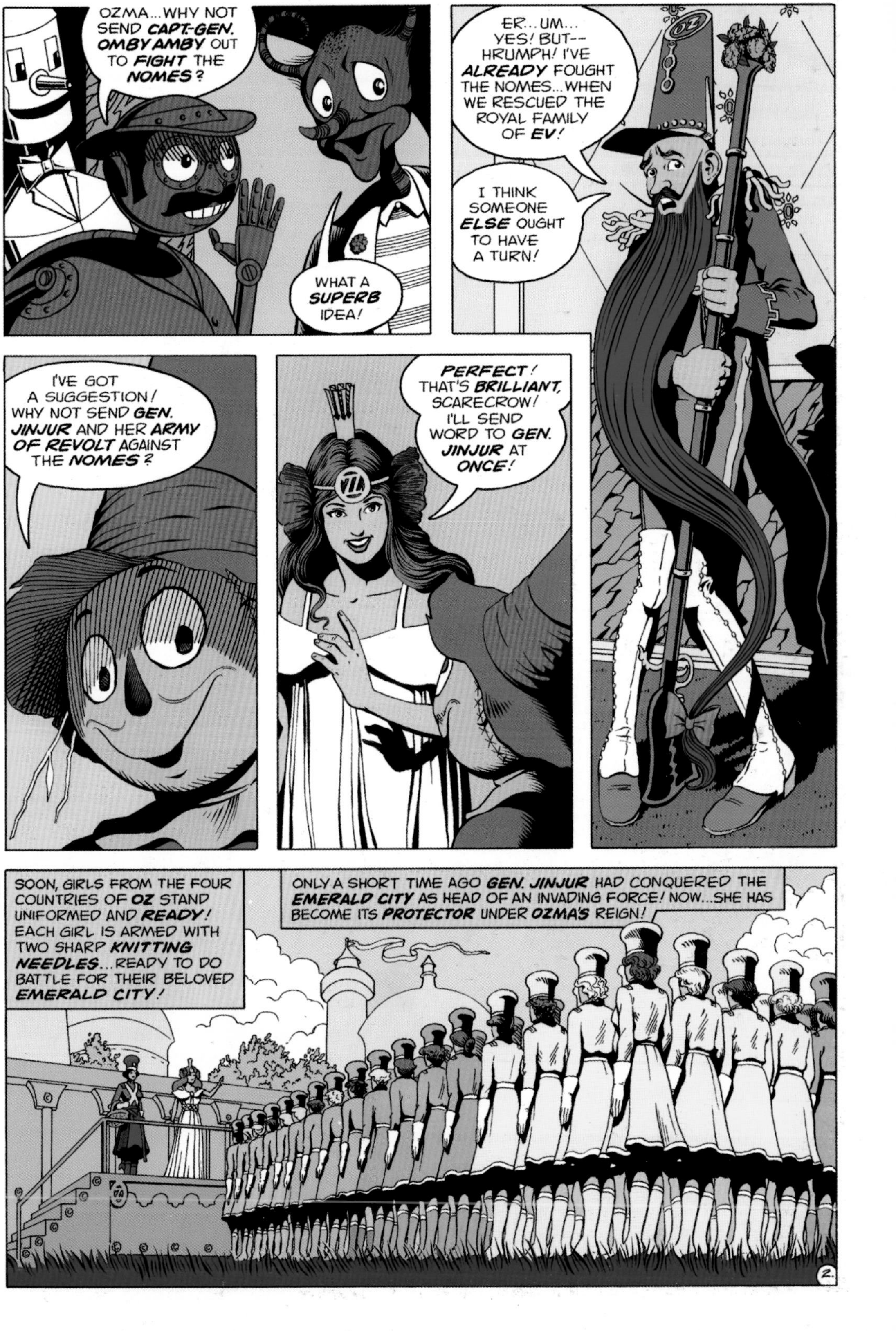
OZMA...WHY NOT SEND CAPT.-GEN. OMBY AMBY OUT TO FIGHT THE NOMES?
WHAT A SUPERB IDEA!
ER...UM... YES! BUT-- HRUMPH! I'VE ALREADY FOUGHT THE NOMES...WHEN WE RESCUED THE ROYAL FAMILY OF EV!
I THINK SOMEONE ELSE OUGHT TO HAVE A TURN!
I'VE GOT A SUGGESTION! WHY NOT SEND GEN. JINJUR AND HER ARMY OF REVOLT AGAINST THE NOMES?
PERFECT! THAT'S BRILLIANT, SCARECROW! I'LL SEND WORD TO GEN. JINJUR AT ONCE!
SOON, GIRLS FROM THE FOUR COUNTRIES OF OZ STAND UNIFORMED AND READY! EACH GIRL IS ARMED WITH TWO SHARP KNITTING NEEDLES...READY TO DO BATTLE FOR THEIR BELOVED EMERALD CITY!
ONLY A SHORT TIME AGO GEN. JINJUR HAD CONQUERED THE EMERALD CITY AS HEAD OF AN INVADING FORCE! NOW...SHE HAS BECOME ITS PROTECTOR UNDER OZMA'S REIGN!
2.

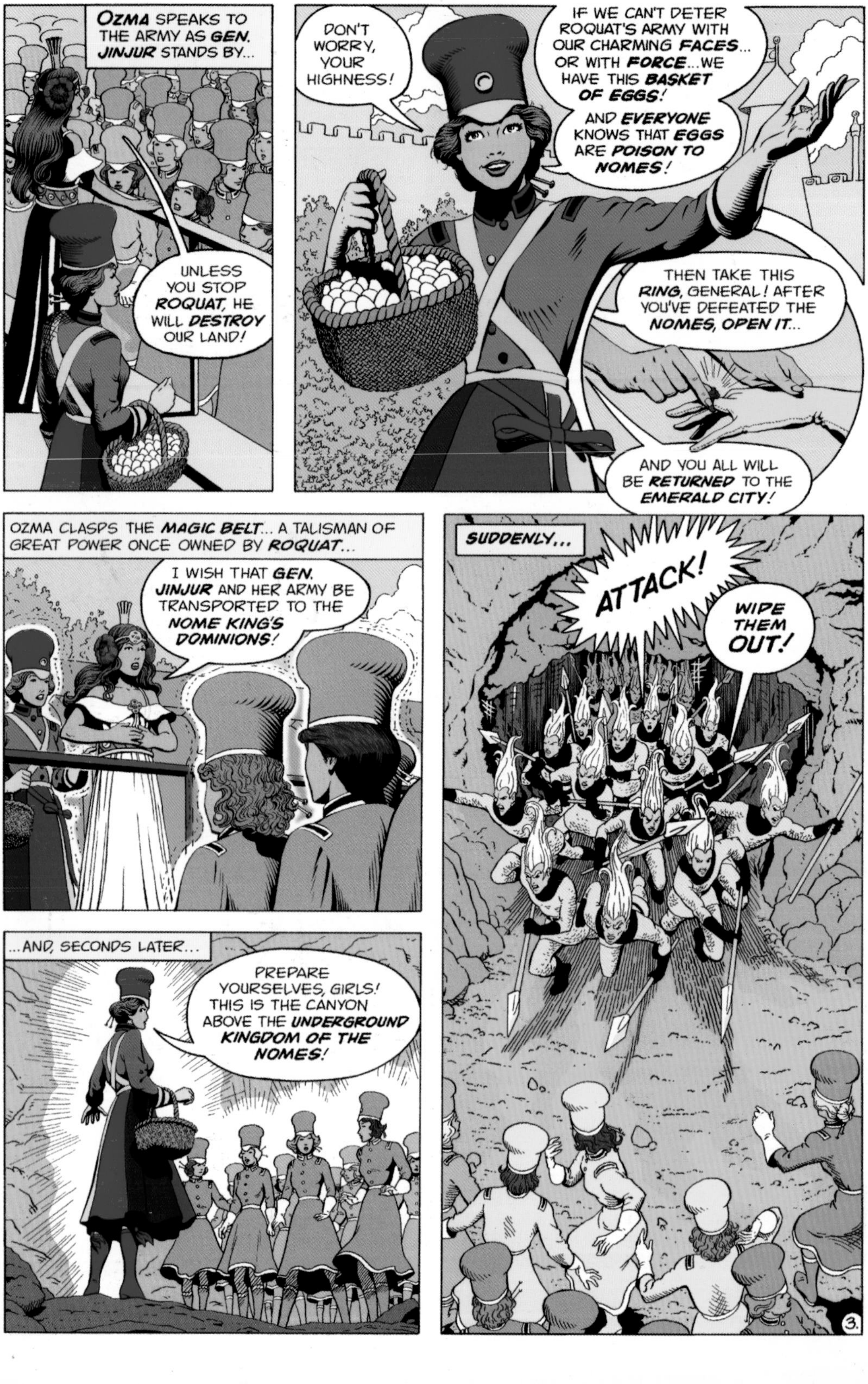
OZMA SPEAKS TO THE ARMY AS GEN. JINJUR STANDS BY...
UNLESS YOU STOP ROQUAT, HE WILL DESTROY OUR LAND!
DON'T WORRY, YOUR HIGHNESS!
IF WE CAN'T DETER ROQUAT'S ARMY WITH OUR CHARMING FACES... OR WITH FORCE...WE HAVE THIS BASKET OF EGGS!
AND EVERYONE KNOWS THAT EGGS ARE POISON TO NOMES!
THEN TAKE THIS RING, GENERAL! AFTER YOU'VE DEFEATED THE NOMES, OPEN IT...
AND YOU ALL WILL BE RETURNED TO THE EMERALD CITY!
OZMA CLASPS THE MAGIC BELT... A TALISMAN OF GREAT POWER ONCE OWNED BY ROQUAT...
I WISH THAT GEN. JINJUR AND HER ARMY BE TRANSPORTED TO THE NOME KING'S DOMINIONS!
...AND, SECONDS LATER...
PREPARE YOURSELVES, GIRLS! THIS IS THE CANYON ABOVE THE UNDERGROUND KINGDOM OF THE NOMES!
SUDDENLY...
ATTACK!
WIPE THEM OUT!
3.

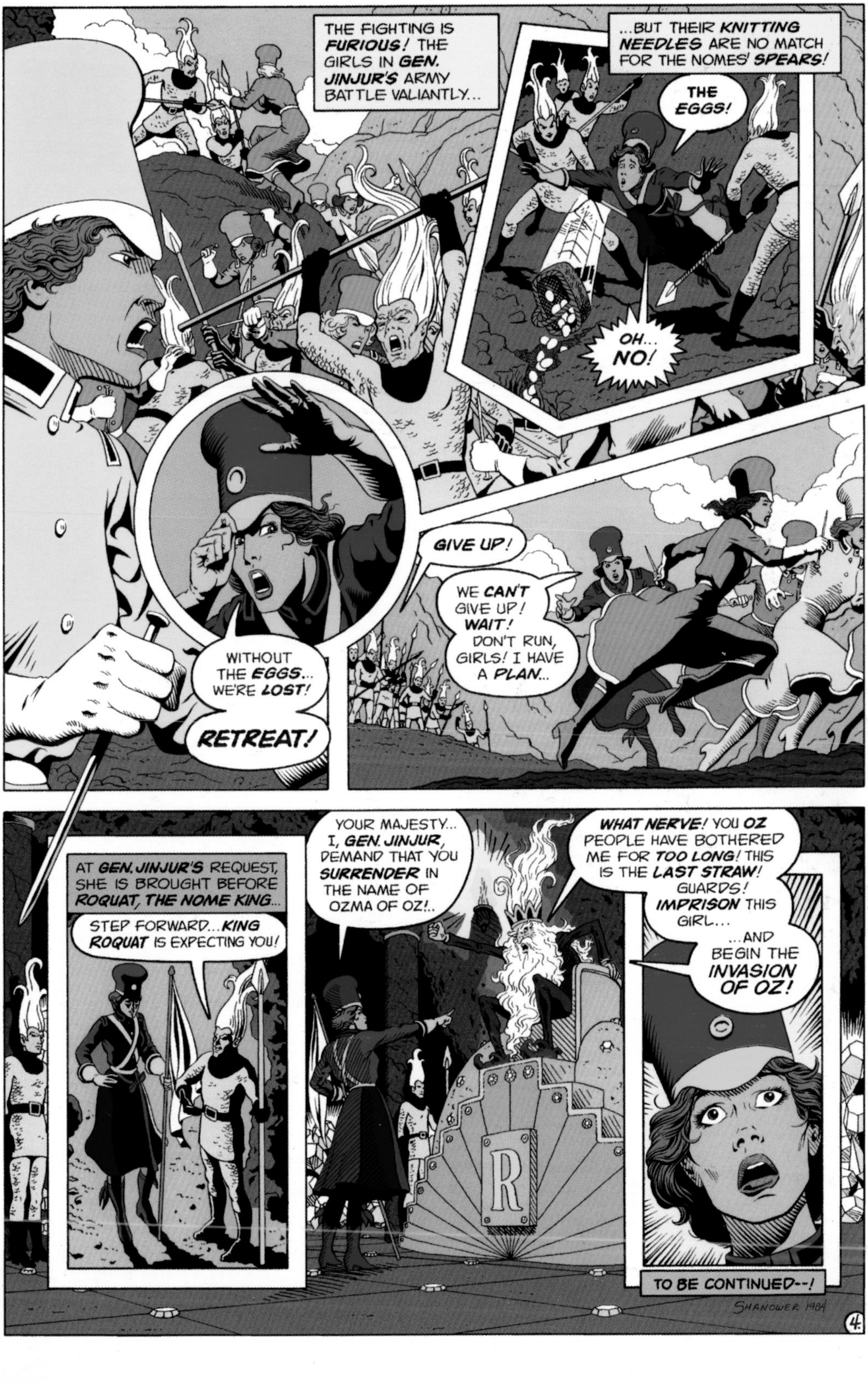
THE FIGHTING IS FURIOUS! THE GIRLS IN GEN. JINJUR'S ARMY BATTLE VALIANTLY...
...BUT THEIR KNITTING NEEDLES ARE NO MATCH FOR THE NOMES' SPEARS!
THE EGGS!
OH... NO!
GIVE UP!
WITHOUT THE EGGS... WE'RE LOST!
RETREAT!
WE CAN'T GIVE UP! WAIT! DON'T RUN, GIRLS! I HAVE A PLAN...
AT GEN. JINJUR'S REQUEST, SHE IS BROUGHT BEFORE ROQUAT, THE NOME KING...
STEP FORWARD... KING ROQUAT IS EXPECTING YOU!
YOUR MAJESTY... I, GEN. JINJUR, DEMAND THAT YOU SURRENDER IN THE NAME OF OZMA OF OZ!..
WHAT NERVE! YOU OZ PEOPLE HAVE BOTHERED ME FOR TOO LONG! THIS IS THE LAST STRAW! GUARDS! IMPRISON THIS GIRL...
...AND BEGIN THE INVASION OF OZ!
R
TO BE CONTINUED--!
SHANOWER 1984
4.

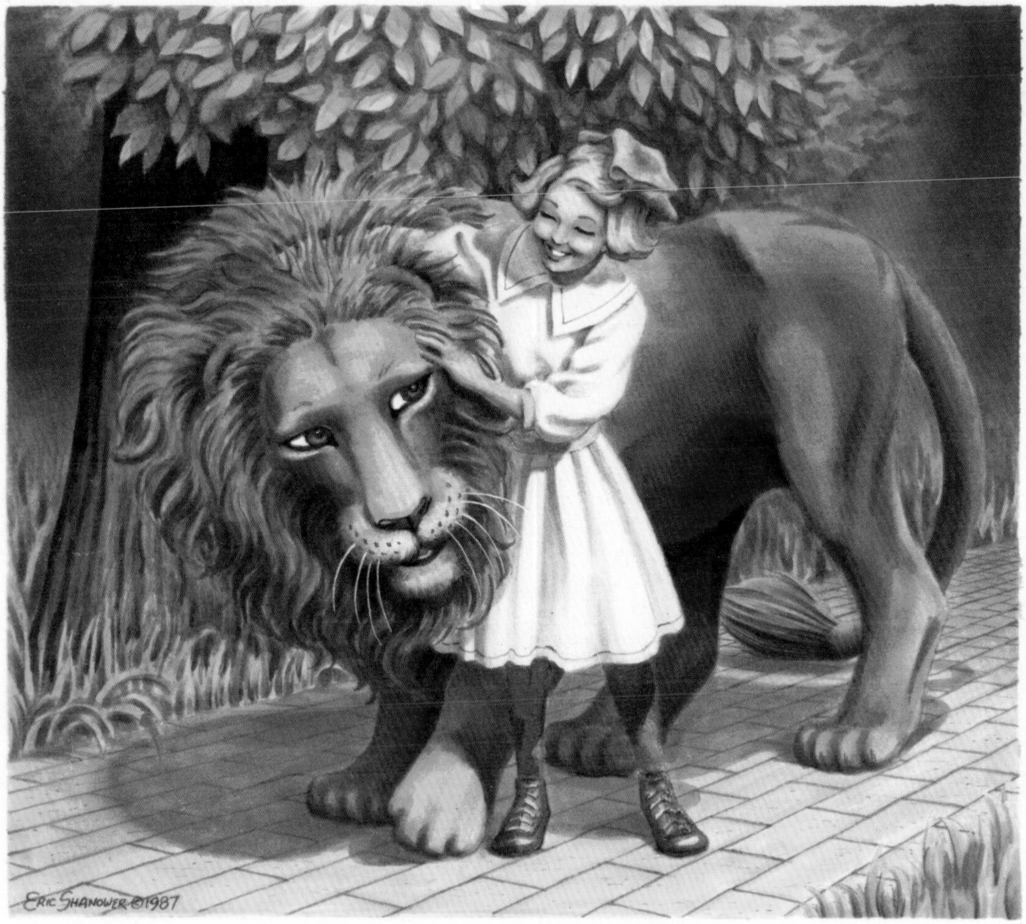
ERIC SHANOWER ©1987

Previous four pages:
"General Jinjur of OZ" was originally planned for publication in DC Comics' *Sgt. Rock,* but was withdrawn and never completed.

Next five pages:
Pencil art for an early version of *The Enchanted Apples of OZ.*

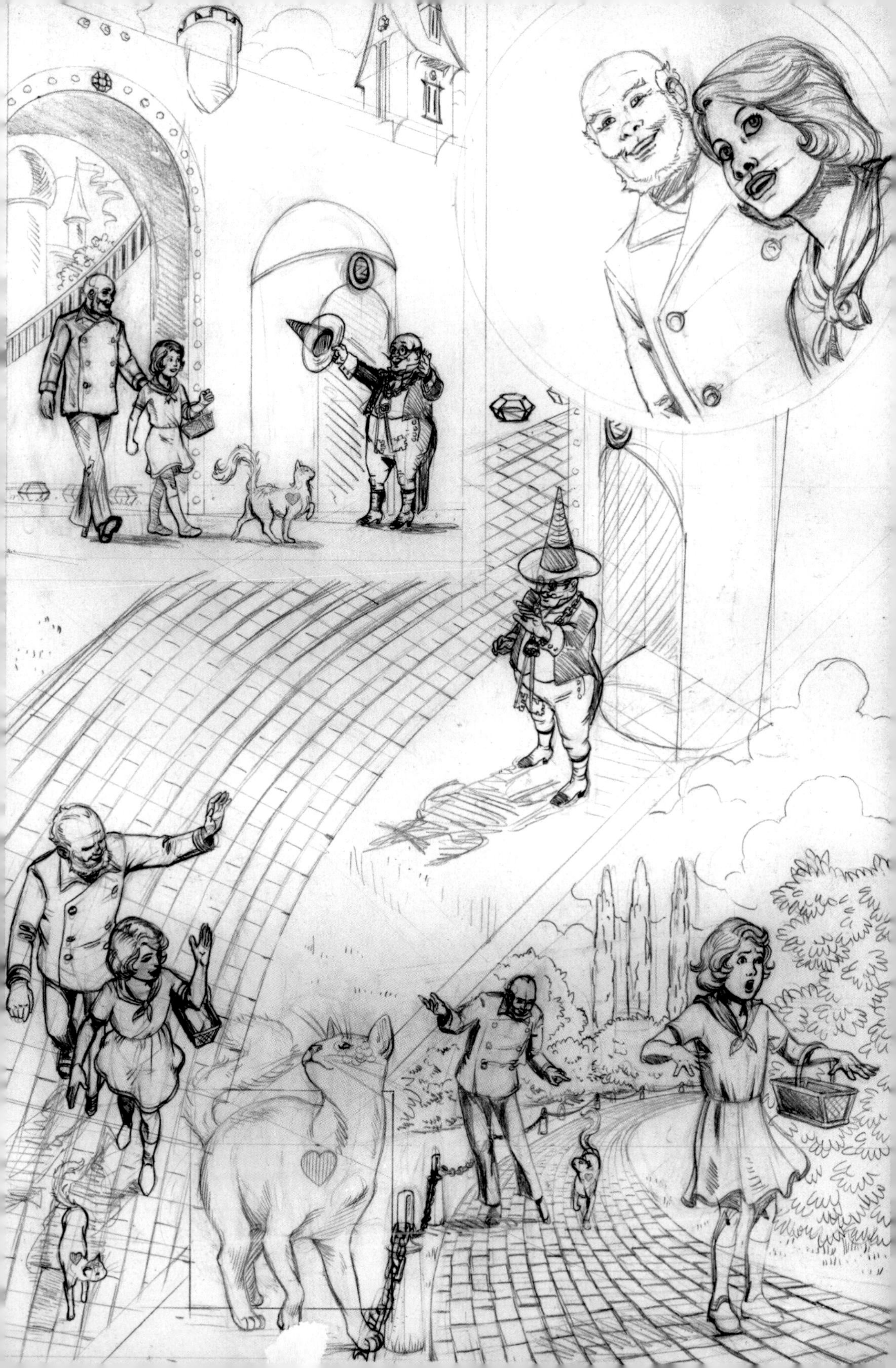

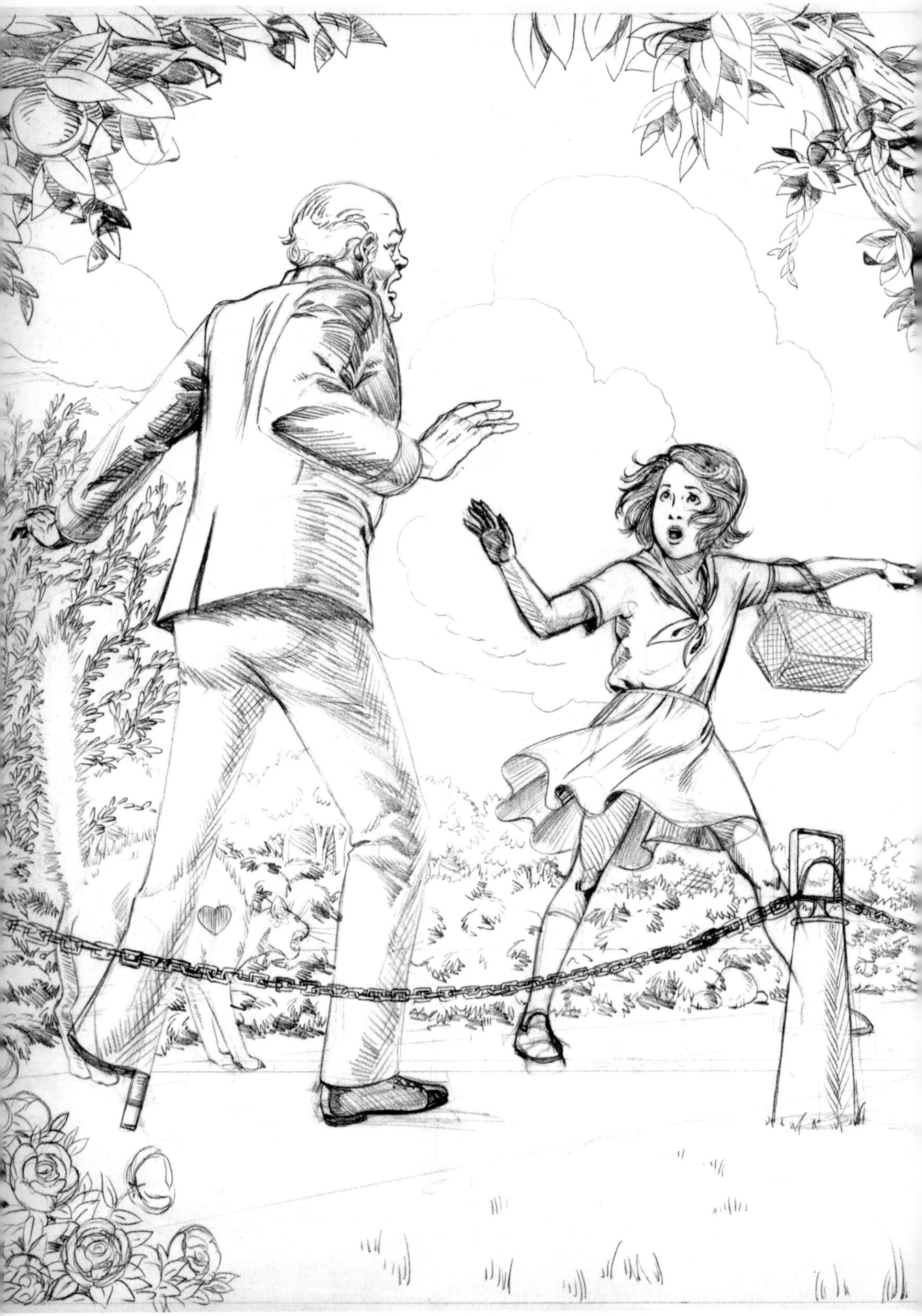

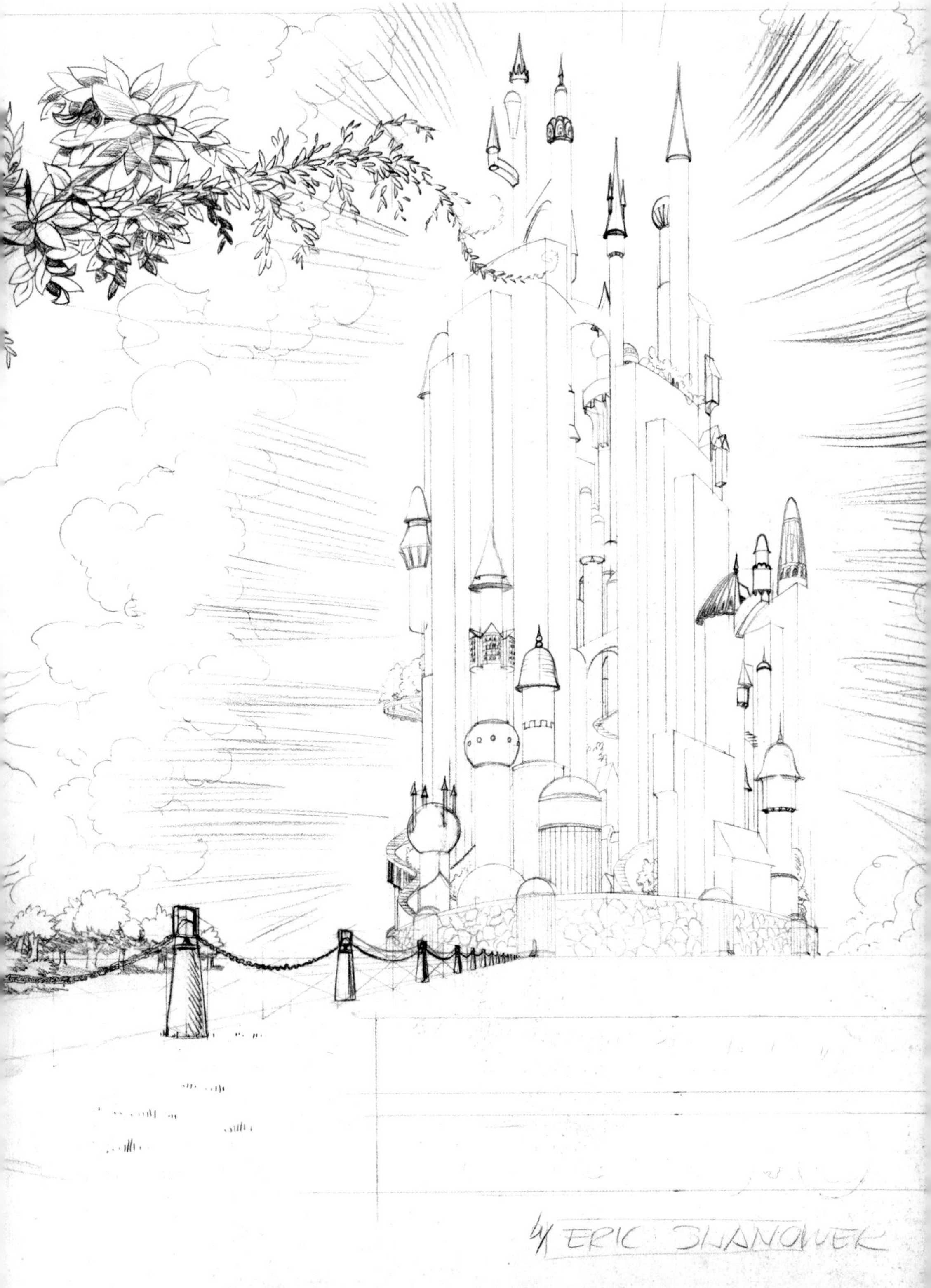
by ERIC SHANOWER

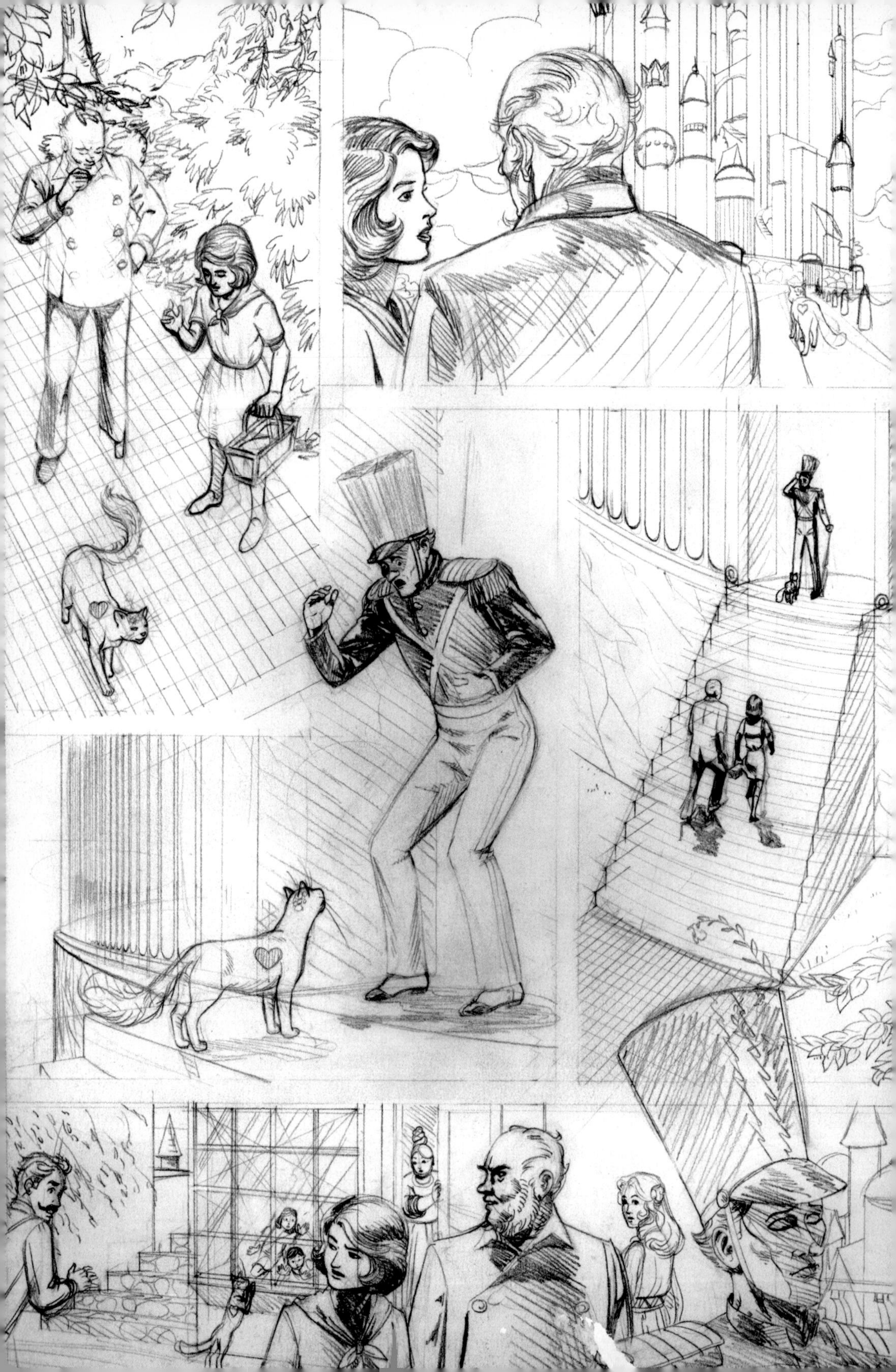

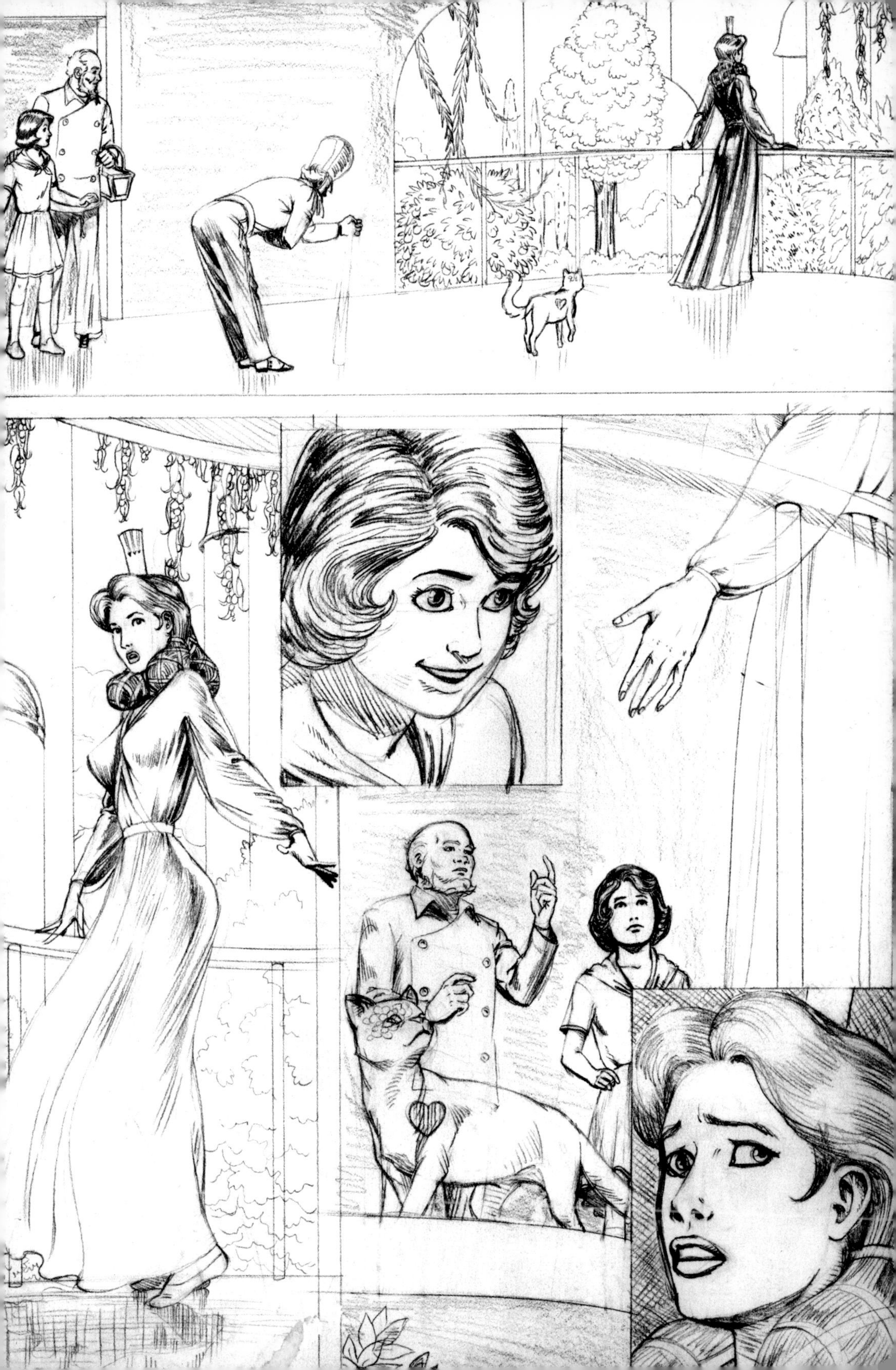

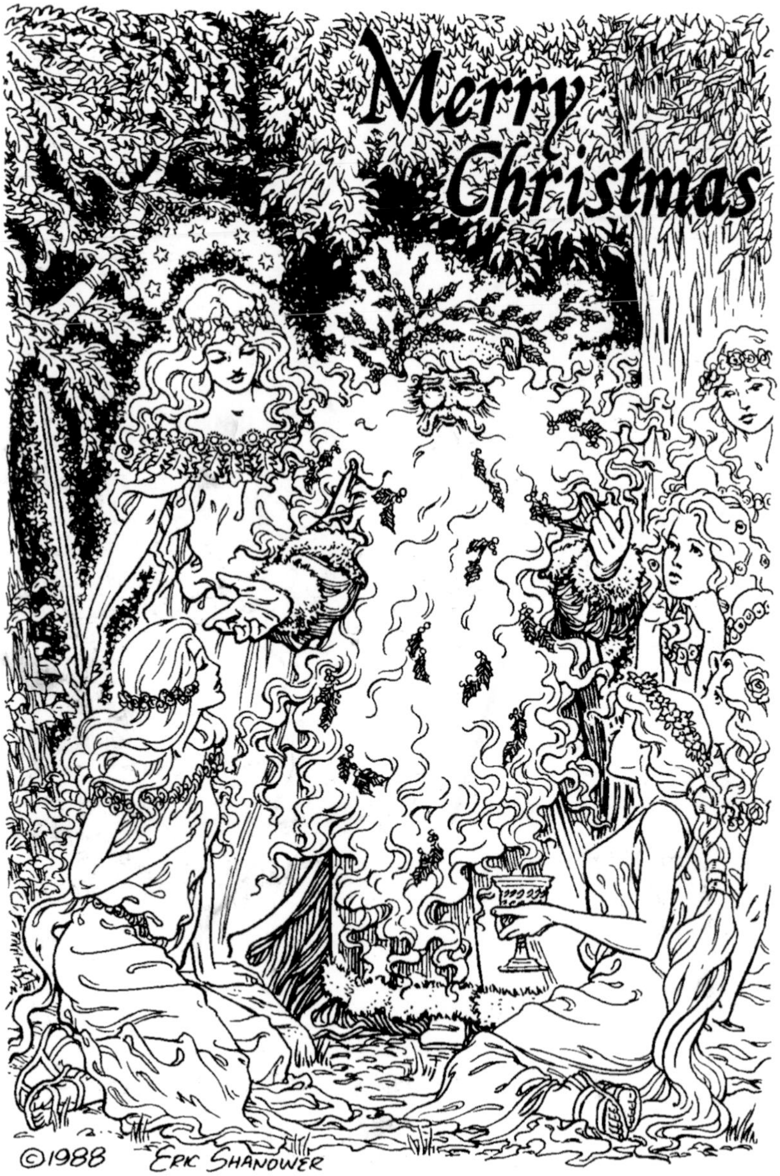
Merry Christmas
©1988 ERIC SHANOWER

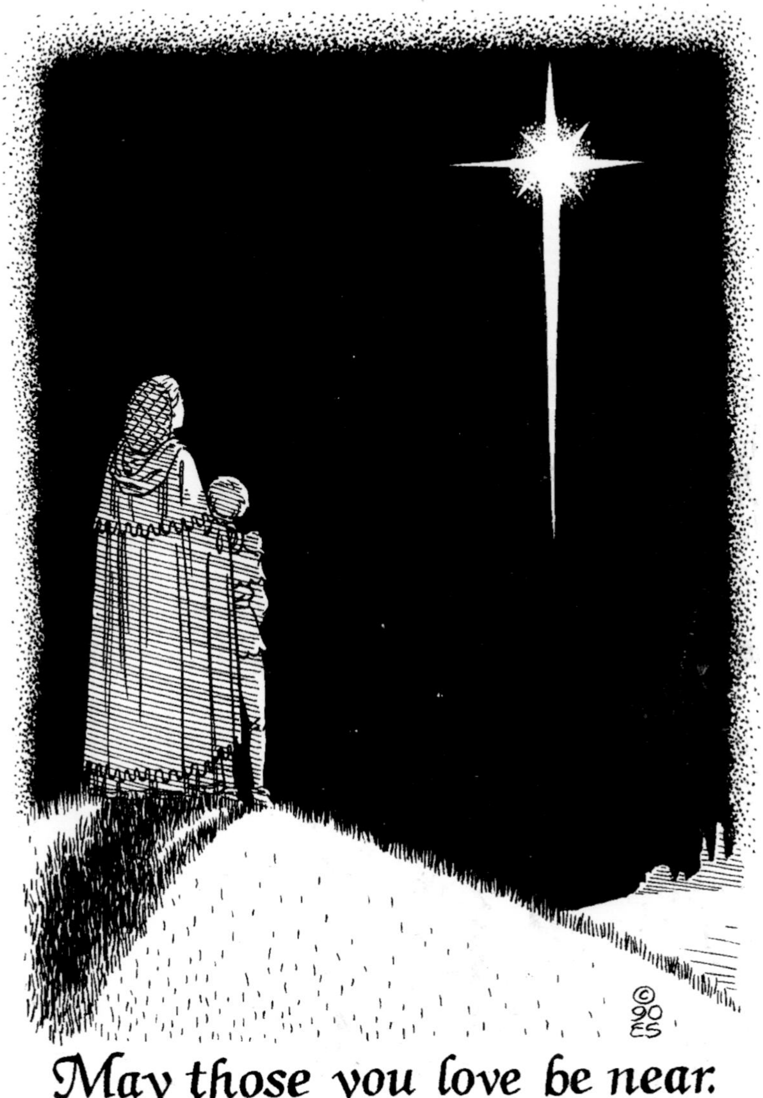
©
90
ES

May those you love be near.
Merry Christmas.

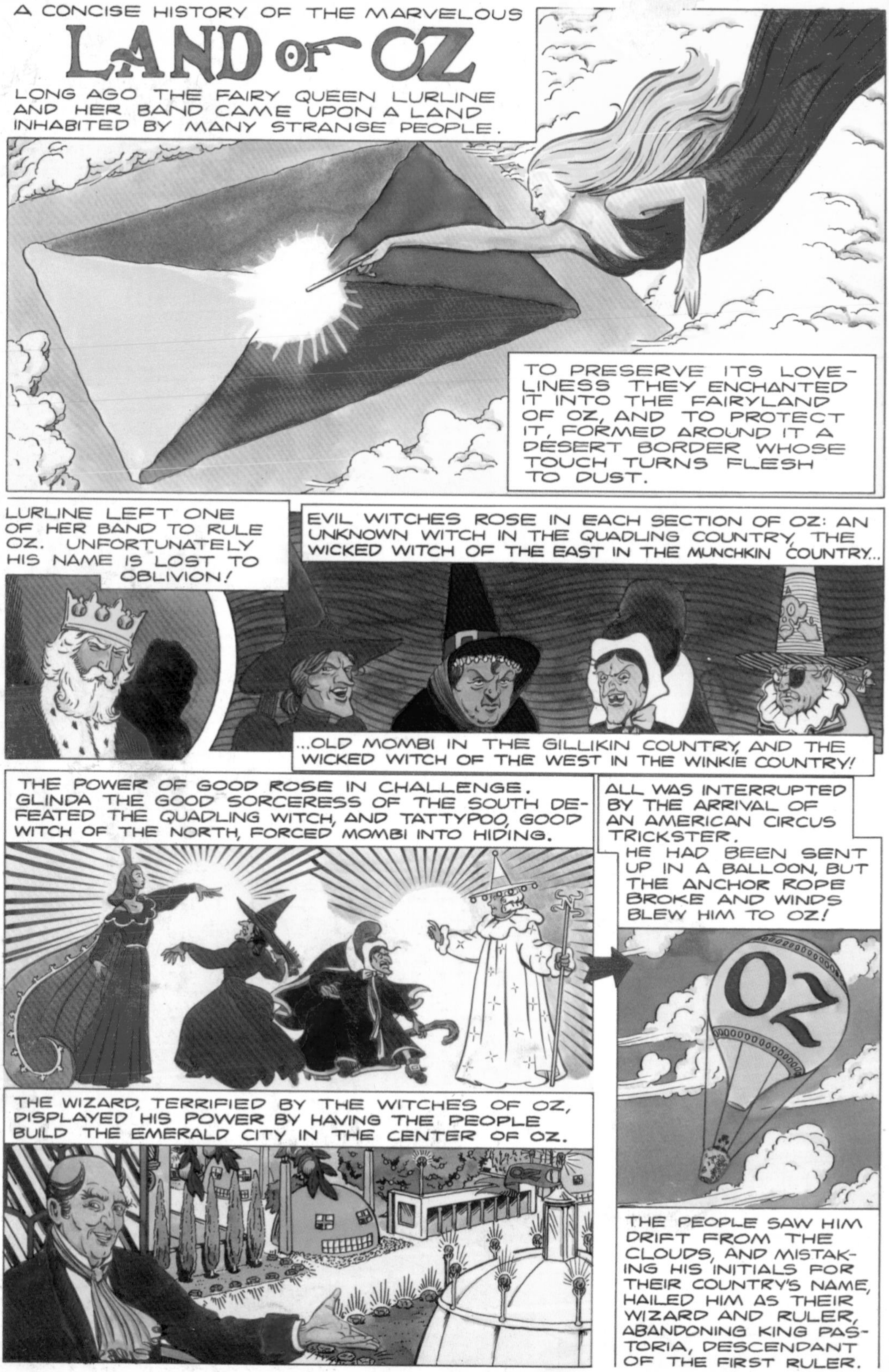
A CONCISE HISTORY OF THE MARVELOUS
LAND OF OZ
LONG AGO THE FAIRY QUEEN LURLINE AND HER BAND CAME UPON A LAND INHABITED BY MANY STRANGE PEOPLE.
TO PRESERVE ITS LOVE-LINESS THEY ENCHANTED IT INTO THE FAIRYLAND OF OZ, AND TO PROTECT IT, FORMED AROUND IT A DESERT BORDER WHOSE TOUCH TURNS FLESH TO DUST.
LURLINE LEFT ONE OF HER BAND TO RULE OZ. UNFORTUNATELY HIS NAME IS LOST TO OBLIVION!
EVIL WITCHES ROSE IN EACH SECTION OF OZ: AN UNKNOWN WITCH IN THE QUADLING COUNTRY, THE WICKED WITCH OF THE EAST IN THE MUNCHKIN COUNTRY...
...OLD MOMBI IN THE GILLIKIN COUNTRY, AND THE WICKED WITCH OF THE WEST IN THE WINKIE COUNTRY!
THE POWER OF GOOD ROSE IN CHALLENGE. GLINDA THE GOOD SORCERESS OF THE SOUTH DE-FEATED THE QUADLING WITCH, AND TATTYPOO, GOOD WITCH OF THE NORTH, FORCED MOMBI INTO HIDING.
ALL WAS INTERRUPTED BY THE ARRIVAL OF AN AMERICAN CIRCUS TRICKSTER.
HE HAD BEEN SENT UP IN A BALLOON, BUT THE ANCHOR ROPE BROKE AND WINDS BLEW HIM TO OZ!
OZ
THE PEOPLE SAW HIM DRIFT FROM THE CLOUDS, AND MISTAK-ING HIS INITIALS FOR THEIR COUNTRY'S NAME, HAILED HIM AS THEIR WIZARD AND RULER, ABANDONING KING PAS-TORIA, DESCENDANT OF THE FIRST RULER.
THE WIZARD, TERRIFIED BY THE WITCHES OF OZ, DISPLAYED HIS POWER BY HAVING THE PEOPLE BUILD THE EMERALD CITY IN THE CENTER OF OZ.

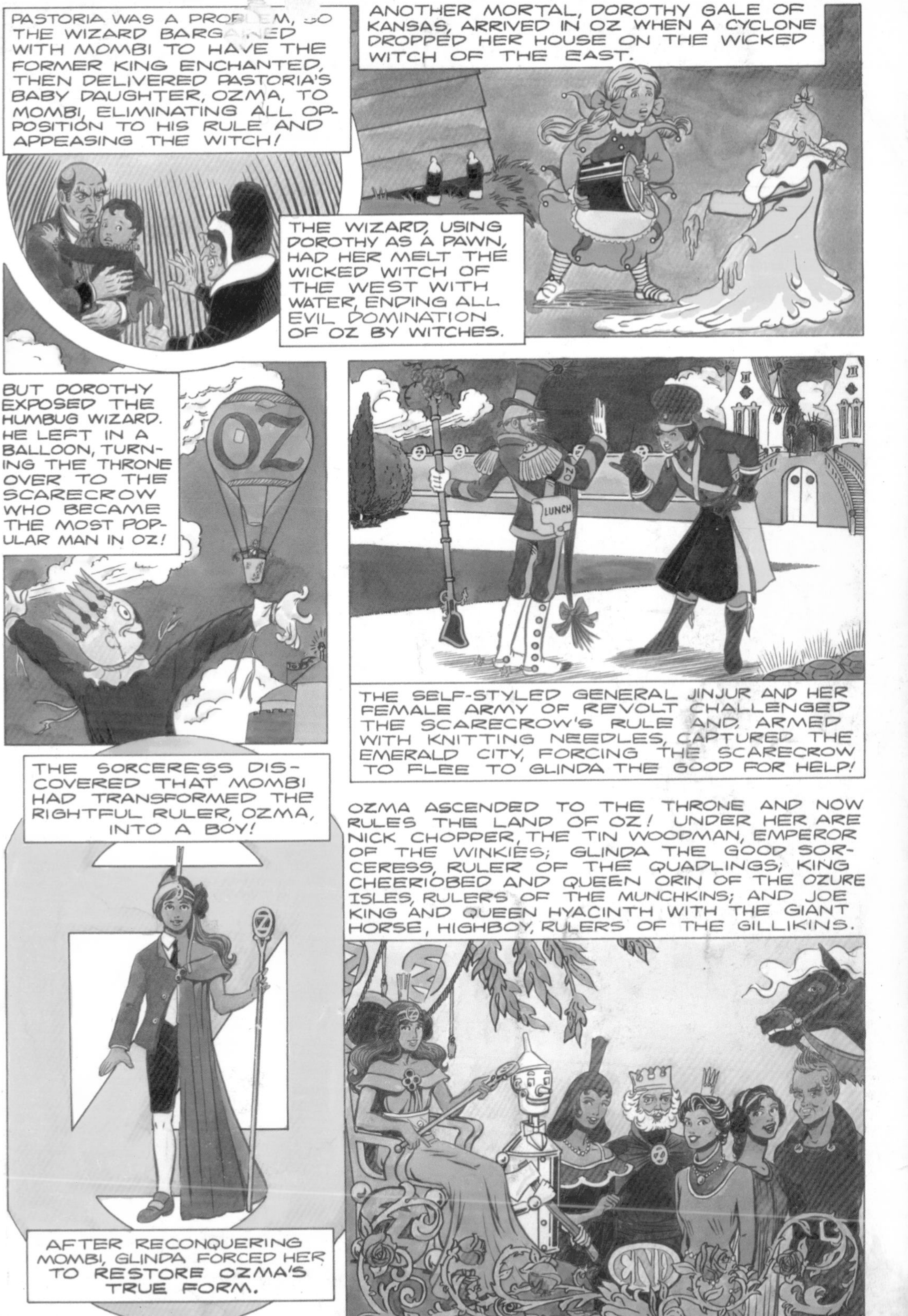
PASTORIA WAS A PROBLEM, SO THE WIZARD BARGAINED WITH MOMBI TO HAVE THE FORMER KING ENCHANTED, THEN DELIVERED PASTORIA'S BABY DAUGHTER, OZMA, TO MOMBI, ELIMINATING ALL OPPOSITION TO HIS RULE AND APPEASING THE WITCH!
ANOTHER MORTAL, DOROTHY GALE OF KANSAS, ARRIVED IN OZ WHEN A CYCLONE DROPPED HER HOUSE ON THE WICKED WITCH OF THE EAST.
THE WIZARD, USING DOROTHY AS A PAWN, HAD HER MELT THE WICKED WITCH OF THE WEST WITH WATER, ENDING ALL EVIL DOMINATION OF OZ BY WITCHES.
BUT DOROTHY EXPOSED THE HUMBUG WIZARD. HE LEFT IN A BALLOON, TURNING THE THRONE OVER TO THE SCARECROW WHO BECAME THE MOST POPULAR MAN IN OZ!
OZ
LUNCH
THE SELF-STYLED GENERAL JINJUR AND HER FEMALE ARMY OF REVOLT CHALLENGED THE SCARECROW'S RULE AND, ARMED WITH KNITTING NEEDLES, CAPTURED THE EMERALD CITY, FORCING THE SCARECROW TO FLEE TO GLINDA THE GOOD FOR HELP!
THE SORCERESS DISCOVERED THAT MOMBI HAD TRANSFORMED THE RIGHTFUL RULER, OZMA, INTO A BOY!
AFTER RECONQUERING MOMBI, GLINDA FORCED HER TO RESTORE OZMA'S TRUE FORM.
OZMA ASCENDED TO THE THRONE AND NOW RULES THE LAND OF OZ! UNDER HER ARE NICK CHOPPER, THE TIN WOODMAN, EMPEROR OF THE WINKIES; GLINDA THE GOOD SORCERESS, RULER OF THE QUADLINGS; KING CHEERIOBED AND QUEEN ORIN OF THE OZURE ISLES, RULERS OF THE MUNCHKINS; AND JOE KING AND QUEEN HYACINTH WITH THE GIANT HORSE, HIGHBOY, RULERS OF THE GILLIKINS.
END

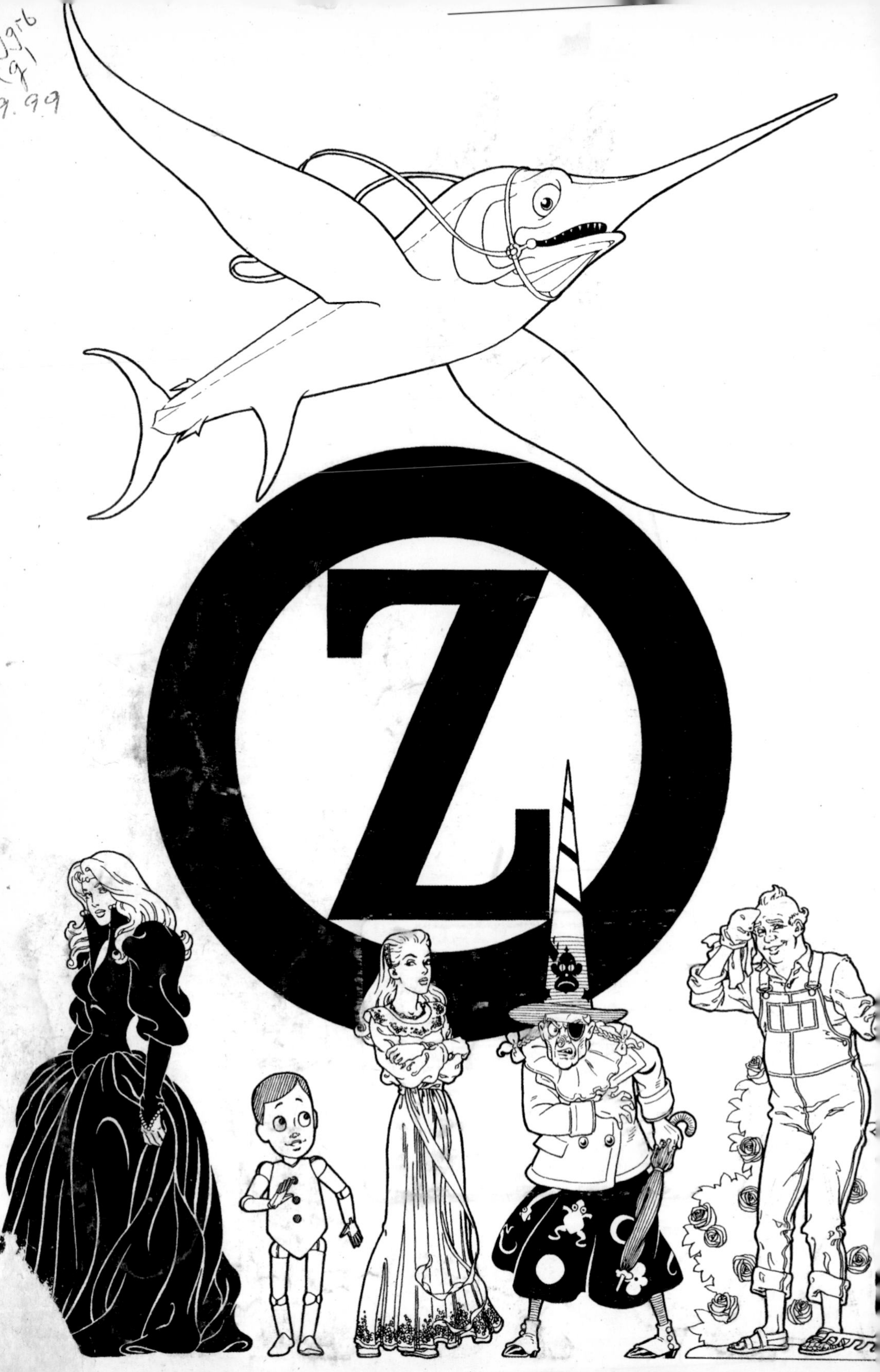
OZ